AF725243

THE THREE ORDERS

A GUIDE TO LACANIAN PSYCHOLOGY

TABLE OF CONTENTS

INTRODUCTION TO JACQUES LACAN'S THEORIES

Preliminary Considerations

Jacques Marie Émile Lacan, a renowned French psychoanalyst, was born on April 13, 1901, in Paris, France. After completing his early education, Lacan enrolled in medical school at the University of Paris, where he developed an interest in psychiatry and psychoanalysis. In his formative years, Lacan was greatly influenced by the works of Sigmund Freud, leading him to delve deeper into the discourses of psychoanalytic theory and practice. This pivotal phase marked the beginning of Lacan's lifelong dedication to revolutionizing the field of psychoanalysis.

Lacan's intellectual journey reached a significant milestone when he encountered the teachings of structural linguistics and the work of Ferdinand de Saussure. These encounters profoundly shaped Lacan's conceptualization of the human psyche and laid the groundwork for his groundbreaking reinterpretation of Freudian theories. His integration of linguistic principles into psychoanalytic discourse would later become a defining feature of his theoretical framework.

After undergoing personal analysis with renowned psychoanalyst Rudolph Loewenstein, Lacan went on to immerse himself in the burgeoning psychoanalytic community. His growing reputation as a charismatic and intellectually formidable figure within this sphere eventually led to his recognition as a formidable force in the evolution of psychoanalysis.

In 1932, Lacan received his psychiatric qualification and subsequently began his clinical practice. During this period, he also participated in the infamous Controversial Discussions at the British Psychoanalytical Society, where his perspectives on psychoanalysis began to crystallize and mature. Throughout his career, Lacan displayed a fervent commitment to advancing the interpretive scope of psychoanalysis, transcending the conventional boundaries of the discipline.

In 1953, Lacan introduced his seminal concept of the "Mirror Stage," which garnered widespread attention and acclaim from the psychoanalytic community. This pivotal concept elucidated the formation of the ego in relation to the idealized image, making significant strides in comprehending the complexities of human identity and subjectivity.

Subsequently, Lacan's increasing disillusionment with the institutionalized psychoanalytic establishment culminated in his divergence from the International Psychoanalytic Association (IPA), prompting him to establish the Société Française de Psychanalyse. This decision marked the inception of Lacan's rousing seminars, where his enigmatic lectures captivated audiences and initiated a paradigmatic shift in psychoanalytic thought.

As an engaging orator and profound thinker, Lacan's discourses traversed diverse disciplines, attracting a wide array of intellectuals, philosophers, and students. His oeuvre of theoretical writings and innovative insights solidified his prominence as a visionary figure in the milieus of psychoanalysis and critical theory. Through his unyielding commitment to challenging conventions and reshaping traditional psychoanalytic dialogues, Jacques Lacan has indelibly etched his legacy as one of the most influential figures in the history of psychoanalysis.

Fundamental Concepts in Lacanian Psychoanalysis

Jacques Lacan's psychoanalytic framework is underpinned by several fundamental concepts that are central to understanding his theories. One of the most crucial concepts is the idea of the unconscious as structured like a language, originally formulated as *l'inconscient est structuré comme un langage*. According to Lacan, the unconscious is not a repository of repressed thoughts and desires but rather a system of signifiers that shape an individual's subjectivity and experience. This linguistic framework posits that our unconscious desires and experiences are mediated through language, revealing the deeply symbolic nature of human psychology. Additionally, Lacan introduced the concept of the mirror stage, which explores the formation of the self and its relationship with the external world. The mirror stage highlights the pivotal role of identification and the formation of the ego through the image of the other, shedding light on the developmental processes of identity and subjectivity. Moreover, Lacan's tripartite model of the psyche, comprising the imaginary, the symbolic, and the real, provides a comprehensive framework for understanding human subjectivity. The imaginary order encapsulates images, illusions, and identifications, while the symbolic order represents the structure of language and cultural systems that govern social interactions and meaning-making. Finally, the real point towards the unfathomable and ineffable aspects of existence that exceed symbolic representation, encompassing traumatic experiences and the limits of language. Central to Lacanian theory is the concept of the *objet petit a*, which signifies the elusive object-cause of desire that propels psychic life and remains perpetually unattainable. This concept underscores the inherent lack and incompleteness within human subjectivity, shaping the endless pursuit of satisfaction and fulfillment. Furthermore, Lacan's emphasis on the Oedipus complex and the role of familial dynamics in shaping the unconscious underscores the significance of intergenerational and cultural influences on subjective experience.

The Relevance of Language in Lacan's Theories

In Lacanian psychoanalysis, language occupies a central position, serving as the primary medium through which human subjectivity is both formed and conveyed. For Lacan, language is not merely a tool for communication, but rather a system that structures how individuals perceive and interpret reality. This belief underscores the significance of linguistic symbols in shaping the unconscious and conscious mind. Through his reimagining of Freudian concepts, Lacan introduced the idea that the unconscious is structured like a language, with its own grammar and syntax. This perspective reframes the understanding of unconscious desires and drives, anchoring them within linguistic frameworks. As such, the study of language becomes integral to uncovering the underlying mechanisms of the human psyche. Furthermore, Lacan emphasized the pivotal role of signifiers, or linguistic units, in mediating individuals' interactions with the world. According to his theory, subjectivity is constituted through the interplay of signifiers that give meaning to experiences and emotions. Consequently, our perception of self and others is intertwined with the linguistic constructs through which we articulate our thoughts and feelings. Beyond individual psychology, language also influences the nature of human social dynamics. Lacan proposed that language shapes social relationships and power structures, attributing symbolic significance to societal norms and institutions. By highlighting the ways in which language mediates interpersonal interactions, Lacan's theories offer insights into the nuances of human behavior within broader cultural contexts. Moreover, Lacan's emphasis on language extends into the therapeutic sphere, where verbal expression becomes a conduit for analyzing and unraveling unconscious processes. Through linguistic discourse, patients engage in introspection and narrative construction, enabling the exploration of hidden meanings and subconscious patterns. Consequently, therapists utilize language as a tool for deconstructing and reconstructing the narratives that shape their patients' realities. In this way, language functions as a gateway to uncovering and addressing psychological complexities within the clinical setting. Overall, the centrality of language in Lacanian theories underscores its multifaceted role in shaping individual subjectivity, interpersonal dynamics, and therapeutic interventions.

Lacan's Return to Freud

Drawing from the foundational works of Sigmund Freud, Jacques Lacan embarked on a pioneering endeavor to reinterpret and revitalize psychoanalytic theory. His return to Freud represents a significant departure from mainstream psychoanalytic thought, as he sought to reinvigorate the discipline by re-examining and refocusing on Freud's original insights. Lacan's reimagining of Freudian concepts was not mere replication but a process of re-invention that aimed to uncover deeper layers of meaning and significance. Through his innovative perspective, Lacan introduced a fresh understanding of the unconscious, emphasizing its linguistic and symbolic nature. In essence, Lacan's return to Freud can be seen as a transformative journey that revitalized and reconfigured psychoanalytic discourse, setting the stage for a new era of theoretical engagement and clinical practice.

Core Tenets and Their Significance

As previously stated, one of the central tenets of Lacanian theory is the concept of the unconscious as structured like a language. This departure from traditional views of the unconscious as a repository of repressed desires or traumatic memories represents a paradigm shift in psychoanalytic thinking. By emphasizing the symbolic nature of the unconscious, Lacan posits that our deepest drives and fantasies are not simply chaotic impulses but are organized according to linguistic and symbolic structures. This insight has profound implications for the practice of psychoanalysis, transforming the therapeutic approach from unearthing hidden content to interpreting language and its underlying structures. Another cornerstone of Lacanian theory is the notion of the "mirror stage," which elucidates the formation of the ego and the individual's relationship with their sense of self. According to Lacan, during the mirror stage, an infant recognizes themselves as a unified and coherent entity through a process of identifying with their mirror image. This pivotal moment not only marks the emergence of the ego but also engenders a fundamental alienation as the individual internalizes an idealized image that they can never fully attain. The significance of the mirror stage extends beyond individual development, shedding light on the nature of subjectivity and the perpetual quest for wholeness and recognition. Lacan's emphasis on the role of signifiers and their effects on subjectivity and desire constitutes another key aspect of his work. In the milieu of language, signifiers take precedence over signifieds, leading to a constant deferral of meaning and the elusive nature of truth. This insight into the slippery nature of language has profound implications for understanding human communication, identity formation, and the construction of reality. Moreover, Lacan's rethinking of desire as fundamentally interwoven with lack and perpetually unsatisfied speaks to the existential condition of human beings, offering a compelling framework for examining the intricacies of motivation and fulfillment. These core tenets of Lacanian theory illuminate the intersections of language, subjectivity, and desire, inviting scholars and practitioners to grapple with profound questions about the self, society, and the human experience.

The Influence of Structuralism

Structuralism has played a pivotal role in shaping the trajectory of Jacques Lacan's theories and psychoanalytic practice. Building on the foundation laid by notable structuralists such as Ferdinand de Saussure and Claude Lévi-Strauss, Lacan deftly integrated structuralist principles into his conceptual framework, subsequently fostering a paradigm shift within the field of psychoanalysis. At the heart of structuralism lies an emphasis on systems, relationships, and the underlying structures that dictate meaning and behavior. This profound orientation towards the study of underlying structures has resonated deeply with Lacan's endeavor to elucidate the workings of the human psyche and language. Central to Lacanian thought is the notion of the unconscious as structured like a language, intrinsically entwined with the premises of structuralism. By viewing the unconscious as a structured system governed by the interplay of signifiers and signifieds, Lacan effectively aligned psychoanalysis with the prevalent structuralist discourse of his time. Lacan's engagement with structuralism extended beyond theoretical intersections, permeating into his therapeutic techniques and clinical approaches. His utilization of linguistic and symbolic structures to decode and address the unconscious further underscored the far-reaching impact of structuralist influences on his work. Furthermore, Lacan's appropriation and adaptation of structuralist concepts bolstered his quest to reconceptualize the nature of subjectivity and identity, reshaping the contours of psychological inquiry. The reverberations of structuralism within Lacanian theory are palpable in his reconfiguration of the Oedipus complex, which he framed in terms of structural and symbolic dynamics rather than solely as a developmental stage. Moreover, Lacan's formulation of the 'mirror stage' and his articulation of the 'imaginary' as a site of alienation and misrecognition bear the indelible imprint of structuralist insights. In essence, the infusion of structuralist tenets fortified Lacan's intellectual edifice, ensconcing his ideas within the intellectual zeitgeist of structuralist thought. Ultimately, the influence of structuralism on Lacan's oeuvre is testament to the symbiosis between structuralist inquiries and the evolution of psychoanalytic discourse.

Major Works and Contributions

Jacques Lacan's seminal oeuvre encompasses a diverse array of writings, lectures, and seminars that continue to shape the discourse of contemporary psychoanalytic theory. One of Lacan's most renowned works, 'Écrits', stands as a monumental testament to his intellectual prowess, presenting an extensive collection of his essays and theoretical expositions. Within this compendium, Lacan delves into the intricacies of human subjectivity, language, and the unconscious, propounding radical ideas that have spurred countless debates and scholarly investigations. His relentless pursuit of reinterpreting and enriching the philosophical foundations of psychoanalysis permeates through 'Écrits' and lays the groundwork for many of his future endeavors.

Lacan's contributions extend beyond 'Écrits' to encompass his provocative seminars, where he expounded on his ever-evolving theories and concepts. These seminars, such as the famous 'The Four Fundamental Concepts of Psychoanalysis' and 'The Ethics of Psychoanalysis', offered a platform for Lacan to engage in captivating dialogues with his audience, dismantling traditional psychoanalytic paradigms and laying bare the profound implications of his thought. Unraveling the enigmatic nuances of desire, drive, and the unconscious, Lacan's seminars stand as testaments to his extraordinary ability to captivate, challenge, and inspire his listeners.

Lacan's conceptual innovations and their impact on the practice of psychoanalysis reverberate through his notable contributions to the understanding of the mirror stage, the symbolic order, and the role of language in the construction of subjectivity. With incisive clarity, Lacan forefronts the dialectic between the ego and the Other, illuminating the inherently fraught nature of identity formation and the perennial quest for selfhood. His relentless interrogation of the signifier and signified not only revitalized psychoanalytic discourse but sparked new interpretive frameworks within the wider arena of cultural studies, literary analysis, and critical theory.

Reception Among the Psychoanalytic Community

Jacques Lacan's theories and contributions have not been devoid of controversy and debate within the psychoanalytic community. Although there are fervent supporters and proponents who laud Lacanian psychoanalysis for its innovative approach and theoretical depth, there also exist skeptical voices and detractors who contest the validity and applicability of Lacan's ideas. The reception of Lacanian theory has been somewhat polarized, as it elicits passionate responses from both advocates and critics.

One point of contention revolves around Lacan's divergence from traditional Freudian psychoanalysis, as he infused Freudian concepts with elements of structural linguistics, semiotics, and post-structuralist philosophy. This departure from established psychoanalytic norms raised skepticism and resistance among some in the field. Critics argue that Lacan's work deviates too far from the empirical and clinical foundations of Freudian psychoanalysis, thereby challenging the legitimacy of his contributions to the discipline.

Conversely, proponents of Lacanian theory assert that Lacan's reimagining of Freudian psychoanalysis offers profound insights into the nature of human subjectivity, language, and unconscious processes. They see his emphasis on the symbolic order and the role of language as pivotal in advancing the understanding of the human psyche and social dynamics. For these proponents, Lacan's departure from classical psychoanalysis represents an evolution rather than a deviation, heralding a new era of theoretical exploration and clinical practice.

The impact of Lacanian theory extends beyond traditional psychoanalysis, influencing diverse fields such as literary criticism, film studies, gender studies, and cultural theory. This interdisciplinary reach has broadened the discussion surrounding Lacan's ideas, attracting scholars from various disciplines who seek to engage with his complex conceptual framework.

It is essential to note that the reception of Lacan's ideas varies across different geographical regions and academic communities. His work has garnered significant attention and acclaim in some intellectual circles, while encountering skepticism and disapproval in others. This diversity of reception further underscores the complex and nuanced nature of Lacanian theory and its implications for contemporary psychology and critical thought.

Ultimately, the reception of Lacanian theory within the psychoanalytic community reflects the ongoing dialogue between tradition and innovation, between continuity and rupture. It encapsulates the fervent intellectual discourse that characterizes the evolution of psychoanalytic theory and practice, underscoring the significance and relevance of Lacan's contributions in shaping the landscape of modern psychoanalysis.

THE ORIGINS OF THE THREE ORDERS

Historical Context and Intellectual Background

In the early 20th century, Europe was undergoing significant cultural, social, and political transformations that would indelibly shape the intellectual landscape. The aftermath of World War I left profound scars on the collective psyche of the continent, leading to a pervasive sense of disillusionment and a fervent quest for new meaning and understanding. This intellectual climate, characterized by existential questioning and the search for deeper insights into human consciousness, provided fertile ground for the burgeoning field of psychoanalysis. Sigmund Freud, with his revolutionary theories on the dynamics of the unconscious mind, had already begun to evoke widespread interest and controversy in academic circles. It was within this context that Jacques Lacan embarked on his exploration of psychoanalytical thought.

Lacan was coming of age amidst a time of great upheaval. French society was grappling with the legacy of World War I, the rise of fascism in neighboring countries, and the advent of surrealism as a potent artistic and intellectual movement. These multifaceted influences converged to shape Lacan's early intellectual development, fostering an environment of deep introspection and critical inquiry. He immersed himself in the study of medicine and psychiatry, laying the groundwork for his later integration of these disciplines with psychoanalysis. Moreover, Lacan's exposure to the works of Freud during this formative period ignited a profound intellectual awakening. He was captivated by Freud's pioneering investigations into the human mind, which challenged established notions of rationality and consciousness.

With the growing popularity of Freudian ideas in academic and clinical circles, Lacan found himself drawn to the profound potential of psychoanalysis as a tool for understanding the complexities of human subjectivity. However, it was not merely the intellectual appeal of Freudian theory that captivated Lacan; rather, it was the revolutionary implications of psychoanalysis for redefining the very nature of human identity and experience. These early encounters with psychoanalytic concepts laid the foundation for Lacan's enduring commitment to unraveling the enigmas of the human psyche. As he delved deeper into the works of Freud and contemporaneous thinkers, Lacan began to discern the interplay between psychic processes, language, and societal norms.

Overall, his encounters with Freudian theory, coupled with the existential angst permeating European society, kindled a passionate engagement with the mysteries of the human mind, propelling him on a trajectory that would eventually yield his contributions to the field of psychoanalysis.

Lacan's Early Influences in Psychoanalysis

Jacques Lacan's early influences in psychoanalysis can be traced back to his formative years and academic pursuits. Having studied medicine and subsequently delving into psychiatry, Lacan underwent a transformative period where he engaged with the works of renowned figures in the field of psychoanalysis. Sigmund Freud's groundbreaking theories and concepts profoundly impacted Lacan's intellectual development. The foundational principles of the unconscious, repressed desires, and the complex interplay between conscious and unconscious mental processes laid the groundwork for Lacan's own theoretical explorations. Additionally, the emergence of key Freudian concepts, such as the Oedipus complex, served as catalysts for Lacan to embark on his distinct psychoanalytic journey. Moreover, the works of Karl Abraham, one of Freud's earliest followers, played a pivotal role in shaping Lacan's early understanding of psychoanalysis. Abraham's contributions to the study of infantile sexuality and the dynamics of the unconscious left an indelible imprint on Lacan's evolving theoretical framework. Furthermore, the influence of Melanie Klein, particularly her innovative interpretations of child psychology and her emphasis on the significance of early developmental experiences, resonated deeply with Lacan's burgeoning interest in understanding the intricacies of the human psyche. Lacan's exposure to these formative thinkers within psychoanalysis not only broadened his intellectual horizons but also set the stage for the fusion of diverse perspectives that would come to define his own unique contributions to the field.

Development of Theoretical Framework

At the heart of Lacan's theoretical framework lies a fusion of psychoanalytic principles, linguistic theory, and structuralist philosophy. Central to this framework is the re-interpretation and re-conceptualization of Freudian concepts within a linguistic and cultural context. Lacan's departure from traditional Freudian psychoanalysis led to the formulation of a novel theoretical framework that continues to provoke and inspire discourse in contemporary scholarship. Throughout his career, Lacan synthesized insights from various disciplines, crafting a multifaceted approach rooted in the understanding of the human psyche as deeply entwined with language and symbolic systems.

A crucial milestone in Lacan's theoretical development emerged with his conceptualization of the unconscious as structured like a language. This pivotal concept anchored his theoretical framework, framing the unconscious as a sphere governed by its internal logic and symbolism, akin to the syntax and semantics of a language. Drawing upon Saussurean linguistics, Lacan posited that the unconscious operates through a system of signifiers, where meaning is derived from the interplay of linguistic elements akin to the formation of sentences in language. This innovative perspective reframed the understanding of the unconscious, shifting focus from latent content and repressed drives to the intricacies of symbolic communication and language.

Lacan's exploration of the mirror stage and the formation of the ego marked a significant juncture in the development of his theoretical framework. By intertwining developmental psychology with phenomenological insights, Lacan elucidated the role of the imaginary in the formation of subjectivity. This exploration not only contributed to the understanding of identity formation but also underscored the pervasive influence of visual imagery and fantastical identification processes in psychological development.

As Lacan's theoretical framework continued to evolve, its overarching aim became increasingly pronounced: to uncover the underpinnings of subjectivity, desire, and the construction of reality through linguistic and symbolic structures. This trajectory culminated in the articulation of the three orders—Real, Imaginary, and Symbolic—each delineating distinct dimensions of human experience and subjective constitution. The interplay among these orders constitutes the bedrock of Lacanian theory, offering a framework for comprehending the complexities of the human psyche and social interactions.

Philosophical Underpinnings and Inspirations

Lacan's theoretical framework draws deeply from a diverse range of philosophical and intellectual traditions, integrating concepts from phenomenology, structuralism, and post-structuralism. Central to Lacan's thinking are the works of renowned philosophers such as Hegel, Heidegger, and Sartre, whose existential and ontological inquiries provided crucial insights into the nature of human subjectivity and language. Lacan's engagement with these philosophical traditions is marked by a rigorous interrogation of the relationship between language, consciousness, and the formation of identity. Moreover, Lacan's reinterpretation of Freudian psychoanalysis through the lens of these philosophical currents led to the development of innovative concepts that continue to shape contemporary discourse in psychology and cultural theory. The influence of phenomenological thought, particularly the ideas of Husserl and Merleau-Ponty, is evident in Lacan's emphasis on lived experience and embodied subjectivity. Lacan's appropriation of structuralist theories, notably from Saussure and Levi-Strauss, reflects his commitment to exploring the underlying structures and systems that govern human signification and social dynamics. Furthermore, the existential concerns of thinkers like Sartre resonate in Lacan's articulation of the fragmented and alienated self in the symbolic order.

The Emergence of the Orders Concept

In tracing the emergence of Jacques Lacan's concept of the three orders, it is essential to delve into the critical junctures that shaped his intellectual journey. The exploration begins with Lacan's deep engagement with structural linguistics, particularly the works of Ferdinand de Saussure and Roman Jakobson. This theoretical engagement laid the groundwork for Lacan's reconceptualization of psychoanalysis, drawing from linguistic structures to elucidate the complexities of the human psyche. Moreover, Lacan's voracious exploration of philosophical discourses, encompassing existentialism, phenomenology, and Hegelian thought, significantly contributed to the gestation of his seminal theories. These philosophical underpinnings provided the scaffolding for his reconfiguration of Freudian concepts into a novel framework that transcended traditional psychoanalytic paradigms.

As Lacan grappled with the rich tapestry of philosophical and linguistic influence, he underwent a profound reassessment of Freudian theory, recognizing both its indispensable foundational principles and its potential for reinterpretation and expansion. Lacan's meticulous scrutiny of Freud's oeuvre led to a critical reappraisal of key Freudian constructs, prompting him to discern the interplay between language, desire, and subjectivity. It was within this fertile intellectual milieu that the seeds of the three orders concept were sown, germinating through a synthesis of linguistic, philosophical, and psychoanalytic insights.

Lacan's immersion in the surrealist movement and interactions with eminent artists such as Salvador Dali and Pablo Picasso engendered a deeper understanding of the interconnections between symbolism, representation, and the unconscious. The surrealist ethos of tapping into the unconscious mind resonated deeply with Lacan, emboldening him to excavate the enigmatic terrain of human subjectivity. From these multifaceted explorations, the conceptual architecture of the symbolic, imaginary, and real orders acquired greater substance and nuance, offering a profound reimagining of the foundational elements of psychoanalysis.

The emergence of the three orders concept represents the culmination of Lacan's intellectual odyssey, synthesizing diverse strands of knowledge into a cohesive theoretical framework that continues to reverberate across disciplines. By elucidating the intricacies of human experience through an innovative tripartite structure, Lacan broadened the horizons of psychoanalytic inquiry, providing a powerful lens through which to comprehend the complex interplay of language, representation, and the unconscious.

Contributions from Freudian Thought

The development of Jacques Lacan's Three Orders theory was significantly influenced by the foundational concepts of Sigmund Freud's psychoanalytic framework. Freud's groundbreaking work, particularly in uncovering the dynamics of the unconscious mind and the role of human instincts, laid the groundwork for Lacan's subsequent theories. Central to Freudian thought was the notion of the unconscious as the repository of repressed desires, fears, and unresolved conflicts. These formative concepts became pivotal in Lacan's conceptualization of the three orders, as he sought to understand the complex interplay between conscious and unconscious processes within the human psyche. Moreover, Lacan subscribed to Freud's emphasis on the role of early childhood experiences in shaping an individual's psychological development. This shared perspective is evident in Lacan's incorporation of Freudian ideas pertaining to the Oedipus complex, the stages of psychosexual development, and the significance of familial and societal influences. Lacan's engagement with Freud's work also led him to refine and expand upon the concept of libido, invoking it as a vital force that underpins psychic life and fuels the pursuit of desires and pleasures. Furthermore, Lacan drew from Freud's examination of dreams and symbolism, integrating these observations into his elucidation of the symbolic order within his three-orders framework.

Integration with Structural Linguistics

Jacques Lacan's integration of structural linguistics into his psychoanalytic framework was not merely an intellectual exercise but a profound reimagining of the ontological foundations of subjectivity and language. At its core, this integration sought to elucidate the relationship between unconscious desire and linguistic signification, thereby recasting the very essence of human subjectivity within the framework of language. To comprehend the significance of this integration, it is imperative to explore its theoretical underpinnings.

Structural linguistics, as epitomized by Ferdinand de Saussure's seminal work, provided Lacan with a radical departure from traditional conceptions of language and meaning. Saussure's dyadic model of the sign, comprising the signifier and signified, underpinned Lacan's conceptualization of the unconscious as structured like a language. This parallelism served as the linchpin for Lacan's thesis that the unconscious operates through the same structural principles as language itself, opening new vistas for understanding psychic processes.

The implications of this integration reverberated across Lacan's constructs, particularly in the formulation of the symbolic order. By imbuing language with a fundamental role in the constitution of subjectivity, Lacan's structuralist turn recast the symbolic order as the domain within which the subject's identity and desires are mediated and articulated through signifiers. Furthermore, the structuralist lens provided Lacan with a framework to elucidate the mechanisms underlying the formation and function of the unconscious, shedding light on the complex interplay between linguistic structures and the formation of symptomatology and unconscious fantasies.

Lacan's amalgamation of structural linguistics with psychoanalysis led to profound reconceptualizations of key Freudian concepts. For instance, the Oedipus complex, viewed through the prism of structural linguistics, became a discourse on the acquisition of language and the subject's alignment with the symbolic order. Likewise, the role of signifiers in the process of transference gained new significance, emphasizing the centrality of linguistic mediation in the therapeutic context.

This integration was not devoid of controversy, however, as it triggered debates regarding the reduction of the unconscious to linguistic structures and the potential neglect of non-linguistic aspects of subjectivity. Critics argued that such an emphasis on language risked effacing the corporeal, affective, and pre-linguistic dimensions of the unconscious, dubbing it as excessively linguistic-centric. Nevertheless, Lacan's integration with structural linguistics stands as a testament to the profound impact of interdisciplinary dialogue and the fecundity of cross-pollination between diverse academic domains.

Influence of Surrealism and Art Movements

The influence of surrealism and art movements on Jacques Lacan's development of the three orders is a multifaceted aspect of his theoretical framework. Surrealism, with its emphasis on the power of the unconscious mind, dreams, and the irrational, had a significant impact on Lacan's conceptualization of the human psyche. The surrealist movement, spearheaded by figures such as André Breton and Salvador Dalí, sought to liberate the unconscious and explore the depths of human experience beyond rational constraints. This exploration resonated deeply with Lacan, who was drawn to the enigmatic and symbolic nature of the unconscious. The surrealist emphasis on symbols, dream imagery, and free association directly informed Lacan's understanding of symbolism, the imaginary, and the unconscious as integral components of his three orders. Moreover, the provocative and often subversive nature of surrealist art challenged societal norms, encouraging Lacan to confront the complexities of identity, desire, and meaning. This influence is evident in Lacan's recognition of the symbolic order as the milieu of language, cultural symbols, and social norms that shape individual subjectivity. In addition to surrealism, broader art movements such as cubism and abstract expressionism also fueled Lacan's exploration of visual representation, perception, and the construction of reality. These movements revolutionized artistic depictions of the world, often portraying fragmented, multi-perspective realities that parallel Lacan's conceptualization of the fragmented self and the multiplicity of perspectives within the human psyche. The interplay between art, perception, and the unconscious captivated Lacan, prompting him to investigate the mechanisms through which individuals construct and interpret their realities. This fascination found expression in Lacan's elaboration of the imaginary order, where the formation of ego, identification, and mirroring processes are linked to visual representations and artistic expressions. By integrating insights from surrealism and various art movements, Lacan expanded the scope of psychoanalytic inquiry, enriching his theoretical framework with an appreciation for the symbiotic relationship between art, the unconscious, and the construction of subjective experience.

Initial Reception and Scholarly Debate

Upon the publication of his groundbreaking work, Lacan's conceptualization of the three orders faced a diverse array of reactions from scholars, clinicians, and intellectuals. Many were captivated by the innovative nature of his approach, while others were initially critical or skeptical. The revolutionary nature of Lacan's ideas led to lively discussions and incited considerable curiosity about the potential implications for various disciplines. The notion of the three orders spurred interdisciplinary exchanges that extended beyond the milieus of psychology and psychoanalysis. In addition to generating attention within the academic sphere, Lacan's theories also captured the imagination of prominent figures in the arts, philosophy, and cultural studies. The widespread interest in Lacanian thought propelled diverse inquiries into the theoretical underpinnings and practical applications of the three orders. As the layers of Lacan's theories began to unfold, they elicited both fervent support and rigorous critique. Scholars engaged in extensive discourse regarding the compatibility of Lacan's framework with existing psychological paradigms, the verifiability of his claims, and the potential impact on clinical practice. The implications of the three orders for understanding human subjectivity and the nature of reality itself became pivotal topics of investigation. The burgeoning interest in Lacanian theory fostered an atmosphere rife with intellectual exchange, debates, and reevaluation of established assumptions. Moreover, the incorporation of Lacan's ideas into various fields prompted a broader examination of the intersections between language, culture, and cognition. Through these debates, Lacan's conceptualization of the three orders underwent a process of refinement and transformation, as scholars sought to validate its theoretical robustness and practical utility.

Refinements Leading to Canonical Formulation

With its initial inception, Lacan's concept of the Three Orders faced significant scrutiny and generated impassioned scholarly debate. Following this extensive dialogue, Lacan diligently embarked on a process of refinement, characterized by meticulous introspection and rigorous philosophical inquiry, ultimately leading to the canonical formulation that would come to define his theoretical framework. This phase of refinement was marked by an unwavering commitment to precision and coherence, as Lacan sought to elucidate the interplay between the symbolic, imaginary, and real orders.

Central to this process was Lacan's deep engagement with the works of influential thinkers such as Freud and Saussure, from whom he drew crucial insights and foundational principles. As he delved into psychoanalytic theory and structural linguistics, Lacan meticulously sought to synthesize and reconcile divergent perspectives, thereby enriching and solidifying the underpinnings of his theoretical edifice.

Lacan's refining efforts were informed by an acute awareness of the evolving intellectual landscape, acknowledging and engaging with complementary disciplines such as philosophy, anthropology, and literary theory. This multidisciplinary dialogue not only lent nuance and depth to his formulations but also served to align his conceptual schema with broader currents of thought, reinforcing its philosophical robustness and existential relevance.

Crucially, the path to canonical formulation entailed a rigorous reassessment of Lacan's earlier conjectures and propositions, compelling him to explore the depths of his own theoretical terrain. Through a process of dialectical critique and self-interrogation, Lacan honed and polished the contours of the Three Orders, elucidating their connections and interdependencies while ferreting out potential ambiguities or inconsistencies.

Simultaneously, Lacan's engagement with clinical praxis and case studies afforded invaluable insights, allowing him to ground his theoretical abstractions in the concrete reality of psychological phenomena. This continual dialogue between theory and praxis engendered a holistic refinement that not only refined the abstract tenets of the Three Orders but also enriched their practical utility in the context of psychoanalysis and therapeutic intervention.

In sum, the refinements leading to the canonical formulation of the Three Orders represent a testament to Lacan's unrelenting pursuit of theoretical precision, philosophical coherence, and clinical applicability. Through a web of intellectual endeavors, dialogues, and critical reflections, Lacan transmuted the incipient seeds of his conceptual framework into an enduring edifice that continues to resonate across diverse domains of knowledge and practice.

KEY IDEAS AND POSTULATES

Introduction to Lacan's Foundational Concepts

1. The Lacanian Subject:

The notion of the subject in Lacanian psychoanalysis presents a departure from traditional understandings, constituting a pivotal element in the reconfiguration of psychoanalytic discourse inaugurated by Lacan's seminal work. For Lacan, the subject is not a fixed, autonomous entity but rather an elusive construct, perpetually enigmatic and fluid in nature.

At the crux of Lacan's conceptualization lies the assertion that the subject is inexorably entangled within the web of language and culture. In contrast to the ego-centric model advanced by Freudian psychoanalysis, Lacan posits the subject as a product of linguistic and socio-cultural influences, intrinsically bound to the symbolic order. This pivotal shift discerns the Lacanian subject as fundamentally enmeshed within the symbolic framework, thereby unravelling its underlying implication for the analysis of human subjectivity.

The Lacanian subject emerges as a site of perpetual lack, perpetuating a relentless quest for wholeness and unity. The foundational Lacanian concept of 'lack' delineates the intrinsic sense of incompleteness and yearning inherent to the subject, establishing desire as an inherent constituent. As such, Lacan's formulation of the subject engenders a profound reorientation of psychoanalytic praxis, emphasizing the centrality of desire and lack in the constitution of human subjectivity.

Crucially, the Lacanian subject cannot be elucidated outside the purview of the unconscious, encapsulated by the interconnected triad of the Real, the Imaginary, and the Symbolic. The Lacanian conception of the subject invariably intersects with these three dimensions, manifesting in a continual negotiation between conscious and unconscious registers. This dynamic interplay between the conscious and unconscious not only underscores the complexity of the subject position but also establishes the underpinnings for the Lacanian approach to psychic functioning.

In essence, the introduction to the Lacanian subject unfurls a transformative reimagining of the human psyche, contoured by the interplay of language, desire, and the dialectics of lack. It inscribes the subject as a multifaceted entity, inextricably tethered to the vicissitudes of the symbolic order and the enigma of the unconscious. Consequently, grasping the intricacies of the Lacanian subject propels an incisive interrogation of the construction, perpetuation, and destabilization of individual subjectivity, charting new frontiers in the landscape of psychoanalytic inquiry.

2. 'The Unconscious is Structured like a Language':

The assertion that *l'inconscient est structuré comme un langage* reorients our perception of the psyche, positioning language as the primary medium through which unconscious desires, conflicts, and drives find expression. Herein lies the crux of Lacan's departure from conventional psychoanalytic perspectives, advocating for a linguistic turn in approaching the depths of the unconscious. This conceptual shift illuminates the web of signifiers that constitute the unconscious, mirroring the syntax and semantics inherent in linguistic systems. It prompts us to consider the unconscious not as a reservoir of repressed instincts, but as a symbolic network governed by the rules of language.

Delving into the structural analogy between language and the unconscious unveils the pivotal role of signifiers in mediating our experiences and identities. The understanding that our unconscious processes unfold within a linguistic framework calls for a reevaluation of the nature of meaning and representation in human existence. Signifiers, imbued with both conscious and unconscious significations, become the focal points through which our subjective realities are constituted. In essence, the unconscious is not a chaotic sphere devoid of order, but a system permeated with the logic and arrangements akin to language.

In engaging with the implications of this foundational dictum, we confront the profound reverberations it engenders in the spheres of interpretation and psychoanalytic practice. The recognition of the unconscious as linguistically structured transfigures the very nature of the analytic dialogue, emphasizing the interpretive value of language in deciphering hidden meanings and subconscious manifestations. Through this lens, the analytical encounter unfolds as a dialogue of signifiers, where the nuances of language unravel the enigmatic fabric of the unconscious.

In conclusion, the dictum that "the unconscious is structured like a language" emerges as a pivotal tenet in comprehending Lacan's psychoanalytic paradigm. Its profound implications extend beyond theoretical discourse, permeating the very essence of human subjectivity and the praxis of psychoanalysis. By embracing this principle, we explore the interconnections between language, the unconscious, and subjective identity, unveiling the profound impact of linguistic structures on the depths of the human psyche.

3. The Triadic Structure - Real, Imaginary, and Symbolic:

Lacan's conceptualization of the human psyche revolves around the triadic structure comprising the Real, Imaginary, and Symbolic orders. Each order plays a crucial role in shaping an individual's perception of reality and understanding of the self within a socio-cultural context. The Real, as posited by Lacan, denotes the unmediated reality that exists beyond linguistic and symbolic representations. It represents the raw, unfiltered experiences that elude linguistic apprehension but nonetheless exert a profound influence on one's psychic constitution.

In contrast, the Imaginary order is characterized by the formation of the ego through identifications and the 'mirror stage.' Here, individuals develop a sense of self through their perceived reflection in others, resulting in a process of identification and ego formation. Lacan emphasizes the pivotal role played by this narcissistic phase in shaping subsequent psychological development and interpersonal relationships.

The Symbolic order, encompassing language, culture, and social norms, constitutes the register where meaning is constructed and communicated. Language, according to Lacan, not only mediates our interaction with the external world but also shapes subjective understandings and desires. Through the acquisition of language, individuals gain access to social signifiers that organize their experiences and position them within broader societal frameworks.

Central to Lacanian theory is the assertion that the three orders are interdependent and mutually constitutive. The Symbolic order necessarily mediates our encounters with the Real, imposing linguistic and cultural filters that shape our perceptions and interpretations of raw experiences. Likewise, the Imaginary order intertwines with the Symbolic, as our identifications and ego formations are inherently tied to culturally conditioned symbols and representations.

4. Critiques and Misconceptions:

Lacanian psychoanalysis, like any influential theoretical framework, is not immune to criticism or misunderstanding. One prevalent critique revolves around Lacan's perceived opacity and esoteric language, with detractors claiming that his work is needlessly convoluted and incomprehensible. However, it is crucial to recognize that Lacan's intentional use of complex terminology is not meant to veil his ideas but rather to mirror the nature of human subjectivity. By engaging with Lacan's concepts in earnest, one can unravel the richness of his formulations and witness the acute insights they offer into the human condition. Another often-misunderstood aspect is Lacan's rejection of the ego, leading to the assumption that his approach disregards individual agency and autonomy. On the contrary, Lacan's deconstruction of the ego serves to underscore the fragmented and constructed nature of identity, emphasizing the role of unconscious forces that shape human behaviors and desires. This does not diminish individual agency but rather elucidates the interplay between conscious intentions and unconscious motivations. Additionally, Lacan has been criticized for focusing excessively on language and the symbolic register, seemingly neglecting material and historical realities. However, such critiques overlook Lacan's profound awareness of the essential dialectical relationship between the symbolic and the material, contending that the symbolic register not only shapes our perception of reality but also molds the very fabric of our experiences. It is crucial to distinguish Lacan's emphasis on the symbolic as an avenue to investigate the intricacies of human subjectivity rather than a denial of material realities. Furthermore, misconceptions often arise regarding Lacan's views on gender and sexuality, with some interpreting his phallic symbol as an endorsement of phallocentrism. However, a more nuanced examination reveals that Lacan's conceptualization of the phallus transcends mere gender binaries or biological determinism, instead alluding to a complex symbolic signifier that operates within the broader framework of desire and lack.

5. The Evolution of Lacan's Theory Over Time:

Lacan's psychoanalytic theory has undergone a fascinating evolution over time, marked by significant shifts and refinements that have shaped its contemporary form. At its inception, Lacan's theory bore strong resemblance to traditional Freudian psychoanalysis, with an emphasis on the centrality of the unconscious and the dynamics of human desire. However, as Lacan delved deeper into linguistics, structuralism, and other intellectual movements, his conceptual framework underwent a profound metamorphosis. This evolution is evident in the development of key concepts such as the mirror stage, the triadic structure of the psyche, and the symbolic order, each representing a pivotal moment in Lacan's theoretical progression. As Lacan engaged with diverse disciplines and expanded his interdisciplinary approach, these evolving influences infused his work with new dimensions of complexity and richness. Moreover, Lacan's evolving stance on the role of language, signification, and the unconscious served as a catalyst for transformative reinterpretations within the field of psychoanalysis. Embracing the linguistic turn, Lacan's integration of Saussure's structural linguistics and the concept of the signifier facilitated a paradigm shift that redefined the understanding of subjectivity and representation within his framework. Concurrently, Lacan's engagement with philosophy and sociology contributed to a refined articulation of his ideas, rendering them both more comprehensive. Furthermore, Lacan's consistent revision of his earlier formulations exemplifies his dedication to continual introspection and refinement, demonstrating an unwavering commitment to the advancement of his psychoanalytic theories.

The Symbolic - Language and Law

1. Introduction:

The concept of the Symbolic Order, central to organizing human experience and consciousness, represents the milieu of language, law, and culture, serving as the framework through which meaning and signification are established. It encompasses the systems of language and communication that enable humans to symbolically represent their experiences and desires, thus mediating their relationship with the external world and other subjects. Moreover, the Symbolic Order plays a pivotal role in the development of social structures, norms, and institutions, thereby influencing the ways in which individuals interact within society. By understanding the Symbolic Order as a fundamental determinant of human existence, we gain insight into the web of symbolic meanings that underpin our subjective realities. Furthermore, the Symbolic Order introduces the notion of 'the Other' as a crucial component in the formation of an individual's identity. This 'Other' is not merely an external entity but a symbolic representation of societal norms, expectations, and ideals that individuals internalize and seek to attain. Through the processes of identification and differentiation within the Symbolic Order, individuals situate themselves within social contexts and construct their sense of self in relation to others. Additionally, the Symbolic Order imposes a system of law and prohibition, represented by the 'paternal metaphor', which governs and regulates human behavior through the establishment of norms, taboos, and moral codes. This legalistic dimension of the Symbolic Order instills a sense of order and structure within the psyche, influencing the formation of individual desire and ethical conduct.

2. The Primacy of Language:

In Lacanian theory, the primacy of language is a foundational concept that underpins the entire psychoanalytic framework. Language, as understood by Lacan, does not merely serve as a tool for communication, but rather constitutes the very structure through which human subjectivity and social relations are organized. This departure from traditional understandings of language places it at the core of the individual's psychic development and the formation of their identity. According to Lacan, the entry into the milieu of language is a decisive moment in an individual's life, marking the transition from the pre-linguistic, imaginary stage to the symbolic order, where language becomes the primary medium through which reality is constructed and communicated. Central to this transition is the acquisition of the symbolic function, symbolizing absence and lack, which shapes the individual's relationship to desire and the world. Furthermore, Lacan emphasizes that language operates not only as a means of expression, but also as a determinant of thought, signifying a close interrelation between language, perception, and cognition. This perspective challenges conventional psycholinguistic views and underscores the profound impact of language on human subjectivity. Moreover, Lacan's understanding of the unconscious as structured like a language points to the inherent connection between linguistic structures and the workings of the psyche. In this regard, the unconscious is not simply a reservoir of repressed desires, but rather a linguistic and symbolic network that governs the individual's experience and behavior. The significance of language in Lacanian theory extends beyond the individual to encompass the social milieu. Language, through its symbolic nature, establishes the framework for intersubjective relations, creating shared meanings and cultural norms that shape collective identities and societal structures. This socio-linguistic dimension highlights the role of language in perpetuating power dynamics, ideological formations, and the construction of truth within a given society. Hence, language is not confined to individual psychology, but serves as a crucial link between the personal and the social, mediating both subjective experience and communal existence.

3. Structural Linguistics and Its Influence on Lacan:

Structural linguistics, a theoretical framework founded by Swiss linguist Ferdinand de Saussure, exerted a profound influence on Jacques Lacan's development of psychoanalytic theory. Saussure, renowned for his groundbreaking work in the field of semiotics, introduced the concept of the linguistic sign as a fundamental unit of language, comprising a signifier and a signified. This pivotal notion served as a cornerstone for Lacan's conceptualization of the unconscious and the construction of subjectivity. Central to structural linguistics is the idea that meaning is generated through differences within the language system rather than inherent connections between words and their referents. Lacan adopted this view and transposed it into the milieu of psychoanalysis, positing that human subjectivity is similarly structured through symbolic systems and the play of difference.

Saussure's dichotomous conception of langue (language system) and parole (actual speech acts) resonated deeply with Lacan's differentiation between the 'symbolic' and the 'imaginary'. By aligning the symbolic order with langue, the system of differential linguistic signs, and the imaginary with parole, the individual's concrete, situational use of language, Lacan elucidated how the interplay between these levels shapes subject formation and desire.

In addition, Saussure's emphasis on the arbitrary nature of the linguistic sign, wherein there is no inherent connection between the signifier and the signified, profoundly informed Lacan's delineation of the 'lack' at the heart of the symbolic order. According to Lacanian theory, this lack is built into the structure of language, engendering a fundamental absence that propels the subject's search for meaning and identity. Moreover, Saussure's notion of the 'diachronic' and 'synchronic' dimensions of language evolution provided Lacan with a framework for understanding the temporal dimension of the unconscious and the coexistence of multiple historical layers within the psyche.

Overall, the marriage of structural linguistics and psychoanalysis in Lacan's work yielded a rich tapestry of insights into the nature of human subjectivity, the functioning of the unconscious, and the dynamics of signification. Through an exploration of these intertwined domains, Lacan opened up new avenues for understanding the complexities of language, the constitution of the self, and the enigmatic terrain of the psyche.

4. The Role of the Father - Law and Prohibition:

In the Lacanian framework, the pivotal function of the father figure relates to the concept of law and prohibition, which plays a crucial part in shaping the subject's entry into the symbolic register. The father is emblematic of the Law, representing a figure of authority and imposition of norms and prohibitions that structure the subject's experience of reality. Through the paternal function, the individual becomes acquainted with societal and cultural rules, setting the stage for their recognition of the constraints and norms governing social existence. The father's presence or absence and the nature of his influence greatly impact the formation of the individual's subjective world. Lacan emphasizes the father's dual role as both the enforcer of law and the object of desire, elucidating the dialectical tension between acceptance of social norms and the pursuit of forbidden desires. This duality creates an internal conflict within the subject, leading to a complex negotiation with the symbolic order. The father's position represents not only the embodiment of authority but also serves as an exemplar for the subject's own aspirations and identifications. Moreover, the father's perceived power shapes the subject's understanding of their position within the broader socio-cultural context. In this way, the father becomes a vehicle through which the subject seeks to engage with the rules and expectations of society, reflecting on their own position vis-à-vis societal norms. Furthermore, Lacan proposes that the father's role is instrumental in mediating the Oedipal dynamic, which involves the subject's struggle to position themselves within the familial structure. The Oedipus complex emerges from the child's relationship with the father and the resulting resolution of tensions and identification with parental figures. Through this process, the child gains access to the symbolic order by relinquishing certain desires and accepting social regulations, thereby paving the way for the development of a cohesive sense of self. Overall, the father's symbolic significance lies in his ability to reinscribe the laws of the society onto the subject, thereby guiding the individual's integration into the cultural fabric while also fueling their yearning for transgression and independence.

5. Symbolic Identification and Subject Formation:

In Lacanian theory, the concept of symbolic identification plays a fundamental role in the formation of subjectivity. The symbolic order, represented by language and law, constructs the framework within which individuals develop a sense of self and identity. As individuals engage with the linguistic and cultural symbols that permeate their environment, they undergo a process of identification that shapes their understanding of themselves and their place within society.

Central to the idea of symbolic identification is the notion of the 'big Other,' which encompasses the social and cultural norms, values, and expectations that individuals internalize as they orient themselves within their social worlds. Through language and communication, individuals are introduced to the symbolic structures that define their reality, and they learn to position themselves within this system. This process of identification is not only a means of aligning oneself with societal conventions but also a mechanism for negotiating desire and its regulation.

Symbolic identification influences the formation of the ego, the ideal-I, and the superego, thereby shaping the subjective experience of the individual. The subject's relationship with the symbolic order is not one of passive acceptance but rather entails complex negotiations and contestations. The tension between conformity to established symbolic norms and the desire for autonomy and self-expression gives rise to the dynamics of subject formation.

Lacan emphasizes the role of trauma and lack in the process of symbolic identification, highlighting how disruptions in the symbolic order can lead to enduring effects on an individual's sense of self. These disruptions may manifest as dissonance between personal aspirations and societal expectations, often precipitating profound psychological turmoil.

The implications of symbolic identification extend to clinical practice, where therapists must remain attuned to the ways in which patients negotiate their identities within the broader symbolic framework. Understanding the nuances of symbolic identification enables clinicians to comprehend the interplay between conscious and unconscious processes, providing valuable insights into the patient's struggles and aspirations.

6. Symbols as Mediators of Desire:

Lacanian desire is a central and complex notion that permeates the psyche, guiding human behavior and shaping individual subjectivity. At its core, desire is not reducible to simple, linear wants or needs – it is intertwined with the structure of the unconscious and the language-based nature of the Symbolic Order. In the Lacanian paradigm, symbols operate as conduits through which desire is both articulated and obscured. It is through the web of linguistic and symbolic representations that desires take shape and are communicated, often in ways that evade direct conscious recognition. The negotiation and expression of desire occur largely within symbols, requiring a nuanced understanding of how these symbols function as mediators between the conscious and unconscious registers. From the Lacanian perspective, desire is inherently bound up with the pursuit and identification with symbolic signifiers – objects, images, words, and cultural constructs that come to represent our most profound longings and unfulfilled aspirations. The inherent inadequacy and elusiveness of these signifiers contribute to the perpetual nature of desire, perpetuating a relentless quest for the unattainable and the ineffable. Moreover, symbols do not merely passively represent desires; rather, they actively shape and construct them, influencing the ways in which individuals conceive, pursue, and experience their desires within the framework of the Symbolic Order. Lacanian theory emphasizes that this complex interplay between symbols and desire extends beyond personal longing and resonates within larger societal structures. Within social and cultural contexts, symbols hold significant power in shaping collective desires and notions of fulfillment, often perpetuating deeply ingrained socio-cultural norms and ideals. Furthermore, the mediated nature of desire through symbols introduces a layer of indirection, wherein individuals engage with desires indirectly, filtered through the symbolic landscape. This interrelationship between symbols and desire underscores the pivotal role of the Symbolic Order in shaping human subjectivity and illuminates the fundamental influence of symbols as mediators of desire.

7. Language as a Structure for Social Relationships:

Language, within Lacan's theory, emerges as a quintessential structure that not only shapes individual subjectivity but also acts as a pervasive force in shaping social relationships. Within this context, the Symbolic Order, of which language is a fundamental constituent, serves as the medium through which human subjects establish and engage with their positions within the socio-cultural landscape. In understanding language as a structure for social relationships, it becomes imperative to delve into the ways in which linguistic systems operate to mediate interactions and organize societal dynamics. Linguistic communication, whether verbal or non-verbal, conveys and reinforces norms, values, and power dynamics within a given community or society. Through the use of language, individuals negotiate their identities, assert their affiliations, and engage in processes of inclusion and exclusion. The formation of social bonds and hierarchies is deeply intertwined with linguistic practices, as individuals position themselves within networks of relationships based on shared meanings and understandings facilitated by language. Furthermore, the symbolic nature of language implicates it in the construction and perpetuation of socio-cultural narratives, defining collective histories, belief systems, and moral codes. Language as a vehicle of discourse shapes the development of social institutions, influencing legal, political, and ethical frameworks that govern interactions among members of a community. It catalyzes the transmission of cultural knowledge and traditions, contributing to the continuity and evolution of social structures. Moreover, language operates as an apparatus for the exercise of power, as it can be employed to reinforce or subvert existing social hierarchies and to mobilize collective action. Analyzing language as a structure for social relationships necessitates addressing issues of access, representation, and voice within diverse linguistic communities, acknowledging the differential impact language has on various social groups. These considerations highlight the multifaceted role of language in constructing, reinforcing, and transforming social relationships, underscoring its centrality within the complex fabric of human interactions.

8. Interplay Between the Symbolic and Other Orders:

The Symbolic Order, primarily defined by language and law, acts as a structuring force that interacts with the other two orders in shaping an individual's psyche and experiences. The Symbolic order, through its linguistic and regulatory functions, imposes a framework of meanings and norms onto the individual, influencing the construction of their identity and perceptions of reality. This interplay between the Symbolic and the Imaginary can be observed in the mirror stage, where the development of the ego is intertwined with language acquisition and societal norms, leading to a sense of recognition and misrecognition. Furthermore, the Symbolic Order also intersects with the Real, as it attempts to symbolize and represent the unattainable aspects of experience, such as trauma and fundamental lack. This intersection often results in conflicts and contradictions, highlighting the inherent tensions within the human psyche. Understanding the interdependence of the Symbolic, Imaginary, and Real Orders is essential in psychoanalytic practice, as it provides insight into the dynamics of unconscious processes and the formation of symptoms. Recognizing how these orders interact allows clinicians to manage the complexities of transference and countertransference, enabling a deeper understanding of the patient's subjective experience and internal conflicts. Moreover, the interplay between these orders underscores the relevance of cultural and societal influences on individual subjectivity, emphasizing the need to consider broader socio-political contexts in clinical work. By exploring the dynamic relationships between the Symbolic and other orders, practitioners can offer more comprehensive and nuanced interventions that address the multifaceted nature of human psychic life.

9. Clinical Implications of the Symbolic:

The clinical implications of the Symbolic in Lacanian theory are profound and far-reaching, influencing the practice of psychoanalysis in numerous ways. One significant implication lies in its role in shaping the structure of the unconscious. By recognizing the centrality of language and its impact on subjectivity, clinicians can gain a deeper understanding of the symbolic framework within which their patients operate. Language not only shapes thought and perception but also structures desires and identifications. Therapists can leverage this understanding to interpret the symbolic manifestations in their patients' speech, dreams, and associations, thereby gaining access to the underlying unconscious conflicts and repressed material.

The Symbolic Order illuminates the nature of transference and countertransference in the therapeutic relationship. Through the lens of the Symbolic, clinicians can comprehend the complex interplay of unconscious identifications and projections that color the therapeutic process. This awareness enables therapists to manage the transference dynamics more effectively, facilitating the analysis of patients' relational patterns and deep-seated emotional entanglements. By grasping the Symbolic underpinnings of transference, therapists can guide patients towards a greater understanding of their unconscious investments in the therapeutic space.

Additionally, the Symbolic Order informs the understanding of symptoms and psychopathology. It underscores the significance of language and social norms in the manifestation of symptoms, emphasizing that symptoms are not merely individual expressions but are embedded in the broader socio-linguistic context. Clinicians can employ this understanding to deconstruct the symbolic meanings encoded in their patients' symptoms, unpacking the layers of signification and uncovering the underlying conflicts and unconscious dynamics.

The Symbolic provides a framework for comprehending resistance and the patient's adherence to the status quo. By recognizing the ways in which the Symbolic Order governs the subject's relation to authority and ideology, clinicians can elucidate the patient's resistance to change and their investment in maintaining the existing symbolic configurations. This insight equips therapists to address and work through resistance more effectively, fostering meaningful therapeutic progress.

10. The Legacy of the Symbolic Order:

The Symbolic Order, constituting the milieu of language, law, and symbolic structures, permeates every aspect of human experience, shaping individual identities and interpersonal dynamics. Its pervasive influence manifests in the ways individuals engage with the enculturation process. From early childhood, individuals are enmeshed in a web of signifiers, norms, and linguistic systems that shape their perceptions and behaviors. The Symbolic Order, with its emphasis on language and social regulations, provides a conceptual apparatus for comprehending the mechanisms through which individuals internalize societal expectations and negotiate their desires within the constraints of the symbolic framework.

The legacy of the Symbolic Order reverberates across clinical settings, offering profound insights for therapeutic interventions. By recognizing the centrality of language and the symbolic in shaping psychological distress and subjective conflicts, clinicians can attend to the ways in which patients articulate their experiences and grapple with unconscious determinants. Understanding the symbolic dimension of human experiences allows for nuanced interpretations of symptoms and facilitates deeper explorations of meaning within the therapeutic encounter.

Furthermore, the implications of the Symbolic Order extend beyond the confines of clinical practice, positioning itself as a critical tool for deconstructing power differentials and societal stratifications. Through examining the functioning of symbolic structures in perpetuating hierarchical relations and normative standards, this framework opens avenues for critical inquiries into social justice, identity politics, and emancipatory movements. By interrogating the symbolic underpinnings of systemic inequalities, scholars and activists can incite transformative change and advocate for more equitable social configurations.

In essence, the legacy of the Symbolic Order beckons us to reckon with the tapestry of symbols, words, and cultural edifices that mold our collective existence. Its relevance persists in unraveling the enigmas of human subjectivity, elucidating the dynamics of power and authority, and fostering empathic engagements that honor the polyphony of voices within our social fabric.

The Imaginary - Mirrors and Misrecognitions

1. Introduction:

The Imaginary Order represents a crucial dimension of human subjectivity and identity formation. It functions as one of the three primary orders, alongside the Symbolic and the Real, in explicating the complexities of the human psyche from a structural standpoint. The term 'Imaginary' in this context does not solely imply the unreal or imaginary in a colloquial sense. Rather, it encompasses images, perceptions, and identifications that mediate individual experiences and understandings of self and other. At the core of the Imaginary Order lies the lacuna or lack inherent in the human condition, contributing to a perpetual quest for wholeness and unity. Introduction to the Imaginary Order seeks to elucidate how early interpersonal relationships and visual representations play a pivotal role in the development of the ego and its subsequent sense of identity. Furthermore, it endeavors to explicate the fundamental tension between the internal subjective idealized self and the external mirrored representations that shape our self-perception.

2. The Mirror Stage - Origins and Implications:

The Mirror Stage elucidates the formative processes of the imaginary order. Coined by Jacques Lacan in 1936, this developmental phase explores the infant's encounter with its own image in a mirror and the ensuing implications for subjectivity and identity construction. The mirror stage is not merely a physical act of looking into a reflective surface; rather, it symbolizes a transformative moment wherein the child becomes cognizant of its own corporeal existence and recognizes itself as a separate entity. This pivotal realization engenders profound consequences for the child's evolving sense of selfhood and interpersonal relations.

The origins of the mirror stage can be traced to Lacan's interdisciplinary approach, drawing inspiration from Freudian psychoanalysis, phenomenology, and infant development research. Lacan posited that the mirror stage represents a critical juncture in the individual's psychic development, wherein the ego begins to take shape through a process of identification and alienation. By apprehending its reflected image as an idealized and coherent whole, the infant enters into a dialectical relationship with its fragmented and uncoordinated body, laying the groundwork for the formation of the ego and its subsequent integration into the symbolic order.

The implications of the mirror stage extend beyond the individual's psychological constitution, permeating various domains of social, cultural, and artistic expressions. Lacan contends that the fascination with one's mirror image and the perpetual pursuit of unity and mastery stemmed from this primordial experience of misrecognition. Consequently, the inherent tension between the idealized self-image and the dissonance with one's actual being gives rise to enduring quests for selfhood and fulfillment, generating manifold consequences for human desires and aspirations.

The mirror stage prompts us to reconsider conventional notions of selfhood and subjectivity within the broader scope of Lacanian theory. While deeply entrenched in early childhood development, the underpinnings of the mirror stage continue to resonate throughout the life course, permeating adult perceptions of identity, relationships, and existential dilemmas. By situating the mirror stage within a broader framework of psychoanalytic inquiry, we gain deeper insights into the complexities of human subjectivity and the effects of early experiences on psychic formations.

3. Concept of Misrecognition in Lacanian Theory:

The concept of misrecognition in Lacanian theory is rooted in the idea that individuals often misunderstand their own identities and perceive themselves through a distorted lens. This misrecognition, or *méconnaissance* in French, occurs within the Imaginary order, where the ego takes shape through identification with external images and ideals. The process of misrecognition is central to Lacan's understanding of the formation of subjectivity and plays a pivotal role in shaping an individual's relationship with the self and the Other.

At its core, misrecognition involves an inherent inability to accurately recognize oneself as a separate entity, distinct from the objects and individuals in the external world. The construction of the ego is intertwined with an illusory sense of cohesiveness and completeness derived from mirroring processes, wherein the subject identifies with an external image, typically manifested in early childhood experiences. This identification establishes a foundation for the development of the ego, yet simultaneously engenders a sense of alienation and fragmentation within the individual.

Lacan contends that misrecognition precipitates a perpetual desire for unity and wholeness, prompting individuals to seek affirmation and validation from external sources, such as peers, authority figures, and societal norms. Consequently, the pursuit of recognition becomes a dominant force driving human behavior, inherently tied to the perpetual quest for a perceived 'ideal-I' that remains elusive. This dynamic underpins Lacan's assertion that the ego's construction is intrinsically flawed, as it hinges on the illusion of self-coherence and completeness perpetuated by misrecognition.

The concept of misrecognition extends beyond the individual level and permeates societal structures, shaping collective perceptions and interactions. Lacan's exploration of misrecognition elucidates the inherent discrepancies and tensions present in interpersonal relationships and social systems, underscoring the pervasive nature of illusions and false assumptions that underpin human interactions. This insight has profound implications for understanding power dynamics, alienation, and the perpetuation of false ideologies within broader socio-political contexts.

4. Formation of the Ego Through Reflection:

When a child undergoes the mirror stage, they encounter a critical juncture in their psychological development wherein the reflection in the mirror becomes a locus for self-recognition and identification. This pivotal encounter with the specular image fosters the embryo of the ego, marking the genesis of individuation and a sense of distinct subjectivity.

Lacan's proposition of the mirror stage posits that the child experiences a form of jubilation as they perceive themselves as a unified, coherent entity in the mirror, thereby creating an idealized, yet illusory, image of themselves. The reflection not only engenders a sense of unity but also imparts a feeling of mastery and autonomy over one's own body. This process contributes to the construction of the ego as the child perceives the mirror image as a more complete and proficient version of themselves.

The mirror stage is not limited to the mere act of visual recognition; rather, it encompasses a profound psychological experience that shapes one's subjective understanding of themselves and their relationship to the external world. The mirroring process instigates an internal dialogical exchange, in which the child evaluates their own physicality and strives to reconcile their inner sensations with the outward reflection. In this evaluative process, the child endeavors to attain a self-image that aligns with the external representation, giving rise to the formation of the ego.

Crucially, Lacan emphasizes the inherently dualistic nature of the mirror stage, wherein the reflected image presents an idealized and cohesive impression that stands in stark contrast to the child's fragmented and incomplete self-experience. This discord between the perceived unity in the mirror and the disarray within the subjective sphere engenders a perpetual sense of inadequacy and alienation, underpinning the subsequent psychological dynamics of desire and lack.

However, it is essential to acknowledge that the mirror stage does not denote the culmination of ego development, but rather initiates a lifelong pursuit for completeness and coherence within the individual's self-concept. It lays the groundwork for the continual negotiation of identity, serving as a foundational aspect in understanding the complexities of subjectivity and the ego's inherent connection to the external gaze.

5. Imaginary Identification and Subjectivity:

In the Lacanian framework, the concept of 'imaginary identification' revolves around the formation of the ego through a complex interplay between internal and external perceptions. As individuals engage with the mirror image during the formative stages of development, they encounter a semblance that becomes integral to their self-concept. The mirroring process fosters a sense of coherence and unity as the individual identifies with the reflected image, thereby initiating the construction of the imaginary ego. This identification is not merely a passive recognition but rather an active assimilation of the visual representation, laying the foundation for subsequent imaginative identifications in social interactions and relationships. The strength of this identification is such that the individual often strives to align their actions and behaviors with the perceived ideal reflected in the mirror. Furthermore, the influence of societal norms and expectations amplifies this process, leading to the internalization of culturally defined ideals and standards of beauty, success, and desirability. Consequently, the imaginary identification perpetuates a continuous pursuit of fulfillment and validation based on these external constructs. Within this context, the subjective experience is deeply intertwined with the imaginary register, as the individual's sense of self is linked to these idealized images and representations. The interplay between the imagined ego and external influences shapes not only the individual's perception of self but also their understanding of others. The implications of imaginary identification extend beyond the individual, impacting interpersonal dynamics and communication patterns. These identifications can lead to an unconscious projection of one's internal desires, anxieties, and conflicts onto others, thus influencing their interpretations and interactions within the social sphere. Additionally, the intersection of the imaginary and symbolic orders significantly contributes to the complexities of subjectivity, as these registers intertwine to shape an individual's sense of identity and meaning-making processes.

6. Role of Duality in the Imaginary:

The role of duality within the Imaginary order draws attention to the fundamental schism that defines subjectivity. At its core, the Imaginary is built upon the dialectics of identification and alienation, which manifest as a fundamental duality within the individual's psychic structure. This duality is epitomized in the concept of the mirror stage, where the infant's self-recognition gives birth to a fractured sense of identity. Here, the image in the mirror both reflects and distorts, creating a dualistic representation that becomes foundational to the construction of the ego.

The duality within the Imaginary order extends beyond mere self-perception, permeating the broader landscape of human experience. It encapsulates the tension between the idealized 'mirror' image, representing the cohesive and perfected self, and the disarrayed 'actual' self, mired in imperfections and vulnerabilities. This fundamental bifurcation engenders a perennial struggle for wholeness and unity, often leading individuals toward the pursuit of unattainable ideals and external validations in an attempt to reconcile this inherent duality.

The dualistic nature of the Imaginary order also resonates within interpersonal dynamics and social relationships. The perpetual quest for recognition and validation stems from the desire to mend the ruptured self-image, leading to complex patterns of projection and introjection that underpin human interactions. The internal division engendered by the Imaginary duality thus echoes through the societal fabric, influencing the collective construction of symbolic meanings and representations.

The influence of duality extends beyond the individual and relational spheres, seeping into the broader cultural and historical contexts. Lacan posited that the Cartesian mind-body dichotomy and the enlightenment's emphasis on rationality are emblematic of the Imaginary duality's pervasive impact. Moreover, societal constructs such as gender binarism and racial dichotomies underscore the deep-seated influence of the Imaginary's dualistic structure on collective discourse and power dynamics.

This profound entrenchment of duality within the Imaginary order prompts an introspective interrogation of its implications on subject formation, interpersonal engagements, and sociocultural paradigms. By delving into the interplay of identifications and alienations, we unravel the complex tapestry of human subjectivity, paving the way for a more nuanced understanding of the mechanisms that propel our experiences and interactions.

7. Intersection of the Imaginary and Symbolic Orders:

In Lacanian psychoanalytic theory, the concepts of the Imaginary and Symbolic orders are linked, forming a complex interplay that significantly influences an individual's subjective experience and understanding of the world. The Imaginary order primarily revolves around visual images, with an emphasis on the formation of ego through identification and mirroring processes. On the other hand, the Symbolic order is rooted in the milieu of language, law, and cultural norms, serving as the domain where meaning is generated and signifiers acquire significance. Despite their apparent differences, these two orders intersect in profound ways, shaping human subjectivity and perception.

At the intersection of the Imaginary and Symbolic orders lies the pivotal concept of the 'mirror stage.' As the child identifies with the idealized image reflected back to them, they begin to construct a sense of self, albeit one that is illusory and fragmented. This process not only signifies the entwinement of the Imaginary and the formation of the ego but also marks the initial entry of the subject into the Symbolic order through language-mediated interactions with others.

The intersection of the Imaginary and Symbolic orders can be observed in the concept of phallic signification. In Lacanian theory, the phallus represents not merely a biological organ but a symbol that encapsulates the lack and desire inherent in human subjectivity. The phallus operates as a key signifier within the Symbolic order, mediating relations of power, authority, and desire. Simultaneously, the phallus also holds significance within the Imaginary register, serving as a symbol of unattainable completeness and engendering feelings of lack and inadequacy within the ego.

The intersection of these orders becomes salient in the analysis of fantasy and imaginary constructs. Within the symbolic register, fantasy is shaped through language and cultural narratives, imbuing it with specific meanings and connotations. However, these fantasies are often deeply rooted in the Imaginary as they stem from early childhood experiences and unconscious formations of self-image. Thus, the intersection between the two orders complicates the analysis of fantasies, requiring a nuanced understanding of both the linguistic and visual dimensions that underpin them.

8. Critical Perspectives on the Imaginary Order:

In scrutinizing the role of the Imaginary, critics have underscored both its significance in understanding human subjectivity and its potential limitations as a theoretical construct. One key critique revolves around the perceived overemphasis on visual identification through the mirror stage, which may neglect other sensory and affective dimensions of human experience. Critics argue that an exclusive focus on visual recognition could overshadow the complexities of human subjectivity, leading to an oversimplified model of identity formation. Additionally, scholars have questioned the universality of the mirror stage's applicability across diverse cultural and historical contexts. This critique calls for a more nuanced understanding of self-identification that accommodates cultural variations and individual differences. Another critical perspective pertains to the inherent dualistic nature of the Imaginary order, which is often depicted as a binary opposition between the subject and the (idealized) other. Critics assert that this binary framework may obscure the interplay of power dynamics, relationality, and multiplicity inherent in human identity construction. Moreover, some scholars have raised concerns about the risk of essentialism in equating the Imaginary with fixed, static representations of the self, overlooking the fluid and contingent nature of subjectivity. Criticism regarding the application of the Imaginary order in clinical practice has also been articulated, with some practitioners advocating for a more integrative approach that acknowledges the complex interweaving of the Imaginary, Symbolic, and Real in psychoanalytic treatment. Despite these critical stances, proponents of Lacanian theory argue that the Imaginary order offers valuable insights into the formation of the ego, intersubjective relations, and the constitution of desire. They contend that the visual metaphor of the mirror stage serves as a potent heuristic device for comprehending the developmental trajectory of subjectivity, albeit acknowledging the necessity of complementing it with other sensory modalities. Furthermore, defenders of the Imaginary defend its conceptual duality as essential for apprehending the structural tensions inherent in human identity negotiation.

The Real - Beyond the Apparent

1. Introduction:

The concept of the 'Real' holds a unique and enigmatic position within Lacanian psychoanalysis, evoking both fascination and perplexity. It serves as a crucial cornerstone in comprehending the dynamics of human subjectivity and plays a pivotal role in shaping Lacan's tripartite model of the psyche. Although the notion of the Real resists precise delineation, its significance is unmistakably profound. Within Lacanian discourse, the Real is not simply synonymous with empirical reality or tangible existence;

rather, it encompasses an elusive, ungraspable domain that transcends perceptual immediacy. It elicits a sense of unease and disquiet, as it challenges our conventional understanding of what is deemed 'real' in everyday experience. The Real, as expounded by Lacan, traverses the terrain of absence and impossibility, defying straightforward categorization. As such, it prompts an ongoing quest for deciphering its complexities and ramifications.

2. Historical Context and Evolution:

The origins of the Real can be traced back to Lacan's radical rethinking of Freudian psychoanalysis in the mid-20th century. Influenced by structural linguistics, anthropology, and philosophy, Lacan sought to redefine traditional psychoanalytic concepts, leading him to introduce the Real as a crucial component of his theoretical framework.

The early development of the Real can be linked to Lacan's engagement with the works of prominent thinkers such as Saussure, Levi-Strauss, and Hegel. These intellectual influences provided fertile ground for Lacan to construct a novel understanding of the human subject and its relationship to language, culture, and the unconscious. Through a dialectical process of synthesis and critique, Lacan gradually articulated the concept of the Real as distinct from the Symbolic and the Imaginary, thereby laying the groundwork for its subsequent exploration and elaboration.

As Lacanian theory evolved, the concept of the Real underwent significant refinement and elaboration. It became increasingly evident that the Real transcended mere physical or empirical reality, extending into symbolic, linguistic, and existential dimensions. This expansion of the Real's scope paralleled broader developments in poststructuralist philosophy and critical theory, further embedding it within the interdisciplinary discourse of the time.

In the trajectory of Lacanian thought, the concept of the Real continued to evolve, intersecting with diverse intellectual currents and theoretical paradigms. From its foundational articulation as a gap or lack in the Symbolic order to its more nuanced conceptualizations informed by mathematics, topology, and quantum physics, the historical trajectory of the Real reflects a rich tapestry of intellectual exchange and theoretical innovation.

The international dissemination of Lacanian psychoanalysis facilitated cross-cultural encounters and dialogues, engendering diverse interpretations and applications of the Real within different cultural and clinical contexts. This global diffusion contributed to the enrichment and diversification of perspectives on the Real, expanding its relevance beyond the confines of Western intellectual traditions.

3. The Interplay between the Real, Symbolic, and Imaginary:

The interplay between these three registers forms the basis of the human psyche as delineated by Jacques Lacan. The Real, often considered enigmatic and ineffable, stands as the foundational register that eludes symbolization and representation. It operates outside the planes of language and meaning, existing as an ungraspable presence that disrupts the coherence of the Symbolic order. In contrast, the Symbolic encompasses the milieu of language, law, and societal norms, where signifiers and signifieds construct the fabric of meaning and cultural reality for the subject. Importantly, the Symbolic mediates the subject's interaction with the social world and sets the stage for the internalization of identity through linguistic and symbolic structures. Additionally, the Imaginary, characterized by identifications and imaginings, serves as the site of ego formation and narcissistic identifications, particularly through the mirror stage. This register is intertwined with visual images and illusions that contribute to the construction of the subject's self-image and idealized representations of the 'other.' The dynamic interplay among these registers constitutes the fundamental framework through which human subjectivity is constituted and mediated. It is within this interplay that the tensions and conflicts arising from the coexistence of these registers come into play. The Real constantly destabilizes the Symbolic order, introducing ruptures and disturbances that resist integration and symbolization. Simultaneously, the Symbolic structures and regulates the Real, imposing sociocultural frameworks upon the ungraspable nature of the Real. The Imaginary, in turn, bridges and complicates the relationship between the Real and the Symbolic by offering semblances and identifications that seek to stabilize and solidify experiences. These continuous negotiations among the registers precipitate the complexities of psychic life, marking the terrain on which desires, fantasies, and resistances unfold. Moreover, the interplay between these dimensions elucidates the mechanisms underlying the formation of symptomatology and the intricacies of therapeutic interventions within the Lacanian framework.

4. Representations of the Real in Psychoanalytic Practice:

The Real, as elucidated by Lacan, exists beyond language and symbolic representation, making its presence felt through gaps, fractures, and disruptions in the symbolic order. Consequently, representations of the Real in clinical settings often emerge in paradoxical and enigmatic ways. This phenomenon can be observed when patients express unarticulated feelings or experiences that resist symbolization and linguistic capture. Such ineffable manifestations of the Real pose a fundamental challenge for psychoanalysts, who strive to engage with the contours of the unconscious and confront the limits of verbal expression. Moreover, the Real frequently surfaces in moments of rupture within the therapeutic process, compelling practitioners to acknowledge the inherent limitations of interpretation and meaning-making. These instances demand a heightened sensitivity to non-verbal cues, affective tonalities, and bodily gestures, as they may serve as conduits for encounters with the unassimilable Real. Furthermore, the Real materializes in the transference dynamics between analyst and analysand, often disrupting the carefully constructed semblance of the symbolic rapport. This disruption can destabilize established power dynamics and authority structures, requiring the practitioner to grapple with their own subjective implication in the analysand's subjective reality. By recognizing these representations of the Real, clinicians can cultivate a nuanced sensitivity to the complexities of human subjectivity, paving the way for a more attuned and responsive psychoanalytic praxis. Integration of the Real into clinical work extends beyond merely acknowledging its existence; it necessitates the cultivation of a reflexive mode of engagement wherein the analyst remains vigilant about the continual intrusion of the Real into the analytic space. Developing an awareness of how the Real permeates the clinical encounter enables practitioners to manage uncertainty and ambiguity with humility and openness, acknowledging that some facets of human experience may defy rational comprehension. This process invites a dynamic reconfiguration of the therapist–patient relationship, one that thrives on a willingness to engage with the ungraspable dimensions of psychic life. As such, representations of the Real in psychoanalytic practice beckon analysts to foreground receptivity, attunement, and reverence for the unfathomable aspects of human subjectivity.

5. Challenges in Engaging with the Real:

Engaging with the concept of the Real within psychoanalytic practice presents a myriad of challenges that practitioners must manage. One of the foremost difficulties lies in the very nature of the Real itself – as Lacan famously posited, the Real is inherently elusive and resistant to symbolization. This fundamental resistance poses a significant challenge for analysts who seek to apprehend and work with the underlying realities of their patients' experiences. Moreover, the very act of attempting to represent the Real inevitably leads to its distortion, as it transcends linguistic and conceptual limitations.

Another key challenge arises from the daunting task of distinguishing between the Real and its imbrication with the Imaginary and the Symbolic. Given that these three dimensions are inextricably intertwined, disentangling the pure Real from its interplay with the other psychic registers is a complex and delicate endeavor. Additionally, the Real often manifests through phenomena that defy traditional modes of rational comprehension, rendering it an enigmatic and perplexing aspect of human subjectivity.

Practitioners also face the challenge of effectively integrating the insights gleaned from encountering the Real into their clinical practice. The transformative potential of engaging with the Real necessitates a reevaluation of conventional therapeutic approaches, demanding a nuanced understanding of the ways in which the Real disrupts and reshapes established treatment paradigms. Furthermore, the ethical considerations surrounding the revelation of the Real in clinical contexts cannot be overlooked, as such encounters may provoke profound existential upheaval for both the analyst and the analysand.

Another crucial obstacle emerges from the inevitable limitations of language and discourse in capturing the essence of the Real. Language, being grounded in the Symbolic order, inherently veils the raw intensity of Real experience, evoking a tension between articulating the ineffable and acknowledging its inherent resistance to representation. This linguistic impasse raises critical questions about the communicability of the Real and the potential distortions imposed by the very act of verbalizing it.

The pervasive influence of cultural and societal constructs adds further complexity to the engagement with the Real. The ways in which socially constructed norms and expectations shape individuals' encounters with the Real exemplify the interconnections between the personal and the collective dimensions of human existence, adding layers of complexity to the already labyrinthine terrain of the Real.

6. Philosophical Underpinnings of the Real:

The notion of the Real intersects with fundamental inquiries that have preoccupied philosophers across civilizations and epochs, inviting an interdisciplinary dialogue that enriches its comprehension. From the ancient metaphysical musings on the nature of reality to the existential contemplations on authenticity and existence, the philosophical tapestry woven around the Real embodies a rich reservoir of intellectual discourse. Within this web of ideas, Lacan's conceptualization of the Real holds resonance with diverse philosophical paradigms, offering a lens through which to engage with perennial questions about human consciousness, perception, and truth. Central to this inquiry is the ontological delineation of the Real as distinct from both the Symbolic and the Imaginary. Drawing from phenomenological traditions, the Real necessitates a departure from representation and language, evoking considerations of lived experience, embodiment, and the ineffable dimensions of being. Existentialist inquiries into subjectivity and the apprehension of the external world converge with Lacanian insights, gesturing towards the profound implications of the Real for individual selfhood and intersubjective encounters. Furthermore, the dialectical tensions inherent in the encounter with the Real evoke resonances with Hegelian thought, prompting contemplation on the fluid interplay between absence and presence, negation and affirmation. Such explorations serve to illuminate the ways in which the Real disrupts conventional modes of comprehension, destabilizing entrenched frameworks and demanding a reorientation of philosophical conceptions. Additionally, engagements with the Real resonate with poststructuralist interrogations of power, knowledge, and discourse. Intersecting with Foucauldian analyses of the operation of power within systems of representation, Lacan's Real unveils the fractures and aporias in discursive formations, intimating at the disruptions that rupture the fabric of symbolic order. It is within these liminal spaces that the philosophical significance of the Real unfolds, nurturing an expansive terrain of inquiry that reverberates far beyond the confines of psychoanalytic discourse.

7. The Real's Role in Lacanian Diagnostics:

In Lacanian diagnostics, the concept of the Real exerts a profound influence on the psychoanalytic process. Grounded in the tapestry of Lacanian theory, the Real serves as a conceptual cornerstone, transcending mere theoretical abstraction to permeate the lived experiences of both analysts and analysands. It necessitates a nuanced exploration to decipher its implications within diagnostic frameworks.

Central to Lacan's diagnostic approach is the recognition of the limitations of language and symbolism in encapsulating the totality of human subjectivity. Unlike the Symbolic and the Imaginary, which are imbued with representational elements, the Real resists symbolization and remains beyond linguistic capture. Its indescribable essence poses a formidable challenge for clinicians seeking to engage with the raw, unmediated aspects of their patients' psyches. As such, the Real prompts a reconfiguration of traditional diagnostic paradigms, calling for a departure from conventional interpretative methods to engage with the enigmatic terrain of subjective realities.

Within Lacanian diagnostics, the Real functions as an elusive yet indispensable compass, steering clinical inquiry towards uncharted depths of the unconscious. It dismantles the illusory façade constructed by the Imaginary and disrupts the semblance of order perpetuated by the Symbolic, unraveling the inherent dissonance and ineffable truths that underpin human existence. The clinician's encounter with the Real engenders a transformative reorientation, inviting a radical reconsideration of assumed certainties and entrenched interpretations.

The Real's impalpable nature confronts clinicians with the unfiltered expressions of trauma, desire, and existential anguish that evade symbolic articulation. This exposure to the unadulterated core of human suffering necessitates a vigilant attunement to non-verbal cues, affective resonances, and somatic manifestations that emanate from the Real. It compels clinicians to adopt a receptive stance that transcends verbal dialogue, fostering an environment where the unspeakable can find resonance and validation within the therapeutic space.

Consequently, the clinical integration of the Real demands a recalibration of diagnostic sensitivity, urging practitioners to exquisitely attune themselves to the disquieting disturbances and aporias that surface within the therapeutic encounter. This entails a departure from diagnostic reductionism, eschewing the temptation to prematurely confine complex psychic phenomena within familiar taxonomies or predefined categories. Instead, it invites an embrace of uncertainty and openness to the latent revelations afforded by confronting the ineffable magnitude of the Real.

Ultimately, the Real's role in Lacanian diagnostics unfolds as a transformative odyssey, engendering a humbling recognition of the irreducible alterity and primal authenticity inherent to each analysand's subjective universe. Embracing the Real beckons clinicians to traverse the liminal spaces of human experience, charting a path through the uncharted terrains of psychic disruption and existential vulnerability. With its profound implications for clinical praxis, the Real emerges as a potent force that animates the continual evolution of Lacanian diagnostics, reshaping the contours of therapeutic engagement and enriching the tapestry of human understanding.

8. Implications for Clinical Practice:

The implications of the Lacanian concept of the Real for clinical practice are manifold, as this fundamental component of human subjectivity carries significant weight in psychoanalytic treatment. Perhaps one of the most profound implications lies in the acknowledgment of the Real's pervasive presence in the patient's psyche, often manifesting as unspoken, unprocessed traumas and unresolved conflicts. Recognizing the impact of the Real on the analysand's subjective experience is crucial for the analyst, as it directs attention to the underlying factors influencing the individual's symptoms, behaviors, and interpersonal relationships.

The Lacanian view of the Real calls for an expanded understanding of resistance in clinical settings. The Real, characterized by its resistance to symbolization, challenges the conventional therapeutic approach, necessitating a nuanced framework to address the unspeakable and the inaccessible within the patient's psychic structure. Therapists must manage this uncharted territory with sensitivity and finesse, encouraging a reevaluation of traditional techniques and interventions that may not adequately engage with the profound impact of the Real.

Embracing the implications of the Real for clinical practice involves redefining the nature of therapeutic transference. The Real's disruptive influence on the symbolic order often manifests in non-verbal, affect-laden communications, altering the dynamics of transference and countertransference. Understanding the ways in which the Real permeates these relational dynamics allows for a more comprehensive grasp of the patient's unconscious processes, shedding light on otherwise concealed aspects of their internal world.

In a broader sense, the implications of the Real extend beyond the confines of the consulting room, reverberating through the socio-cultural and political dimensions of psychoanalysis. The recognition of the Real prompts a critical examination of societal constructs, power differentials, and systemic injustices, urging practitioners to consider the broader socio-political context in which their patients are situated. This necessitates a reorientation of clinical praxis that acknowledges the intersectionality of the patient's experiences and the potent influence of the Real on their lived realities.

Ultimately, grappling with the implications of the Real underscores the imperative for ongoing reflexivity and self-interrogation within the therapeutic dyad. By acknowledging the complexities of the Real and its ramifications for clinical work, therapists are propelled into a deeper engagement with the intricacies of human subjectivity, paving the way for more holistic and profound healing processes.

The Role of Jouissance in the Three Orders

1. Introduction:

Jouissance, a concept central to Lacanian psychoanalysis, rends the fabric of traditional understanding of pleasure. It transcends the mere pursuit of hedonistic satisfaction outlined in Freud's Pleasure Principle, edging towards an enigmatic domain punctuated by excess and even pain. In delving deeper into the intricacies of Jouissance, one ventures on a journey that unsettles conventional psychological paradigms and beckons the exploration of the intrinsic desires that operate beyond conscious cognition. This vantage point invites a departure from the conventional dichotomy of pleasure and unpleasure. Instead, it introduces a nuanced comprehension of subjective experiences that exist at the interstices of delight and anguish, traversing boundaries conceptualized in the Pleasure Principle. Jouissance disrupts the established equilibrium posited by the pleasure-seeking inclination highlighted in Freudian theory, for it encompasses a terrain where gratification intersects with discomfort in convoluted ways. By unraveling this complex interplay, individuals gain insight into the elusive nature of their aspirations and the underlying tensions that punctuate human experience. Within this paradigm, one encounters an uncharted dialectic between enjoyment and suffering that defies the simplistic binaries of pleasure and pain, demanding a recalibration of perceptual frameworks. Discerning the inscrutable contours of Jouissance requires an acknowledgment of its multi-faceted dimensions, provoking an interrogation of the very essence of pleasure itself. As we embark on this expedition, it becomes imperative to explore through the corridors of human desire, expanding our consciousness to encompass the immeasurable nuances that transcend traditional understandings of gratification. Imperceptible to the untrained eye, the phenomenon of Jouissance unravels a rich tapestry of human emotions that eludes the linearity underpinning the Pleasure Principle. Hence, it is incumbent upon us to acknowledge the profound implications inherent in venturing 'beyond pleasure,' embracing the disquieting allure of Jouissance that heralds a departure from conventional modes of psychological inquiry.

2. Jouissance in the Symbolic Order - The Law and its Transgressions:

In Lacanian theory, jouissance within the symbolic order is intertwined with the concept of law and transgressions. The symbolic order constitutes the domain of language, culture, and societal norms – the network of signifiers that govern human subjectivity. Here, jouissance is entangled with the restrictions and regulations imposed by the law, constituting a complex interplay between desire and its regulatory mechanisms.

Lacan posits that the symbolic order imposes a set of laws and rules that circumscribe the boundaries of individual desire. Jouissance, as a form of excess beyond pleasure, often emerges as a site of transgression against these symbolic laws. It embodies an excessive, overwhelming experience that both entices and terrifies the subject. The pursuit of jouissance can thus lead to clashes with societal norms, ethical constraints, and the accepted codes of conduct, resulting in what Lacan terms as 'the underside of law.'

Jouissance in the symbolic order is linked with the notion of lack. The never-ending quest to attain jouissance stems from this inherent lack, perpetuating a cycle of desire and frustration. Individuals seek to fill this void through various means, often resorting to transgressive behaviors in an attempt to breach the limits enforced by the symbolic law. Lacan's exploration of jouissance unveils its paradoxical nature – it is both the source of pleasure and the cause of suffering, existing at the intersection of acceptance and defiance of the symbolic order.

The symbolic order constructs a framework of language and signifiers that shape the subject's identity and desires. Jouissance, in this context, disrupts the linguistic structure and challenges the established meanings, leading to moments of rupture and dissonance. The very act of articulating jouissance necessarily involves a destabilization of the symbolic edifice, pushing the subject towards the forbidden territories where laws are breached and taboos shattered.

3. Jouissance within the Imaginary Order - Illusions and Desires:

Within the Imaginary order, jouissance manifests as a constant pursuit of unattainable ideals, compelling individuals to strive for an imagined completeness or fulfillment that is forever beyond reach. At the core of the Imaginary order lies the formation of the ego through the mirror stage, where the individual's sense of self is shaped through identification with external images and symbols. Within this framework, jouissance emerges as a key driving force behind the incessant quest for idealized self-images, leading to a perpetual cycle of desire and unfulfilled yearnings.

4. The Real Order and Jouissance - Encounters with the Impossible:

In Lacanian theory, the concept of jouissance refers to a complex and often enigmatic form of satisfaction that is inextricably linked to impossibility. The Real is characterized by its resistance to symbolization and representation, rendering it an elusive terrain that lies beyond conscious comprehension. Within this order, jouissance is experienced as encounters with the impossible, where the individual grapples with the limits of language and meaning. The pursuit of jouissance in the Real is marked by a relentless quest for unattainable gratification, transcending the boundaries of traditional pleasure-seeking tendencies. As we engage with the landscape of the Real, we encounter the paradoxical nature of jouissance, wherein the yearning for fulfillment is inherently intertwined with the experience of lack and impossibility. This tension gives rise to a unique form of satisfaction that defies conventional logic, prompting individuals to confront the inherent inadequacies of symbolic representations. Through clinical illustrations and theoretical elaborations, the enigmatic nature of jouissance in the Real becomes palpable, offering a profound exploration of the inherent contradictions and tensions within the human psyche. Furthermore, an examination of the interplay between jouissance and the Real lays bare the intricacies of psychic functioning, illuminating the ways in which individuals negotiate their interactions with the unattainable and the inexplicable. By confronting the impossible within the Real, we are confronted with the very essence of human subjectivity and the perennial quest for fulfillment amidst the recognition of inherent limitations.

5. Interconnections between Three Orders:

Jouissance, often described as a form of excessive enjoyment or traumatic pleasure, manifests differently in each of these domains, yet its influence permeates the entire psychoanalytic landscape. The dialectical approach to jouissance facilitates a comprehensive examination of its nuanced manifestations across the three orders. Within the Symbolic order, jouissance intersects with the law and its transgressions, highlighting the paradoxical nature of pleasure and constraint. This intersection evokes questions of desire, prohibition, and subversion, underscoring the complex relationship between societal norms and individual gratification. Moving into the Imaginary, jouissance becomes entwined with illusions and desires. Here, we encounter the mirroring mechanisms and fantasies that shape subjective experiences of pleasure, longing, and insatiable yearning. The juxtaposition of idealized self-images and the underlying lack contributes to a web of jouissance within the Imaginary order. As we venture into the Real order, the encounters with jouissance delve into the impossible. This domain reveals the raw, unmediated experiences that transcend symbolic representations and imaginary constructs. Jouissance in the Real exposes the inherent tension between the search for unattainable bliss and the unsettling confrontation with the limits of representation. It is within the interstices of these three orders that the dialectical approach illuminates the dynamic interplay of jouissance, offering a profound exploration of human subjectivity and its entanglement with pleasure and pain. Through this lens, the elusive nature of jouissance is encapsulated within a framework that acknowledges the intricacies of psychic life, inviting further inquiry and introspection. The dialectical approach to jouissance not only unravels its interwoven threads but also underscores its relevance in deciphering the complexities of human experience.

6. Cultural Interpretations - Jouissance in Literature and Arts:

Literature, being an arena where the nuances of human experience are poignantly depicted, offers insightful glimpses into the manifestations of jouissance. From the seductive allure of forbidden pleasures in classic works of fiction to the explorations of unattainable desires in contemporary novels, the theme of jouissance often serves as a pivotal element shaping the narrative landscape. Through in-depth analysis of select literary masterpieces, we unravel the interplay between characters' pursuit of jouissance and the inevitable pitfalls that accompany such relentless quests.

The arts, encompassing visual, performing, and cinematic mediums, provide a canvas for the embodiment and portrayal of jouissance. Paintings, sculptures, and other visual art forms capture the essence of jouissance through evocative imagery and symbolism, inviting viewers to contemplate the enigmatic nature of pleasure and pain. Similarly, in the domain of performing arts, the enactment of jouissance on stage or screen becomes a riveting exploration of human emotions and vulnerabilities, serving as a mirror to society's collective fascination with the complexities of pleasure and suffering.

By delving into cultural artifacts spanning diverse historical and sociocultural contexts, we discern the subtle yet pervasive presence of jouissance as a motif that transcends temporal and spatial boundaries. Through meticulous scrutiny of renowned literary works, artistic creations, and cinematic productions, we endeavor to illuminate the ways in which jouissance operates as a thematic motif, unveiling profound insights into the human psyche and societal constructs.

7. Gendered Perspectives on Jouissance - Feminine and Masculine Complexities:

Lacanian theory posits that jouissance is not simply a matter of pleasure or pain, but a deeper form of satisfaction that transcends traditional notions of hedonism. When exploring the feminine experience of jouissance, it becomes essential to consider the ways in which cultural representations and societal norms have influenced the construction of feminine desire and satisfaction. Likewise, the masculine experience of jouissance is entwined with societal expectations and the manifestation of power dynamics. Lacan's conceptualization of phallic jouissance and its relation to masculine identity sheds light on the interplay between gender and psychoanalytic experiences. Moreover, through a critical analysis of the role of the Other and its influence on the construction of jouissance, we can discern the nuanced ways in which gender shapes the subjective experience of this fundamental concept.

8. Critiques and Debates:

Lacanian jouissance has been a subject of extensive debate and critique in contemporary psychoanalytic discourse, reflecting the evolving understanding of human subjectivity and desire. One prevalent critique revolves around the ambiguous nature of jouissance as posited by Lacan, with some scholars arguing that its abstraction renders it too elusive to be adequately defined or operationalized within clinical practice. This skepticism often stems from the inherent challenges in translating theoretical constructs into tangible therapeutic interventions. Critics also question the universal applicability of Lacanian jouissance, contending that its emphasis on language and symbolic structures may overlook the diversity of individual experiences and cultural contexts.

Additionally, the gendered dimension of jouissance has sparked fervent discussions, with some commentators highlighting Lacan's predominantly phallocentric framework and its implications for understanding female subjectivity and pleasure. This critique underscores the need for an inclusive and intersectional approach to jouissance that acknowledges the complexities of gender identity and sexual orientation. Despite these criticisms, proponents of Lacanian theory counter by emphasizing the transformative potential of jouissance in illuminating unconscious processes and uncovering repressed desires. They argue that the enigmatic nature of jouissance mirrors the inexhaustible depths of human subjectivity, offering a radical perspective on psychic phenomena that transcends traditional pleasure paradigms. Moreover, contemporary psychoanalysts have sought to integrate Lacanian concepts with advancements in neuroscience and affective studies, aiming to establish empirical foundations for understanding jouissance within the neural networks of the brain. This interdisciplinary dialogue expands the horizons of jouissance beyond purely theoretical debates, fostering a more nuanced comprehension of its neurobiological underpinnings and clinical implications. As such, the contemporary discourse on Lacanian jouissance prompts a critical reevaluation of psychoanalytic praxis and calls for an integrative approach that reconciles theoretical elaborations with the practical demands of therapeutic engagement.

The 'Other'

1. Introduction:

The concept of the 'Other' encapsulates multifaceted dimensions that extend beyond conventional understandings of external entities. Its delineation epitomizes a departure from traditional perceptions of the 'other' as merely an external entity or separate individual. Within Lacanian theory, the 'Other' transcends mere alterity, delving into the interplay of subjectivity, language, and desire. At its essence, the 'Other' embodies not only the external world one confronts but also the symbolic order that delineates the parameters of human experience. Furthermore, it encapsulates the internalized ideals and identifications that shape one's self-conception and relational dynamics. This expansive conceptualization underscores the centrality of the 'Other' in shaping human subjectivity and illuminates its pivotal role in the psychical development of individuals. Moreover, by elucidating the dialectical relationship between the Self and the 'Other', Lacan introduced a paradigm-shifting perspective that reframed the very fabric of psychoanalytic inquiry. In understanding the 'Other' as a constitutive force in the dynamics of subject formation, Lacanian theory underscores the intrinsic intertwinement of selfhood with the larger socio-cultural milieu. By foregrounding the 'Other' as a mediating construct through which subjects orient themselves within their existential journey, it reconfigures traditional psychoanalytic terrains, imbuing them with an enriched dimensionality. Consequently, this comprehensive understanding lays bare the interconnectedness of subjective experience with the 'Other', seeding fertile ground for an in-depth exploration of identity formation, desire, and intersubjective relations.

2. Historical Context and Evolution:

The historical context and evolution of the concept of the 'Other' within Lacanian theory are deeply entrenched in the intellectual milieu of post-structuralist and psychoanalytic discourses. Arising in the wake of Freudian psychoanalysis, Jacques Lacan's rethinking of the 'Other' marked a pivotal shift in the understanding of subjectivity and the construction of reality. Central to comprehending this evolution is an exploration of Lacan's engagements with linguistic and philosophical currents that heavily influenced his conceptualization of the 'Other.' The linguistic turn in the mid-20th century, particularly the works of Ferdinand de Saussure and Roman Jakobson, played a crucial role in shaping Lacan's thoughts on the symbolic dimension of the 'Other.' Additionally, the influence of Hegelian philosophy, particularly the dialectical interplay of self and other, provided a fertile ground for Lacan to develop his ideas regarding subjectivity and intersubjectivity. Furthermore, the evolution of Lacanian theory in relation to the

'Other' can be traced through the various phases of Lacan's work, from his early seminars to his later writings. The evolving significance of the 'Other' reflects Lacan's own intellectual journey and the refinement of his theoretical framework over time. As Lacanian theory gained momentum in the milieus of psychology, literary studies, and cultural theory, scholars have further elaborated on the historical and intellectual underpinnings of the 'Other' within Lacanian discourse. The application of Lacanian concepts in diverse fields has also contributed to the continued evolution and reinterpretation of the 'Other,' echoing the dynamism inherent in Lacanian thought.

3. The 'Other' in Relation to the Symbolic Order:

The 'Other' is not merely an external entity but encompasses a complex network of linguistic, cultural, and social frameworks that shape individual identity and perception. Within the Symbolic Order, the 'Other' functions as a repository of shared symbols, norms, and signifiers that regulate human experiences and interactions.

When delving into the 'Other' in relation to the Symbolic Order, it is crucial to recognize that this construct transcends mere individuals and extends to encompass broader societal constructs. The Symbolic Order, as posited by Lacan, represents the milieu of language and culture, wherein the 'Other' plays a central role in mediating subjectivity. Through language and symbolic systems, individuals come to engage with their existence and construct meaning within the framework of the 'Other's' influence.

The 'Other' in relation to the Symbolic Order introduces notions of authority, law, and inter-subjective dynamics. This dynamic interplay is essential for understanding how individuals internalize societal norms and expectations, often unconsciously conforming to the dictates of the 'Other.' Thus, the Symbolic Order, through its connection with the 'Other,' becomes a site for the regulation of social conduct and the formation of subjectivity.

Lacan emphasizes that the 'Other' within the Symbolic Order also instills a sense of lack or incompleteness in the human subject. This inherent lack, stemming from the recognition of the 'Other' as a locus of authority and knowledge, propels individuals to strive for identification and recognition within the symbolic framework. Consequently, the 'Other' emerges as a fundamental determinant in the development of desire and identity within the Symbolic Order.

Notably, the 'Other' in the Symbolic Order engenders a dialectical relationship, whereby individuals both resist and assimilate its influence. This dialectic leads to the negotiation of personal agency and social conformity, as individuals seek to assert their subjectivity while being shaped by the norms and conventions prescribed by the 'Other.' Such negotiations reveal the power dynamics inherent in the 'Other's' function within the Symbolic Order.

4. Imaginary Versus Symbolic - The Dual Aspect of the 'Other':

The symbolic 'Other' represents the milieu of language, law, and societal norms that structure our understanding of reality and govern our interactions. It is through the symbolic 'Other' that individuals come to recognize themselves as separate entities within the larger social framework. This recognition is pivotal in the development of subjectivity, as it establishes the basis for the formation of one's own identity. Conversely, the imaginary 'Other' emanates from perception, imagery, and idealized representations. It embodies the mirroring aspect of human experience, where individuals construct their self-image and desires through identification with others and internalized images. The imaginary 'Other' plays a crucial role in the formation of ego and narcissistic tendencies, as individuals strive to align themselves with idealized reflections. However, this idealization often leads to misperceptions and alienation from the true self. Understanding the duality of the 'Other' sheds light on the dynamics of subject-object relations within the Lacanian framework. It underscores the simultaneous presence of both external societal influences and internal psychological projections in shaping individual identities. Moreover, the interplay between the symbolic and the imaginary 'Other' reveals the inherent tensions and contradictions inherent in the constitution of subjectivity. By delving into the dual aspect of the 'Other', we gain insight into the complexities of human subjectivity and the nuanced interplay between societal structures and internal psychological processes.

5. Subjectivity and the Role of the 'Other':

In focusing on the role of the 'Other' in shaping subjectivity, we delve into the core of Lacanian psychoanalysis and its implications for understanding the human psyche. The 'Other' serves as a pivotal construct in the formation of subjectivity, as it represents the external forces that influence one's sense of self. Through the lens of Lacanian theory, subjectivity is not viewed as an autonomous, self-contained entity, but rather as dynamically constructed in relation to the 'Other'. This relational aspect underpins the interplay between the individual and the external world, emphasizing the profound impact of social and cultural dynamics on the formation of subjectivity. As such, the 'Other' becomes an essential mediator in the constitution of one's identity and subjective experience. Furthermore, the 'Other' operates within the Symbolic order, contributing to the internalization of social norms, language, and cultural ideals that shape individual subjectivity. Lacan posits that the 'Other' acts as a repository of meanings and signifiers which individuals draw upon to structure their understanding of self and reality. This appropriation of the 'Other's' symbolic resources serves to anchor one's sense of identity and provides a framework for traversing the complexities of existence. Moreover, the 'Other' plays a fundamental role in the development of desire and the construction of linguistic and symbolic representations. It is through the 'Other' that individuals gain access to the symbolic register, thereby establishing a framework for articulating and expressing their desires within the constraints of language and societal norms. This interdependence between subjectivity and the 'Other' underscores the dynamic and complex nature of human experience, elucidating the profound impact of external influences on the constitution of the self.

6. The 'Other' as a Mirror:

In the Lacanian framework, the concept of the 'Other' is deeply intertwined with the individual's experience of language and desire. The 'Other' functions as a profound mirror through which individuals perceive themselves and their place within the symbolic order. This mirroring process occurs both linguistically and in desire, playing an instrumental role in shaping subjectivity and identity.

Language, as a system constructed by the 'Other,' serves as a reflective mechanism through which individuals form their sense of self. The linguistic symbols and signifiers provided by the 'Other' not only enable communication but also mediate the subject's understanding of their own identity. Thus, the 'Other' becomes the agent through which individuals internalize and engage with the symbolic order, ultimately influencing their self-perception and relation to the external world.

The 'Other' reflects desires back to the subject, constituting a crucial aspect of Lacanian psychoanalysis. The subject's desires are inevitably entwined with the perceived desires of the 'Other,' leading to a complex interplay that influences the individual's aspirations and sense of fulfillment. The 'Other' acts as a mirror wherein the subject's desires are both reflected and shaped, profoundly impacting their understanding of what is valued and sought after within the social and cultural context.

This reflective function of the 'Other' extends beyond the individual, permeating societal dynamics and power structures. The mirroring process inherent in language and desire perpetuates certain norms, values, and ideologies sanctioned by the 'Other,' consequently shaping collective identities and societal structures. As such, the 'Other' acts as a reflective force that not only molds individual subjectivities but also contributes to the construction and reinforcement of broader social frameworks.

However, within this mirroring relationship lies the potential for resistance and subversion. Individuals can challenge the reflections presented by the 'Other,' leading to reconfigurations of identity and desire that diverge from the established norms. This dynamic tension between conformity and resistance underscores the multifaceted nature of the 'Other' as a mirror, demonstrating its capacity to both solidify and unsettle the foundations of identity and desire within the Lacanian framework.

7. Interplay Between the 'Other' and Identity Formation:

In understanding this relationship, it becomes evident that the 'Other' serves as a crucial determinant in the construction of individual subjectivities. Through the lens of Lacanian psychoanalysis, the 'Other' functions as a dynamic force in shaping and influencing the development of an individual's sense of self.

In the Lacanian framework, identity formation is inherently linked to the recognition and internalization of external influences, primarily emanating from the 'Other.' This process unfolds within the symbolic order, where language and societal norms act as conduits for the transmission of cultural, familial, and ideological paradigms. Individuals orient themselves within the symbolic network by assimilating the perceptions and expectations projected onto them by the 'Other,' thereby contributing to the continuous negotiation of their own identities.

The 'Other' operates as a crucial agency in the establishment of social roles and norms, thereby exerting considerable influence on the manner in which individuals perceive themselves and are perceived by others. The mediation of societal expectations, moral codes, and cultural values by the 'Other' significantly shapes the contours of individual identity. Lacan's emphasis on the role of the 'Other' elucidates that self-perception and social positioning are inherently interconnected, underscoring the relational nature of identity.

Identity formation, as construed within Lacanian discourse, is not solely an internally driven process; rather, it is fundamentally intertwined with the external reflections received from the 'Other.' The complex dynamics between self-perception and external validation are integral to comprehending the tapestry of identity construction. The 'Other' operates as a mirror through which individuals encounter and negotiate their own images, discerning themselves amid the web of societal expectations, desires, and linguistic constructs.

Lacanian theory posits that the 'Other' does not merely reflect pre-existing identities but actively participates in their ongoing constitution. As individuals engage with the dictates of the 'Other,' they partake in a continual process of identity negotiation, oscillating between compliance and resistance. This dialectical interplay perpetuates the ever-evolving nature of identity construction, challenging static conceptions of selfhood and highlighting the indispensable involvement of the 'Other' in this iterative formation.

To fully grasp the intricacies of identity formation in the Lacanian paradigm, one must carefully unravel the convoluted relationship between the 'Other' and the constitution of subjectivities. This interplay transcends mere introspection, venturing into intersubjective negotiations and societal entanglements. Ultimately, the 'Other' emerges as a pivotal axis around which the fabric of individual and collective identities unfolds, necessitating sustained scrutiny and theoretical elucidation.

8. The 'Other' and Its Influence on Social Structures:

Social structures are inherently intertwined with the dynamics of the 'Other' in Lacanian theory, playing a critical role in shaping individual subjectivity and societal norms. The concept of the 'Other' extends beyond individual interactions to permeate the fabric of social institutions, hierarchies, and power dynamics. Within social contexts, the 'Other' acts as a pivotal force in delineating boundaries between self and other, cultivating a sense of belonging or alienation, and influencing collective behaviors. By scrutinizing the interdependence between the 'Other' and social structures, a deeper understanding of the complexities inherent in human communities emerges.

The 'Other' operates as an implicit presence that informs cultural paradigms, ethical codes, and normative standards within communities. It conveys a set of implicit expectations and norms that dictate acceptable behaviors, beliefs, and identities. Consequently, individuals engage with these societal expectations and construct their identities in relation to the 'Other.' Through the mechanisms of recognition and misrecognition, the 'Other' molds the social environment by perpetuating certain ideals while marginalizing others.

The influence of the 'Other' is manifest in the establishment of social hierarchies and power differentials. It gives rise to systems of privilege and oppression ingrained in societal institutions, perpetuating unequal distributions of resources, opportunities, and agency. Consequently, the 'Other' plays a pivotal role in sustaining and reproducing social inequalities, often reinforcing dominant narratives while suppressing marginalized voices. This complex interplay between the 'Other' and social structures highlights the transformative impact of the 'Other' on societal power dynamics and collective consciousness.

Lacanian theory prompts critical reflections on the implications of the 'Other' within social structures, urging an interrogation of the underlying power relations and normative frameworks. By shedding light on the repressive and regulatory functions of the 'Other,' this lens exposes how social structures enforce conformity and shape individual subjectivities. Moreover, it invites a reevaluation of prevalent social discourses and practices, propelling the examination of hidden prejudices and biases embedded within societal norms.

In essence, the pervasive influence of the 'Other' on social structures underscores the web of influences that underpin collective behaviors, power dynamics, and identity constructions within societies. Understanding the nuanced interconnections between the 'Other' and social structures opens avenues for critical analysis and transformative interventions to foster more inclusive and equitable social frameworks.

9. Critiques and Reinterpretations of the Lacanian 'Other':

Critiques and reinterpretations of the Lacanian concept of the 'Other' have been instrumental in shaping contemporary discourse within psychoanalysis and beyond. As we delve into this critical analysis, it becomes evident that scholars and practitioners have raised valid concerns regarding the limitations and applicability of Lacan's conception of the 'Other.' One prominent critique revolves around Lacan's somewhat rigid and deterministic view of the 'Other' within the symbolic order. Critics argue that this portrayal neglects the nuanced complexities of individual experiences and agency, potentially overshadowing the diversity of subjective realities. Furthermore, some scholars have highlighted the binary nature of Lacan's delineation between the 'Other' and the self, suggesting that such clear-cut divisions may not adequately capture the intricacies of human relationships and sociocultural dynamics. In light of these critiques, various reinterpretations have emerged, aiming to refine and expand upon Lacan's original framework. For instance, contemporary psychoanalytic thinkers have proposed more relational and contextual understandings of the 'Other,' emphasizing the interconnectedness and mutual constitution of subjectivities. Additionally, intersecting perspectives from feminist, postcolonial, and queer theory have prompted reevaluations of the 'Other' as intertwined with power differentials, social constructions, and intersectional identities. These interdisciplinary dialogues have enriched the discourse on the 'Other' by foregrounding issues of diversity, inclusivity, and social justice within the Lacanian paradigm. Beyond academia, clinical practitioners have also contributed to the reimagining of the 'Other' through their experiential insights and therapeutic innovations. By critically engaging with Lacan's concepts, therapists have developed more personalized and inclusive approaches that acknowledge the multidimensionality of the 'Other' in the therapeutic relationship. Moreover, the ethical implications of the 'Other' in mental health practice have been underscored, leading to reflective discussions on cultural competence, empathy, and the deconstruction of hegemonic norms. These interdisciplinary collaborations and reinterpretations reflect a dynamic engagement with Lacanian theory, demonstrating its ongoing relevance and adaptability within evolving social, cultural, and clinical landscapes.

Lack and Desire

1. The Lacanian Notion of Lack:

Within Lacan's theory, the notion of lack holds a central position in understanding human subjectivity and desire. Rooted in the psychoanalytic tradition, lack is not merely an absence or a void but rather a fundamental component that shapes individual experiences and motivations. At its core, lack extends beyond the tangible and material; it operates within symbolic and imaginary frameworks, exerting a profound influence on the construction of human identity and desire. Lacan's conceptualization of lack emerges as a pivotal concept that underpins the structure of the unconscious and elucidates the intricacies of human desire. To fully grasp the significance of lack in Lacanian theory, it is essential to delve into its multifaceted conceptualizations and implications. Firstly, lack is linked to the formation of the subject within the Symbolic order. It signifies the inherent incompleteness and fragmentation that characterizes human existence. Rather than perceiving lack as a mere deficit, Lacan posits it as a foundational element that propels individuals towards seeking fulfillment and completeness. This dialectical interplay between lack and desire forms the bedrock of Lacanian psychoanalysis, illuminating the compulsive nature of human desires driven by the perpetual quest to fill the void engendered by lack. Moreover, lack extends beyond individual subjectivity and permeates the social and cultural milieu, shaping collective ideologies and aspirations. Lacan's emphasis on lack as a universal condition underscores its omnipresence in societal structures and the construction of meaning. By scrutinizing the role of lack in societal discourses and collective imaginaries, Lacanian theory offers insightful perspectives on the dynamics of power, language, and social norms. Furthermore, the apprehension of lack extends into clinical praxis, where analysts engage with the complex manifestations of lack in their patients' narratives. Understanding how lack operates as a fundamental drive and source of discontentment enables clinicians to unravel the layers of unconscious conflict and repressed desires, fostering a deeper comprehension of the patient's subjective experience. Hence, lack unfolds as a foundational cornerstone in Lacanian theory, permeating individual subjectivity, collective phenomena, and clinical practice with its pervasive influence.

2. Lacan's Concept of Desire:

In Lacanian theory, the concept of desire transcends simple biological or instinctual inclinations. Desire operates within a complex framework that encompasses both conscious and unconscious elements, posing a significant departure from conventional understandings of human needs. On a foundational level, Lacan's articulation of desire reflects a departure from traditional psychoanalytic models, as it nuances desire not as a mere quest for satisfaction but as an elusive trajectory shaped by linguistic and symbolic forces.

Central to this exploration is the differentiation between need and desire. While needs foreground biological imperatives crucial for survival, desire extends beyond these immediate requirements and involves a yearning for unattainable, often symbolic objects. This divergence underlines the nature of human subjectivity, wherein desire becomes intertwined with the unconscious, rooted in language, and deeply enmeshed within the symbolic order.

Unraveling the multifaceted layers of desire necessitates an acknowledgment of its dialectical relationship with lack. Lacan posits that desire emerges as a response to lack, permeating the very fabric of human subjectivity. This turn elucidates desire's perpetual state of incompleteness, forever linked to an inherent absence tethered to the unconscious. Consequently, desire exists as a structuring force shaping individual and collective experiences, engendering the ceaseless pursuit of symbolic signifiers that stretch beyond the tangible dimension.

Delving into Lacanian conceptions of desire necessitates grappling with the role of the Other in its formation. The nature of desire becomes intertwined with intersubjective dynamics, where the Other's influence propels the subject's quest for completion and recognition, manifesting in various interpersonal and societal contexts. Additionally, Lacan's conceptualization of desire underscores its entwinement with the symbolic and imaginary registers, highlighting its pervasive presence across diverse domains of experience.

As such, exploring desire according to Lacanian premises demands a nuanced discernment that surpasses simplistic interpretations. It requires engaging with the perturbations between lack, language, and social dynamics, while recognizing desire's paradoxical essence as both a driving force and an enigmatic construct.

3. The Role of the Unconscious in Lack and Desire:

The interplay between lack and desire in Lacanian theory is intrinsically tied to the workings of the unconscious mind. Central to Lacan's conceptualization is the idea that lack and desire are not solely rooted in conscious thought or rational decision-making, but rather, they are deeply embedded in the unconscious psyche.

In Lacanian theory, the unconscious is a sphere of unacknowledged desires, repressed memories, and fragmented experiences that exert a powerful influence on an individual's perceived sense of lack and pursuit of desire. Lacan posits that it is within this unconscious domain that lacks are inscribed, often stemming from early childhood experiences and the formation of the ego. As such, individuals may harbor unconscious feelings of inadequacy, incompleteness, or yearning that propel their engagement with various objects of desire. Whether it be material possessions, social recognition, or intimate relationships, the unconscious plays a pivotal role in shaping one's subjective experience of lack and the relentless quest for fulfillment.

The unconscious also serves as the locus of repressed desires and fantasies that fuel the perpetual cycle of desire. Lacan's notion of the 'desire of the Other' hinges on the unconscious adoption of societal norms, values, and expectations, which subsequently inform an individual's desires. Through the mechanisms of repression and displacement, the unconscious exerts its influence in channeling and distorting one's conscious expressions of desire, oftentimes leading to enigmatic manifestations and seemingly inexplicable longings.

The unconscious is linked to Lacan's understanding of the symbolic order, where language and cultural signifiers shape the individual's perception of lack and engender specific desires. The symbolic register, as mediated by the unconscious, contributes to the perpetuation of socially constructed ideals and norms, molding an individual's aspirations and longings in ways that often elude conscious awareness. Consequently, the unconscious becomes a reservoir of symbolic identifications and internalized societal demands that underpin an individual's pursuit of desire, frequently operating beyond the grasp of conscious introspection.

Ultimately, the role of the unconscious in Lacanian theory extends far beyond mere psychological processes; it forms the bedrock for understanding the dynamics of lack and desire in human subjectivity. By elucidating the complex interplay between the unconscious and these fundamental concepts, Lacanian theory offers a profound lens through which to unravel the enigmatic tapestry of human motivation, aspiration, and fulfillment.

4. Manifestations of Lack in Subjectivity:

The concept of lack, or *manque* in Lacanian theory, holds profound implications for the understanding of human subjectivity. Lack is not merely the absence of something tangible; rather, it pertains to a fundamental incompleteness that characterizes the human condition. In this context, lack is not rooted in any specific material deprivation but instead constitutes a foundational aspect of the psyche.

Lacan posits that lack sets the stage for desire and provides the impetus for the subject's engagement with the world. This lack is not only subjective but also deeply intertwined with the symbolic order. The subject's sense of lack is inextricably linked to language and cultural signifiers, shaping their identity and self-perception.

Within the framework of Lacanian theory, manifestations of lack in subjectivity are multifaceted. It is evident in the perpetual quest for objects of desire, be they material possessions, social recognition, or emotional fulfillment. This relentless pursuit stems from the individual's attempt to fill the void created by lack, often leading to cycles of insatiable yearning and dissatisfaction.

Lack operates at a more profound level, permeating various aspects of the subject's experience. It underpins the dynamics of human relationships, as individuals seek validation and confirmation from others to alleviate their sense of inadequacy. This quest for external affirmation serves as a compensatory mechanism aimed at mitigating the internal experience of lack.

Lack exerts a pervasive influence on the formation of identity and the construction of the self. The subject's self-perception is entwined with an awareness of their deficiencies, fueling aspirations for self-improvement and the acquisition of traits or attributes believed to assuage their sense of lack.

In the clinical milieu, manifestations of lack in subjectivity are paramount in understanding various psychopathologies. Disorders such as narcissism, dependency, and neurosis often reflect nuanced responses to underlying feelings of lack. These conditions can be viewed as complex coping mechanisms deployed by individuals to contend with their subjective experiences of insufficiency.

5. Desire's Interplay with the Symbolic and Imaginary:

In Lacanian psychoanalysis, desire is not restricted to mere surface-level wants or needs but encompasses a deeper, more elusive yearning that extends beyond the individual's conscious awareness.

Within the Lacanian framework, the symbolic order represents the milieu of language, culture, and social norms that shape an individual's understanding of the world. Desire, in this context, is linked to linguistic structures and the ways in which individuals engage with meaning and identity within the symbolic domain. The symbolic mediation of desire highlights how our yearnings are influenced and often constrained by societal conventions and linguistic frameworks, showcasing the pervasive impact of cultural and symbolic systems on subjective desires.

The interplay of desire with the imaginary dimension elucidates the role of images, fantasies, and idealized representations in shaping individual longing and gratification. The imaginary, characterized by the formation of ego and self-imagery, provides a crucial backdrop for understanding how desire is often intertwined with illusory images and projected fantasies. Lacan's emphasis on the imbrication of desire within the imaginary underscores the complex relationship between internal mental representations and the pursuit of fulfillment, as individuals negotiate their desires through a lens of perceived unity and idealized visions.

In exploring the nexus of desire, the symbolic, and the imaginary, it becomes evident that Lacanian theory offers a unique vantage point for comprehending the multifaceted nature of human yearning. This perspective encourages clinicians and theorists to interrogate the ways in which desire is entwined with language, cultural constructs, and imaginative fabrications, ultimately shaping subjective experiences and relational dynamics. By discerning desire's interplay with the symbolic and imaginary, practitioners can cultivate a deeper appreciation for the nuanced underpinnings of human motivation, paving the way for more insightful therapeutic interventions and theoretical advancements.

6. Clinical Implications:

Addressing lack and desire necessitates a profound comprehension of their multifaceted dynamics within an individual's psyche. Therapists must recognize that lack is omnipresent in human experience, manifesting as a sense of incompleteness or inadequacy that underpins desires. It is crucial to acknowledge that these concepts intersect with an individual's subjective reality and have a profound impact on their psychological well-being.

When addressing lack and desire in therapy, it is imperative to create a conducive environment where patients feel safe to articulate their innermost longings and frustrations. Therapists must skillfully work through the dialectic between the symbolic and imaginary registers to unravel the unconscious manifestations of lack and desire. By delving into the patient's discourse, therapists can identify patterns of substitutive behaviors or repeated frustrations that elucidate underlying unmet desires.

Therapeutic interventions aimed at addressing lack and desire should incorporate a nuanced exploration of the patient's historical and cultural context. Understanding the influence of societal norms, familial dynamics, and personal experiences is essential in comprehending the tapestry of lack and desire manifested in an individual's life. Through empathetic listening and astute observation, therapists can decipher the covert expressions of lack and desire embedded in the patient's narratives, dreams, and fantasies.

The therapeutic process should embrace a multifaceted approach that acknowledges the complexities of lack and desire. Integrating psychoanalytic techniques with cognitive-behavioral strategies can offer a comprehensive framework for addressing the intricacies of desire and the underlying sense of lack. By engaging in introspective exercises, symbolic reenactments, and imaginative explorations, patients can gain insights into their deep-seated desires and confront the underlying sense of lack that permeates their existence.

It is also essential for therapists to sensitize themselves to the ethical dimensions inherent in addressing lack and desire. Upholding the principles of confidentiality, respect, and non-judgmental understanding is paramount in fostering a therapeutic alliance wherein patients feel empowered to confront their vulnerabilities and aspirations. Additionally, promoting self-reflection and self-compassion in patients can catalyze transformative processes, enabling them to embrace their lacunae while aspiring for individuation and fulfillment.

The Phallus as a Central Signifier

1. Historical Context and Evolution of the Concept:

The concept of the phallus as a central signifier in Lacanian thought has evolved over time, influenced by historical, cultural, and philosophical developments. To understand its significance within Lacanian theory, it is essential to delve into the historical context that shaped its evolution. Beginning with the early works of Sigmund Freud, the notion of the phallus initially emerged as a symbol of power and authority, representing the male organ and the patriarchal order. However, Lacan's reinterpretation of this concept transcended its literal and biological implications, transforming it into a complex symbolic signifier within the psychic structure. Lacan's engagement with structural linguistics, particularly the works of Ferdinand de Saussure, played a pivotal role in shaping his conceptualization of the phallus as a linguistic construct rather than a biological organ. By grounding his thinking in the structuralist movement, Lacan expanded the understanding of the phallus beyond anatomical or gender-specific definitions. He emphasized the phallus as a symbol imbued with social, cultural, and psychological meanings, operating within the Symbolic order of language and law. Furthermore, the influence of Jacques Derrida's deconstructive philosophy prompted Lacan to contemplate the inherent instability and multiplicity of meaning associated with the phallus, challenging essentialist interpretations. This historical trajectory demonstrates the transformative journey of the phallus from a simplistic representation of male dominance to a complex signifier embedded in the fabric of human subjectivity and desire. The evolution of the concept reflects the broader shifts in intellectual paradigms, moving away from biological determinism towards a more nuanced understanding of symbolic systems and cultural significations.

2. The Symbolic Order - Phallus as a Signifier:

It is essential to recognize that within the theoretical framework of Lacanian psychoanalysis, the concept of the phallus extends beyond its literal or anatomical implications. Instead, it serves as a symbolic representation of power, authority, and lack in the unconscious. The phallus encapsulates a complex web of meanings, and understanding its role as a signifier in the symbolic order is crucial for grasping the nuances of Lacanian theory. When we speak of the phallus within the symbolic order, we are delving into cultural and social constructs that influence the formation of subjectivity. This goes beyond biological or anatomical considerations and dives into the domain of language, law, and societal norms. The phallus, therefore, functions as a symbol of authority and patriarchal power, shaping the dynamics of desire and lack within the unconscious. Through linguistic and symbolic associations, the phallus becomes intertwined with notions of status, dominance, and social hierarchies. Lacan's redefinition of the phallus situates it as a potent signifier that operates within the structure of language and the unconscious. It is not limited to masculine identity but permeates the entire cultural and psychological landscape. The phallus, as a symbolic signifier, exerts its influence through the imposition of norms and values, often leading to the perpetuation of gendered stereotypes and power differentials. Lacanian scholars emphasize the significance of the phallus as a central, organizing principle in the symbolic order, where it structures the subject's relationship to desire and lack. This conceptualization sheds light on the interplay between language, culture, and unconscious drives. Moreover, understanding the phallus as a signifier allows for a nuanced comprehension of how individuals engage with their identities and desires within societal frameworks. Furthermore, the symbolic dimension of the phallus underscores its transcendence beyond individual bodies, highlighting its role in mediating subject-formation and the regulation of social relations. As we explore the implications of the phallus as a signifier, we must consider its far-reaching impact on the construction of meaning, representation, and the negotiation of psychic reality within the Lacanian framework.

3. The Distinction between Symbolic, Imaginary, and Real Phallus:

In Lacanian theory, the concept of the phallus extends far beyond its literal and biological meaning. It becomes a fundamental signifier within the symbolic order, representing power, authority, and a range of other symbolic meanings. The symbolic phallus is not restricted to male anatomy but operates as a signifier within the milieu of language and culture. It represents a lack, an absence that instigates desire and plays a crucial role in the constitution of the subject within the Symbolic. Moving beyond the symbolic, Lacan introduced the imaginary phallus, which pertains to the individual's identification with the image or idea of the phallus. The imaginary phallus is rooted in appearances, images, and identifications, often leading to misinterpretations and misunderstandings. Lastly, the real phallus delves into the non-symbolic, non-imaginary dimension, representing an elusive and ineffable aspect of existence. This real phallus is not tied to anatomical connotations or cultural symbolism but rather embodies a sense of raw, unmediated reality. Distinguishing between these three dimensions of the phallus is essential for grasping Lacan's sophisticated framework and its implications for psychoanalytic practice. While the symbolic phallus operates within the domain of language and culture, shaping unconscious desires and identity formations, the imaginary phallus deals with the perceptual and visual aspects of representation, often giving rise to misconceptions and distortions. In contrast, the real phallus transcends all symbolic and imaginary representations, pointing towards an ungraspable truth that eludes linguistic and visual capture. Understanding the distinctions between these three manifestations of the phallus illuminates the complexity of Lacanian theory and offers profound insights into the intricacies of human subjectivity and desire.

4. Phallus in Relation to Lack and Desire:

The phallus stands as a symbol within the Symbolic order, signifying the unattainable object of desire. Lacan's concept of lack is intrinsically tied to the phallus, as it represents the fundamental absence that drives human desire. This lack is universal and encompasses all individuals, transcending gender or biological differences. The phallus, as a symbolic signifier, embodies this lack and becomes the focal point of desire, situated beyond reach. It serves as a constant reminder of an unfulfilled longing, perpetuating the endless pursuit of satisfaction. This perpetual state of lack and desire forms the core of Lacanian psychoanalysis, shaping the intricacies of human subjectivity and relationships. Understanding the phallus in relation to lack and desire allows for a profound exploration of the complexities underlying human behavior and motivations. Moreover, recognizing the phallus as a symbolic construct rather than a literal anatomical entity provides a more inclusive and nuanced perspective on desire, liberating it from restrictive gender binaries and biological determinism. Lacan challenges traditional notions of gender and sexuality by asserting that the phallus is not synonymous with male dominance or superiority. Instead, the phallus operates within the Symbolic order, exerting a pervasive influence on all individuals, irrespective of their biological sex. The phallus represents an elusive ideal that fuels aspirations and ambitions, perpetually eluding complete attainment. Its omnipresence in the psyche underscores the profound impact of desire on shaping individual identities and interpersonal dynamics. Exploring the phallus in relation to lack and desire unveils the interplay between conscious intentions and unconscious drives, shedding light on the underlying motivations guiding human actions. This conceptual framework provides a transformative lens through which to examine the multifaceted nature of desire and its profound implications for human experiences and relationships.

5. Phallus and Gender Identity - Misinterpretations and Clarifications:

In Lacanian psychoanalysis, the phallus encompasses a complex symbolic signifier that transcends biological definitions. This has significant implications for understanding gender identity within the Lacanian framework. Despite the apparent focus on the masculine in the terminology, it's important to recognize that in Lacanian theory, the phallus symbolizes lack and desire, rather than being exclusively linked to male anatomy. This distinction is crucial in dispelling misinterpretations and broadening our understanding of gender identity. From a Lacanian perspective, individuals of any gender can position themselves in relation to the symbolic phallus, irrespective of their biological sex. Furthermore, Lacan emphasizes that the phallus is not a fixed or stable signifier, but rather a shifting and elusive presence within the Symbolic Order. It serves as a placeholder for the lack that is inherent in all subjects, regardless of gender. Understanding the phallus in this way helps to challenge traditional binary conceptions of gender and opens up possibilities for a more inclusive and nuanced understanding of identity. It provides a foundation for recognizing the complexities of gender expression and the multiplicity of ways individuals relate to the phallic signifier. However, misconceptions often arise when the concept of the phallus is incorrectly equated with biological maleness, leading to oversimplified assumptions about gender identity. This misinterpretation overlooks the interplay between the Symbolic, Imaginary, and Real orders that shape an individual's subjective experience. To address these misinterpretations, it is essential to clarify that the Lacanian phallus operates at the level of representation and meaning, rather than as a concrete anatomical attribute. Consequently, it becomes evident that the phallus is not limited to male subjects; rather, it encompasses a broader symbolic function in the constitution of subjectivity. By acknowledging this distinction, the Lacanian approach invites a reevaluation of how gender identities are constructed within the psychoanalytic framework, paving the way for a more inclusive and expansive understanding of gender beyond traditional binaries.

6. Psychoanalytic Implications for Patients and Practitioners:

The understanding of the phallus as a central signifier in Lacanian thought holds profound implications for both patients undergoing psychoanalysis and practitioners employing this theoretical framework. For patients, the concept of the phallus serves as a pivotal point in uncovering unconscious desires and conflicts embedded within the symbolic order. Through the exploration of phallic signifiers, individuals can gain insight into the structuring of their subjectivity and the complex interplay between lack and desire. This heightened self-awareness often fosters a deeper comprehension of one's own motivations and behaviors, empowering patients to manage their internal dynamics with greater agency and purpose. Moreover, the integration of the phallus into analytic discourse provides a framework for addressing issues related to gender identity, sexual orientation, and societal expectations, thereby offering a comprehensive lens through which patients can examine the complexities of their lived experiences. From the perspective of practitioners, the conceptualization of the phallus necessitates a nuanced approach to clinical practice. It demands a careful consideration of how the phallus operates as a signifier within the subjective experiences of patients, bearing in mind that its significance may manifest differently for each individual. Furthermore, practitioners must remain attuned to the potential anxieties and resistances that may arise when engaging with the phallic dimension, cognizant of the sensitivity surrounding this profound symbol in the psyche. In the therapeutic context, the clinical application of phallic interpretations requires a balance of interpretation and reflexivity, as practitioners facilitate the exploration of unconscious meanings and the negotiation of subjective truths. Additionally, the recognition of the phallus in psychoanalytic treatment extends beyond individual sessions to encompass broader societal discourses and power structures, prompting practitioners to critically engage with issues of privilege, patriarchy, and cultural norms.

7. Critiques and Alternative Perspectives on the Phallus:

The Lacanian concept of the phallus as a central signifier has been the subject of extensive critique and debate within psychoanalytic circles and academic discourse. Critics often point to the phallocentric nature of Lacanian theory, arguing that it perpetuates gender hierarchies and reinforces patriarchal structures within society. This critique raises important questions about the implications of privileging the phallus as the primary symbolic representation of power and desire, particularly in relation to gender identity and sexual difference.

Alternative perspectives on the phallus have emerged from feminist, queer, and post-structuralist thinkers who seek to deconstruct and subvert traditional notions of phallic symbolism. These alternative perspectives challenge the phallus as the exclusive symbol of authority and question its universal applicability in understanding human subjectivity. By reinterpreting the phallus as a fluid and contingent signifier rather than a fixed, essentialized symbol, these critiques aim to disrupt traditional power dynamics and open up new possibilities for exploring diverse expressions of desire and identity.

Some scholars have questioned the phallus-centered approach as inherently limited and exclusionary, particularly for individuals whose experiences do not align with normative conceptions of gender and sexuality. They argue for a more inclusive framework that acknowledges non-binary and non-phallic modes of subjectivity, emphasizing the need to decenter the phallus as the singular locus of psychic structuration.

In response to these critiques and alternative perspectives, proponents of Lacanian theory contend that the phallus should be understood not as a literal anatomical referent, but as a symbolic construct that encompasses broader dimensions of power, lack, and symbolic mediation. They underscore the intrinsic ambiguity and multiplicity of the phallus, emphasizing its capacity to signify not only male dominance but also the pervasive dynamics of lack and desire that shape human subjectivity beyond biological determinism.

Transference and Countertransference in Analytical Practice

1. Historical Context and Evolution of Concepts:

The historical roots of transference and countertransference can be traced back to the early days of psychoanalysis, with Sigmund Freud's pioneering work laying the foundation for these pivotal concepts. Freud initially introduced the concept of transference in his clinical observations, recognizing the unconscious emotional ties that patients formed with their analysts based on past experiences and relationships. This marked a significant departure from traditional medical practice, recognizing the complex interplay of emotions in the therapeutic relationship. Countertransference, on the other hand, emerged as a tacit acknowledgment of analysts' own emotional reactions to their patients, reflecting Freud's recognition of the reciprocal nature of the therapeutic process.

The evolution of these concepts continued as psychoanalytic theories expanded, leading to a deeper understanding of the dynamics at play during the analytic encounter. Key figures such as Carl Jung and Melanie Klein further contributed to shaping and refining these concepts, adding layers of complexity to their theoretical underpinnings. Jungian psychology emphasized the archetypal elements present in transference, extending the scope of exploration beyond personal experiences to encompass collective unconscious dynamics. Meanwhile, Klein's focus on early childhood experiences deepened the understanding of how unconscious conflicts manifest in the transference-countertransference dyad, illuminating the developmental roots of these phenomena.

The emergence of Lacanian psychoanalysis represented a paradigm shift in the conceptualization of transference and countertransference. Drawing from Freud's original insights, Jacques Lacan reinterpreted these concepts within the framework of his own psychoanalytic theory, emphasizing the linguistic and symbolic dimensions of the unconscious. Lacan's conceptualization of transference as a manifestation of the analysand's positioning within the symbolic order and the analyst's role as the object of desire brought forth a novel perspective, challenging conventional interpretations while enriching the discourse on relational dynamics in analysis.

The evolution of these concepts was also influenced by broader shifts in the field of psychoanalysis, including developments in relational and intersubjective approaches. The acknowledgment of intersubjectivity in the analytic relationship highlighted the mutual influence between analyst and analysand, shedding light on the reciprocal nature of transference and countertransference. This evolving landscape widened the scope of inquiry, fostering ongoing dialogues and debates around the ethical and clinical implications of these complex phenomena.

2. Lacanian Interpretation of Transference:

Transference, a fundamental concept in psychoanalysis, takes on a unique significance within the Lacanian framework. Building upon Freud's original conceptualization, Lacan refines and reinterprets transference through the lens of linguistic and symbolic processes. For Lacan, transference is not merely a manifestation of past relational dynamics but an entrance into the symbolic order, where desires intertwine with linguistic structures. Central to this interpretation is the idea that transference is a repetition of unconscious patterns, traced back to the subject's initiation into language and culture. Lacan emphasizes that the analyst becomes the significant Other for the analysand, serving as a locus for the transfer of affect and signification. In this view, transference is inherently bound up in the play of signifiers, reflecting the subject's entanglement in the web of language and desire. Through the process of transference, the analysand's unmet needs, fantasies, and unresolved conflicts are transferred onto the figure of the analyst, shaping the dynamics of the analytic relationship. Lacan highlights the dual nature of transference, which encompasses both a means of resistance and a pathway to accessing the unconscious. He underscores the importance of recognizing transference as a site of resistance, where the analysand's conscious intentions come into conflict with underlying unconscious motivations. From a Lacanian perspective, the analyst's role is to decode these transference phenomena, n tracing the interplay of signifiers and revealing the underlying fantasies and alienations at play. Furthermore, Lacan extends the concept of transference beyond the traditional dyadic relationship between analyst and analysand to encompass the larger cultural and social context. This broadening of transference aligns with Lacan's insistence on viewing the individual psyche as intertwined with broader socio-cultural forces. Consequently, transference is situated within the wider network of symbolic exchange, blurring the boundaries between the personal and the collective unconscious. By emphasizing the symbolic nature of transference, Lacan revolutionizes its clinical implications, urging analysts to engage with the complex tapestry of signifiers and meanings that underpin the analysand's subjective experience.

3. Countertransference - Echoes in Lacanian Analysis:

Countertransference, as perceived within the framework of Lacanian analysis, provides a unique lens through which to understand the intricacies and complexities inherent in the analytic process. Contrary to traditional psychoanalytic perspectives that often pathologize countertransference as an impediment to the therapeutic relationship, Lacanian thought offers a redefined understanding of this phenomenon. In Lacan's view, countertransference is not merely a reaction stemming from unresolved personal conflicts of the analyst but is an inevitable aspect of the dialectical interplay between the analysand and the analyst. It is an echo, a reverberation of the unconscious dynamics at play within the analytic field. Countertransference can serve as a vital tool for gaining insight into the unconscious material being conveyed by the analysand. Through a meticulous exploration of the resonances evoked within the analyst, Lacanian analysis seeks to uncover the latent signifiers and symbolic representations intertwined within the narrative of the analysand. This exploration illuminates the ways in which the analyst becomes entwined in the same web of signification as the analysand, shedding light on the connections between their subjective positions. Rather than viewing countertransference as an obstacle, Lacanian analysis invites the analyst to embrace it as a source of valuable information regarding the unconscious desires, identifications, and conflicts manifesting within the treatment setting. By interrogating the nature of these resonances, Lacanian analysts can better manage the shifting terrain of transference and countertransference, thereby fostering deeper insights into the unconscious movements taking place within the analytic relationship. Integral to this process is the acknowledgment of the analyst's own position as the subject supposed to know within the analytic situation, recognizing that the analyst is not immune to the effects of transference and countertransference. As such, the analyst's subjective positioning becomes a crucial aspect of the analytic work, influencing the ways in which unconscious material unfolds and is processed.

4. Dynamics of the Analytic Relationship:

In the Lacanian framework, the dynamics of the analytic relationship encapsulate a complex interplay of symbolic, imaginary, and real elements, intertwined with the manifestations of transference and countertransference. The analyst, as the figure of the 'Other' within the therapeutic setting, occupies a position that becomes central to the unconscious processes of the analysand. As the dialogue unfolds, the symbolic dimension comes to the fore, permeating the exchange of language, signifiers, and meanings. This sets the stage for the emergence of unconscious desires, repressed traumas, and deeply ingrained fantasies.

Simultaneously, the imaginary aspects of the relationship manifest through the mirroring and identifications that occur between the analyst and the analysand. These dynamic interactions often give rise to profound moments of misrecognition and projection, illuminating the webs of the analysand's ego formation and self-perception. The interplay of these imaginary dimensions serves as a fertile ground for exploring unresolved conflicts and latent psychological tensions, as they unfold within the therapeutic space.

Delving into the real within the analytic relationship unveils the fundamental lack and unattainable aspects inherent in the human experience. The presence of the real disrupts and destabilizes the symbolic and imaginary coordinates, laying bare the raw and disorienting truths that elude linguistic and perceptual capture. Within this tumultuous terrain, the subjectivity of both the analyst and the analysand grapples with the confrontation of the unsymbolizable and the enigmatic.

The analytical relationship manages the balance between unveiling hidden truths and respecting the boundaries of privacy and confidentiality. The choreography of uncovering repressed experiences, while delicately treading on the ethical considerations and preserving the autonomy of the analysand, underscores the complex ethical dimensions that underpin the dynamics of the therapeutic alliance.

5. The Concept of the Subject Supposed to Know:

In Lacanian psychoanalysis, this notion elucidates the position held by the analyst as the supposed repository of knowledge and understanding within the analytical setting. The phrase captures the idea that the analyst is perceived by the analysand as possessing insights into the unconscious that the analysand does not have. This engenders a dynamic in which the analyst is attributed with a certain authority and knowledge, leading to complex implications for the therapeutic relationship.

From a Lacanian perspective, this concept intertwines with the symbolic order, where language and its associated knowledge structures form a crucial backdrop. The analyst becomes the embodiment of the 'Other' in the analytical dialogue, symbolizing an external locus of knowledge and interpretation. Consequently, the analysand invests the analyst with an enigmatic quality of possessing answers and interpretations, thereby placing the analyst in the position of the 'Subject Supposed to Know.'

This positioning engenders a balance within the analytic space, sparking the interplay of unconscious dynamics and power differentials. The analyst must attend to this role with astuteness and sensitivity, cognizant of the influence they hold over the analysand's psyche. Moreover, the concept of the 'Subject Supposed to Know' implicates the analyst in a responsibility to address and interpret the unconscious utterances of the analysand, wielding their purported knowledge to guide the journey towards insight and self-discovery.

However, the Lacanian perspective also underscores the inherent illusion inherent in this presumed knowledge and authority. It emphasizes the constructed nature of this knowledge, rendering it contingent upon the symbolism and discourse at play within the analytical setting. As such, the analyst is constantly challenged to grapple with the elusive nature of their purported knowledge, recognizing that it is fundamentally intertwined with the symbolic constructs and linguistic frameworks that shape its very essence.

The ramifications of the 'Subject Supposed to Know' ripple through the psychoanalytic domain, permeating the tapestry of transference, countertransference, and the dialectics of desire within the analytic dyad. This concept beckons analysts to introspect deeply on their role and the evolving contours of power and knowledge within the therapeutic milieu, urging a constant reevaluation of the nuances inherent in assuming the mantle of the 'Subject Supposed to Know.' In essence, this Lacanian perspective unearths the layers of complexity underscoring the analytic relationship, unveiling the enigmatic dance of authority, knowledge, and unconscious forces that converge within the sacred space of psychoanalysis.

6. Resistances and Unconscious Dynamics:

Understanding and effectively addressing resistances and unconscious dynamics is paramount in Lacanian analytic practice. As we delve into the spheres of the human psyche, we inevitably encounter moments of resistance, hesitation, and defense mechanisms that manifest as barriers to the unfolding of repressed desires and traumas. These resistances often emerge in the form of transference, countertransference, or symbolic obstructions, reflecting the dialectical interplay between the conscious and the unconscious. In the Lacanian framework, these phenomena are pivotal to the analysis, as they offer profound insights into the subject's psychical constitution and the underlying fantasies and conflicts. By skillfully identifying and interpreting these resistances, analysts gain access to the unspoken, the unsaid, and the repressed, thereby unraveling the enigmatic fabric of the analysand's unconscious.

On the other hand, i, it is essential for analysts to manage the intricacies of unconscious dynamics with finesse and empathy. The analyst serves as a guide through the corridors of the analysand's unconscious, embracing the uncertainties, contradictions, and complexities that reside within. Through the discerning application of Lacan's concepts such as the Imaginary, the Symbolic, and the Real, the analyst illuminates the shadows of the unconscious, shedding light on suppressed traumas, unresolved conflicts, and repressed desires. By meticulously untangling these unconscious threads, the analyst engenders a transformative process that cultivates self-awareness, insight, and the emergence of new signifiers that reconfigure the analysand's subjective landscape.

Crucially, the ethical dimension of handling resistances and unconscious dynamics cannot be overstated. The analyst must manage these territories with integrity, sensitivity, and respect for the analysand's autonomy. Engaging in this delicate dance demands vigilance against imposing one's own desires, biases, or interpretations onto the analysand's narrative. Striking a balance between interpretation and restraint is paramount, as it upholds the ethical imperative of fostering an environment where the analysand's agency and subjectivity remain sacrosanct. Furthermore, acknowledging the limitations of interpretation and embracing the ineffable aspects of the unconscious reinforces ethical conduct while fortifying the bond of trust within the analytic relationship.

7. Ethics in Lacanian Analytic Practice:

As practitioners engage with individuals' unconscious desires and drive towards subjective truth, they are confronted with complex ethical dilemmas. Lacanian analytic practice inherently demands a profound respect for the autonomy and subjectivity of the analysand, recognizing their right to self-determination and personal agency. This foundational premise underscores the ethical principles governing Lacanian analysis.

Central to Lacanian ethics is the emphasis on the analyst's position as an agent of neutrality and non-judgment. The analyst must endeavor to maintain a posture of equanimity and refrain from imposing moral or normative frameworks onto the analysand's subjective experience. This necessitates a commitment to suspending one's personal biases and preconceptions, thereby fostering an environment where the analysand's unique truth can unfurl without undue interference.

The concept of 'desire' within Lacanian theory introduces complexities to the ethical terrain. A fundamental tenet of Lacanian ethics involves recognizing the radical nature of desire and the intricacies of managing its manifestations within the analytic setting. As such, analysts are tasked with engaging with the analysand's desire while avoiding exploitation or manipulation. This calls for a vigilant awareness of power differentials and a commitment to fostering an equitable and respectful dynamic.

An ethical concern in Lacanian practice revolves around the concept of 'the analyst's desire.' While traditional psychoanalytic approaches often prioritize identifying and mitigating the analyst's desires, Lacanian ethics reframe this notion. Here, the analyst's desire is acknowledged and deployed as an instrument for promoting the analysand's subjective exploration. This reorientation challenges analysts to introspectively confront their own desires and utilize them in service of the analysand's analytic journey.

The disclosure of the analyst's personal associations and countertransference experiences is approached with discernment in Lacanian practice. Balancing transparency with the preservation of the analysand's autonomy requires thoughtful ethical management, given Lacan's assertion that the analyst's disclosures should not eclipse the analysand's subjective emergence.

Ultimately, Lacanian analytic ethics encapsulate a continual interplay of responsibility, sensitivity, and self-reflexivity, underscoring the balance between intervention and restraint within the boundaries of analytical practice.

THE SYMBOLIC ORDER - STRUCTURE AND FUNCTION

Linguistic Foundations

1. Introduction:

Lacanian theory is deeply rooted in the linguistic principles that form the foundation of his psychoanalytic framework. At the core of Lacan's theory is the belief that language structures our subjective experience and shapes our identity. Semiotics and structuralism serve as the pillars on which Lacan builds his theoretical edifice. Semiotics, the study of signs and symbols, provides a framework for understanding the significance of linguistic systems in shaping meaning and subjectivity. Structuralism, on the other hand, emphasizes the underlying structures and systems that govern language and human behavior. Saussure's influence is particularly noteworthy in shaping Lacan's views on linguistics. He introduced the notion of the signifier and the signified, laying the groundwork for understanding the arbitrary nature of linguistic signs and the role of differences in signification. Within Lacanian theory, this concept of signifier and signified becomes pivotal in elucidating the mechanisms of desire and the formation of unconscious fantasies. Delving further, we encounter the idea of language as a structure of the unconscious. Lacan posits that language not only reflects but also constructs our subjective reality. The unconscious, according to Lacan, is structured like a language, replete with its own set of rules and significations. This perspective offers a unique vantage point to analyze the symbolic formations that underpin psychological phenomena. Phonemes and chains of signifiers signify another crucial area within Lacanian linguistics. The phoneme, as the smallest unit of sound in a language, plays a central role in Lacanian analysis, heralding the fragmented nature of language and pointing towards the gaps and slippages within speech. Chains of signifiers, or signifying chains, allude to the interconnected web of words and meanings that constitute language. Exploring these elements discloses the intricacies of linguistic structures within Lacanian theory, shedding light on the ways in which language operates as a medium for articulating unconscious desires and conflicts.

2. Semiotics and Structuralism:

Semiotics, as developed by Ferdinand de Saussure and Charles Sanders Peirce, offers a framework for comprehending how language operates as a system of signifiers and signifieds. Saussure's seminal work on the nature of linguistic signs posits that a sign is composed of a signifier (the form of the word) and a signified (the concept it represents). This defined relationship forms the basis of structural linguistics, emphasizing the relational and differential nature of language.

Structuralism, stemming from the works of Claude Lévi-Strauss, examines underlying structures and regularities across various phenomena, including language, culture, and social systems. This approach contends that meaning is derived from the interplay of elements within a structure rather than inherent qualities, aligning with the fundamental tenets of semiotics.

The dichotomous nature of the sign, particularly the concepts of binary oppositions and the roles they play in the construction of meaning, is pivotal to understanding the symbolic order. Binary oppositions, such as presence/absence, male/female, or good/evil, not only structure language but also inform our understanding of reality and shape our experiences.

The structuralist approach emphasizes the notion of 'langue' (language system) as distinct from 'parole' (individual speech acts). This differentiation is vital in comprehending the symbolic order as a collective network of signifying practices that regulate social interaction, identity formation, and unconscious desires.

In psychoanalytic discourse, the application of structuralist principles reveals the unconscious as a structured language, governed by the same mechanisms as conscious discourse. The repressed content manifests through symbolic formations, allowing for the interpretation of unconscious processes through the analysis of linguistic signifiers and their interconnectedness.

3. Saussurean Influence on the Symbolic Order:

Ferdinand de Saussure's seminal work in the field of linguistics, particularly his ideas on the nature of linguistic signs and their role in shaping human consciousness, provided a theoretical framework that greatly informed Lacan's development of the symbolic register within psychoanalysis.

Central to Saussure's theories is the distinction between the signifier and the signified, which lays the groundwork for understanding how language operates as a system of differences. In Saussurean terms, the signifier is the perceptible form or sound pattern of a word, while the signified is the mental concept or meaning associated with that form. This dichotomous relationship becomes a key element in Lacan's formulation of the Symbolic Order, wherein the signifier comes to represent the subject and mediates their entry into linguistic and cultural meanings.

Saussure's emphasis on the arbitrary nature of linguistic signs, where the connection between signifier and signified is not based on intrinsic resemblance but rather on conventional social agreement, aligns with Lacan's conception of the Symbolic Order as a domain deeply enmeshed in cultural norms and societal structures. The notion of arbitrariness and the relational nature of language carries through Lacan's exploration of how subjects are constituted and situated within language, highlighting the interplay between signifiers and the construction of identity.

Saussure's structural approach to language as a system of interconnected elements resonates with Lacan's understanding of the unconscious as structured like a language. The hierarchical organization of linguistic units and the rules governing their combinations parallel Lacan's conception of the symbolic as a network of interconnected signifiers producing meaning through their differential relationships. This structural view informs

Lacan's articulation of the symbolic as the locus of shared cultural symbols and norms that shape individual subjectivity and social interactions.

4. The Role of the Signifier and the Signified:

In the Symbolic Order, the notions of signifier and signified play a fundamental role in shaping our understanding of language and its impact on the unconscious. Ferdinand de Saussure introduced the concept of signifier and signified as key components of the linguistic sign. The signifier represents the physical form of a word, whereas the signified is the concept or meaning associated with that form. This duality forms the basis of language and communication, reflecting the intertwined nature of language and thought.

Within the psychoanalytic framework, the Signifier takes on added significance as it becomes a crucial element in the formation of the unconscious. It is through the signifiers present in language that individuals come to understand and engage with their experiences, emotions, and desires. Moreover, the interaction between signifiers shapes the symbolic landscape within which human subjectivity emerges and evolves.

Lacan further elaborated on this relationship, highlighting the dynamic and often complex interplay between signifiers and signifieds. This interplay is not limited to straightforward, one-to-one correspondences, but rather involves a web of associations and connections that contribute to the richness and ambiguity of language and meaning. Linguistic structures abound with overlapping signifiers and multifaceted signifieds, allowing for the potential of multiple interpretations and layered meanings.

The interaction between the signifier and the signified also resonates deeply with Lacan's broader conceptualization of the unconscious. Within the Symbolic Order, these linguistic elements become entangled with unconscious processes, influencing the ways in which individuals perceive themselves and the world around them. The inherent instability of signification mirrors the elusive nature of the unconscious, where meanings constantly shift and transform, often eluding conscious awareness.

This process of signification holds particular relevance within the practice of psychoanalysis, as it underscores the link between language and the unconscious. Analysts and patients alike engage with the terrain of the symbolic, exploring the nuances of signifiers and uncovering the latent meanings embedded within linguistic expressions. As such, understanding the role of the signifier and the signified is pivotal in deciphering the mechanisms at play within the Symbolic Order, shedding light on the complexities of human subjectivity and experience.

5. Language as a Structure of the Unconscious:

In Lacanian theory, language operates as a medium through which the unconscious mind expresses and conceals desires, thoughts, and conflicts. The way in which language shapes our perceptions and cognitions is paramount to understanding the workings of the unconscious. Linguistic elements such as syntax, grammar, and vocabulary influence the formation of thoughts and the encoding of repressed content within the unconscious.

Lacan posited that the unconscious is structured like a language, and it communicates through the use of signifiers and the play of meanings. This implies that the symbolic order, based on linguistic constructs, serves as a template for the organization of the unconscious, regulating the formation of subjectivity and identity. The bridge between language and the unconscious brings forth the significance of interpretation and the role of the analyst in deciphering the latent content encoded within the linguistic formations of the analysand.

The concept of the unconscious as structured like a language underscores the prevalence of ambivalence, contradictions, and slips of the tongue in human communication. These linguistic phenomena serve as manifestations of the underlying unconscious processes, revealing repressed material through parapraxis and other linguistic deviations. Understanding language as a structure of the unconscious enriches the psychoanalytic practice by offering insights into the symbolic resolutions present within linguistic expressions.

The linguistic nature of the unconscious accentuates the influence of culture and social discourse on the formation and articulation of unconscious desires. The unconscious, shaped by the symbolic order, reflects broader societal and cultural norms embedded within language. As a result, psychoanalysis delves into the linguistic nuances of the subject's speech and narratives to unveil the hidden meanings influenced by societal constructs and prevailing discourses.

The examination of language as an essential component of the unconscious leads to a more profound comprehension of how the symbolic order permeates and structures individual subjectivities. By assimilating language as a fundamental paradigm for the unconscious, psychoanalysis gains invaluable insights into the intricacies of human thought processes, interpersonal dynamics, and the symbolic manifestations within the clinical setting.

6. Phonemes and Chains of Signifiers:

Phonemes represent the smallest units of sound that are capable of distinguishing between distinct meanings in a particular language. They form the building blocks of language and play a pivotal role in the formation of signifiers within the symbolic order. As such, they hold significant relevance in the milieu of psychoanalysis and the decoding of unconscious desires.

Lacan emphasized the importance of phonemes in language, considering them as the carriers of unconscious meaning and integral components in the structure of the symbolic. Through his reworking of Saussure's linguistics, Lacan highlighted the role of phonemes in creating meaning through their alignment within chains of signifiers. These chains, or sequences of interconnected phonemes, serve as the manifestations of linguistic structures that govern thought patterns and communication.

The concept of chains of signifiers extends beyond the individual elements of language, encompassing the complexities of how these phonemic structures relate to one another within discourse. This interaction forms the basis for the construction of meaning and drives the symbolic processes that influence human subjectivity. As individuals engage in linguistic exchanges, these chains of signifiers enable the expression and interpretation of ideas, emotions, and desires, all of which are deeply intertwined with the unconscious.

Within the psychoanalytic framework, the manipulation and distortion of phonemes and signifiers hold profound significance. Lacan's exploration of wordplay, puns, and linguistic slippage underscores the potential for multiple meanings and unconscious connotations embedded within language. This fluidity and ambiguity inherent in phonemic structures contribute to the rich tapestry of the unconscious, highlighting the potential for hidden meanings and repressed thoughts to surface through linguistic expression.

The examination of phonemes and chains of signifiers unveils the web of linguistic symbolism that underpins human interaction and the formation of subjectivity. It provides a lens through which the profound impact of language on the unconscious becomes palpable, offering profound insights into the ways in which linguistic structures shape and influence our psyches. By unraveling the complexities of phonemic arrangements and their interplay within linguistic chains, we gain a deeper understanding of the profound significance of language within the symbolic order and its implications for psychoanalytic practice.

7. Metaphor and Metonymy in the Symbolic:

Metaphor and metonymy play a crucial role in how individuals construct and comprehend reality, thereby shaping their subjective experiences. Within the Symbolic Order, metaphor and metonymy operate as fundamental modes of symbolic communication and representation. Metaphor, as a figurative language device, facilitates the association of one concept with another, often in a non-literal or symbolic manner. By juxtaposing seemingly unrelated elements, metaphor enables the expression of abstract or complex ideas, offering a rich tapestry of meaning within the Symbolic Order. In contrast, metonymy functions by establishing associations between contiguous or related elements, representing a more direct and interconnected mode of signification. In doing so, metonymy operates as a mechanism for highlighting the interconnectedness and continuity of concepts within the Symbolic Order. Moreover, these two linguistic constructs not only influence communication but also permeate the unconscious mind. Within psychoanalytic practice, metaphors and metonymies provide insights into the underlying mechanisms of the unconscious and the processes through which desires and conflicts are articulated. They serve as tools for unlocking subliminal meanings and uncovering latent content within discourse, emphasizing the interplay between language, meaning, and the unconscious in the Symbolic Order. Additionally, the cultural and contextual variations in the employment of metaphor and metonymy further accentuate their significance in understanding the Symbolic Order across diverse linguistic and cultural landscapes. The interplay of metaphor and metonymy within different languages and cultures illustrates the adaptability and universality of these symbolic processes, shedding light on how individuals construct and negotiate meaning within their respective social and communicative frameworks. Furthermore, exploring the nuances of metaphor and metonymy in the Symbolic Order allows for a deeper comprehension of how language structures and influences our understanding of reality, identity, and interpersonal relations.

8. Variations Across Languages and Cultures:

Language and culture are intimately linked, and the variations across different languages and cultural contexts offer valuable insights into the complexities of the Symbolic Order. When we examine these variations, we can better understand how language shapes and reflects the symbolic structures that influence individuals and societies. One of the fundamental aspects to consider is the differing structures and grammatical systems present in various languages. For instance, the presence of grammatical gender in some languages, while absent in others, highlights the diverse ways in which linguistic systems categorize and conceptualize the world. Moreover, variations in sentence structure, word order, and phonological patterns demonstrate the ways in which languages encode and convey meaning. These distinctions underscore the importance of studying language diversity within the framework of the Symbolic Order. Beyond structural differences, the vocabulary and lexicon of a language provide unique perspectives on cultural values, social norms, and historical experiences. Through the analysis of linguistic terms and idiomatic expressions, we gain profound insights into the collective psyche and worldview of a particular culture. Furthermore, the presence of untranslatable words in one language but not in another sheds light on the nuances of human experience that may be more salient or implicitly understood in specific cultural contexts. It is crucial to recognize that these linguistic variations do not exist in isolation; they are embedded within broader cultural practices, rituals, and belief systems. As such, the study of language and culture within the Symbolic Order necessitates an interdisciplinary approach that integrates anthropology, sociology, and linguistics. This interdisciplinary lens allows for a deeper understanding of how language both reflects and perpetuates societal structures, power dynamics, and identity formation. Additionally, the examination of multilingual environments and language contact phenomena provides valuable insights into the negotiation of multiple symbolic systems and the impact of language hybridity on individual subjectivity.

9. Linguistic Determinism and its Critiques:

Linguistic determinism, a concept rooted in the Sapir-Whorf hypothesis, proposes that the structure of a language shapes or determines the perception and thought patterns of its speakers. In other words, the linguistic system one is immersed in significantly influences cognition and worldview. This controversial notion has been widely debated within the arenas of linguistics, psychology, and anthropology, particularly due to its potential implications on individual agency, cultural relativity, and cognitive processes. Supporters of linguistic determinism argue that language not only reflects but also molds our understanding of reality, shaping how we perceive and interpret the world around us. They contend that different languages encode distinct conceptual categories and modes of thought, leading to unique cognitive perspectives among speakers of those languages. However, critics of linguistic determinism question the extent of its influence on human cognition, asserting that while language may influence thought, it does not rigidly determine or restrict it. They point to the diversity of human experiences and the ability of individuals to adopt multiple linguistic and cultural frameworks, suggesting that cognitive flexibility transcends linguistic boundaries. Moreover, empirical studies have provided mixed evidence regarding the strength of linguistic determinism, with certain research findings supporting its influence in specific cognitive domains while others demonstrate a more nuanced relationship between language and thought. The critique further delves into the challenge of disentangling linguistic influences from other social, historical, and psychological factors that shape cognition, highlighting the complexity of understanding the role of language in shaping human perception and behavior. By critically examining the premises and implications of linguistic determinism, scholars aim to elucidate the multifaceted interplay between language and cognition, shedding light on the dynamics of human thought processes and cultural diversity.

The Role of Language and Signifiers

1. Introduction:

Human language is a complex and dynamic system that permeates every aspect of our lives, influencing not only how we communicate but also how we perceive and construct reality. In the context of psychoanalytic theory, language holds a foundational role in shaping human consciousness and subjectivity. The significance of language in the Symbolic Order, as elucidated by Jacques Lacan, extends far beyond mere verbal or written expression; it encompasses the web of symbols and signifiers through which individuals engage with their existence. By delving into the depth of linguistic theories and their implications, we can begin to unravel the profound impact of language on the formation of the self and social relations. Through structuralist and post-structuralist lenses, the study of language as a signifying system unveils its capacity to organize and designate meaning within cultural frameworks, thereby affecting the ways in which individuals experience and signify their world. Consideration of the arbitrariness, duality, and relational aspects of linguistic signs, as expounded by Ferdinand de Saussure, underlines how language operates as a potent force in structuring human perceptions and interactions. Moreover, the intricacies of language acquisition and its intrinsic ties to cognition further emphasize the pervasive influence of language on subject formation, where symbolic representations interplay with individual psychical development. Furthermore, the reevaluation of linguistic determinism and its relation to psychological registers marks an essential exploration in understanding the power dynamics inherent in language and its construction of subjectivity. By embarking on a multifaceted exploration of language and its philosophical, sociocultural, and psychoanalytic underpinnings, we can begin to fathom the tapestry of signification and communication woven into the fabric of human existence.

2. The Concept of the Signifier:

In delving into the complex register of the Symbolic Order, we encounter the pivotal concept of the signifier. The signifier, as elucidated by Ferdinand de Saussure and further expounded upon by Jacques Lacan, constitutes a foundational element in understanding the nature of language and its role within the human psyche. At its essence, the signifier is a linguistic entity that encompasses not merely a sound or a written symbol, but rather a fundamental unit of meaning within a system of language. This meaning, however, is not inherent to the signifier itself, but rather emerges from its relation to other signifiers within the linguistic network.

Crucially, the concept of the signifier denotes the arbitrariness of linguistic signs; that is, the lack of inherent connection between the signifier and the signified. This notion disrupts any presumed direct link between language and objective reality, highlighting instead the constructed and symbolic nature of human communication. By recognizing the signifier as a significant building block of language, we are prompted to consider the profound impact of this construction on the processes of subject formation and inter-subjective relations.

Lacan's integration of the signifier into his psychoanalytic framework illuminates its role in the constitution of the unconscious. Here, the signifier does not simply serve as a conveyor of explicit meanings, but also operates in the unconscious, giving rise to the web of desires and identifications that shape an individual's psychic landscape. Through an exploration of Lacanian theory, we come to appreciate the signifier as more than a mere linguistic entity, but as a vehicle for the transmission of meaning and the formation of subjective experience.

The study of the signifier invites us to consider the diverse cultural and historical dimensions of language. Each signifier encapsulates a wealth of social, historical, and cultural resonances, reflecting the collective experiences and interpretations of a particular community. This multifaceted quality of the signifier underscores the dynamic and evolving nature of language, wherein meanings are continually negotiated and reshaped through socio-cultural practices and discourses.

3. Saussurean Linguistics and Lacanian Theory:

Saussurean linguistics forms a foundational basis for understanding language and its role in the construction of meaning within the symbolic order. This paradigm emphasizes the fundamental distinction between signifier and signified, asserting that language operates through a system of differences rather than fixed, inherent meanings. Within the context of Lacanian theory, this framework provides valuable insights into the nature of linguistic structures and their influence on subjectivity. Lacan himself drew extensively from Saussure's work, integrating it into his psychoanalytic framework to illuminate the symbolic dimension of human existence. Through this integration, Lacan explored the ways in which language and signifiers shape our understanding of self and reality, underscoring the pivotal role of language in structuring subjective experience. Within the Lacanian framework, language is not merely a tool for communication, but a fundamental constituent of the unconscious and the mechanisms by which individual subjectivity is formed. By delving into the interplay between Saussurean linguistics and Lacanian theory, scholars and practitioners gain a deeper appreciation of how language functions as a dynamic force within the symbolic order, shaping and mediating our perceptions, desires, and relationships. Moreover, this synthesis underscores the profound implications of linguistic structures on the constitution of social norms, power dynamics, and identity formation. As such, the exploration of Saussurean linguistics within the context of Lacanian theory serves to highlight the rich tapestry of connections between language, subjectivity, and the broader societal fabric. It elucidates the ways in which linguistic systems intersect with the symbolic order, offering profound implications for fields such as psychoanalysis, semiotics, and cultural studies. Understanding this nexus not only enriches our comprehension of human experience but also sheds light on the complexities of discourse, representation, and meaning-making processes within the symbolic.

4. The Function of Language in the Formation of Subjectivity:

As individuals engage with language, they are not merely passive recipients of linguistic symbols; rather, they actively participate in the process of signification and meaning-making. Through language, individuals engage with and interpret their experiences, emotions, and relationships, thereby constructing their subjective realities. The Symbolic Order, as conceptualized by Lacan, encompasses this web of linguistic and symbolic interactions that underpin the formation of subjectivity.

Central to the function of language in subjectivity formation is the concept of the symbolic signifier. Words, phrases, and linguistic symbols act as signifiers that mediate individual experiences and feelings, translating them into coherent and communicable expressions. This process of signification is not only a means of communication but also a fundamental mechanism through which individuals internalize and comprehend their own thoughts and emotions. The interplay of signifiers within language enables individuals to attribute meaning and significance to their lived experiences, thereby contributing to the construction of their subjective identities.

Language serves as a medium through which individuals negotiate their social and cultural contexts, thereby influencing the development of their subjectivity. The linguistic structures and norms prevalent within a given society or community shape the ways in which individuals articulate and understand their thoughts and feelings, consequently molding their subjective perspectives. In this sense, language operates as a primary tool for individuals to situate themselves within societal frameworks and to establish their roles and identities within various social structures.

The function of language in subjectivity formation extends beyond individual experiences to encompass broader societal and historical narratives. Language, as a repository of collective knowledge, myths, and cultural scripts, influences and shapes the very fabric of an individual's subjectivity. Through language, individuals access and internalize the cultural heritage and traditions that inform their understanding of themselves and their place within the world. Additionally, language acts as a conduit for transmitting societal ideologies, power dynamics, and norms, all of which contribute to the ongoing construction of subjectivity within the Symbolic Order.

5. Symbolic Representation in Human Interaction:

In the milieu of psychoanalysis, the concept of the Symbolic Order extends beyond the individual psyche and permeates into human interaction. Through language and symbolic representation, individuals engage in a complex web of communication and social exchange that is deeply embedded within the Symbolic Order.

Symbolic representation in human interaction encompasses various forms of communication, ranging from verbal discourse to non-verbal cues and gestures. Within the context of psychoanalytic theory, these interactions are laden with symbolic meaning, often manifesting through unconscious processes rooted in language, signifiers, and cultural codes. Through conversation, individuals establish and negotiate their place within social structures, reflecting the interplay between the individual and the Symbolic Order.

Within human interaction, symbolic representation serves as a fundamental mechanism for the expression and interpretation of desires, identities, and power dynamics. Language, as a primary medium of symbolic representation, shapes the construction of social reality and the formation of interpersonal relationships. The exchange of signifiers and symbols facilitates the negotiation of meaning and the establishment of shared understandings, allowing individuals to manage the complexities of social encounters.

The dynamics of symbolic representation in human interaction are deeply intertwined with Lacanian concepts such as the Other and the phallus. These notions illuminate the ways in which individuals position themselves in relation to others, grappling with issues of recognition, authority, and desire within the Symbolic Order. The symbolic dimensions of gender, sexuality, and cultural norms also become salient in shaping the dynamics of human interaction, highlighting the influence of symbolic representation on societal structures.

6. The Interrelationship Between Signifiers and Meaning:

The signifier, as conceived within Lacanian theory, encompasses not only linguistic symbols but also any entity that represents or signifies something else. This could range from spoken words and written text to images, gestures, or even cultural practices. What sets the signifier apart is its functioning as a transmitter of meaning, often bearing a complex relationship with the signified. As we explore this interplay, it becomes evident that the significance and interpretation of signifiers are deeply rooted in the socio-cultural context, thus allowing for a multitude of nuanced meanings that contribute to the richness of human communication.

The connotative aspect of signifiers adds an additional layer of complexity to their relationship with meaning. This connotation is shaped not only by individual experiences but also by the collective unconscious, as proposed by psychoanalytic frameworks. Consequently, the same signifier may evoke varying meanings and emotional responses, thereby illustrating the fluid and dynamic nature of this interrelationship. It is through this inherent ambiguity and plurality of meanings that communication thrives, fostering endless possibilities for interpretation and understanding.

A pertinent elucidation on the interrelationship between signifiers and meaning lies in their function within the psychoanalytic setting. Language, laden with signifiers, becomes a conduit for exploring the depths of the unconscious and deciphering the symbolic representations embedded in individuals' thoughts, dreams, and expressions. Deconstructing these signifiers unveils layers of meaning that may have otherwise remained concealed, offering profound insights and facilitating the process of self-discovery and healing.

Considering the ever-evolving nature of language, it is crucial to acknowledge the ongoing reconfiguration and expansion of signifiers and their associated meanings. This adaptability not only reflects societal changes but also underscores the continuous negotiation of meanings within the symbolic order. By recognizing and embracing this flux, we gain a deeper appreciation of the power vested in signifiers and their integral role in shaping our subjective experiences and interpersonal connections.

7. Linguistic Variations Across Cultural Contexts:

Language exhibits fascinating variations across different cultural contexts. One striking aspect of linguistic variations across cultural contexts is the diverse lexicon and semantic nuances present in different languages. For example, the Inuit people have numerous words to describe snow, reflecting the centrality of this phenomenon in their environment and lives. In contrast, English may not encapsulate the same depth of specificity in its terminology related to snow. These variations highlight the profound influence of cultural and environmental factors on language development and usage.

The grammatical structures and syntactic conventions present in various languages can differ significantly, leading to distinct cognitive frameworks and modes of apprehending reality. For instance, the concept of time may be expressed differently in different languages, influencing the temporal orientation and perception of individuals within these linguistic communities.

Consider the difference between languages that primarily use absolute spatial terms (e.g., north, south, east, west) versus those that rely on relative spatial terms (e.g., left, right). Such variances have profound implications for how individuals make sense of and interpret the world around them.

Cultural idioms, metaphors, and proverbs further exemplify the nuanced characteristics of language within specific cultural milieus. These linguistic features often encapsulate deeper cultural values, beliefs, and collective experiences, providing a window into the symbolic underpinnings of a given society. By exploring these linguistic intricacies, we gain a deeper understanding of the symbolic mechanisms that underpin human communication and social interaction across diverse cultural landscapes.

The ways in which languages encode and express social hierarchy, power dynamics, and societal norms vary significantly, reflecting the complex interplay between language and the symbolic order. The use of honorifics, kinship terms, and politeness markers in different languages reflects the social structures and relational dynamics embedded within these linguistic systems. Understanding the cultural and symbolic significance of these linguistic markers is crucial for comprehending the operation of the symbolic order within specific socio-cultural contexts.

8. Challenges and Limitations of Language within the Symbolic:

Language, as a primary medium for communication and symbolic representation, plays an integral role in shaping individual subjectivity and cultural identity. However, despite its significance, language also poses inherent challenges and limitations within the framework of the symbolic order. One of the key challenges arises from the inherently arbitrary nature of language, wherein the relationship between signifiers and signifieds is not fixed but rather contingent upon conventional agreement within a given linguistic community. This arbitrariness can lead to misunderstandings and conflicts, especially when individuals from different cultural contexts attempt to communicate with one another. Moreover, the multiplicity of meanings within a single language further complicates the process of signification, as words and symbols may evoke diverse connotations and interpretations based on individual experiences and social background. Language also faces limitations in adequately capturing the complexity and depth of human emotions and experiences. The ineffability of certain emotions or concepts poses a challenge to the ability of language to fully represent and articulate the intricacies of subjective inner worlds. Furthermore, the structure and grammar of language impose constraints on the expression of abstract and complex ideas, thereby limiting the precision and accuracy of conveying certain thoughts or perceptions. Additionally, the influence of power dynamics within language usage presents another challenge within the symbolic order. Dominant discourses and linguistic norms may marginalize or silence certain voices, leading to the perpetuation of inequality and oppression within society. Furthermore, the biases and prejudices embedded within language can contribute to the reinforcement of social hierarchies and systemic discrimination. These challenges and limitations underscore the relationship between language and the symbolic order, calling for critical examination and reflection on the role of language in shaping individual subjectivities and social structures. Addressing these complexities is crucial for fostering inclusivity and equity within diverse linguistic and cultural contexts, while also recognizing the inherent constraints of language in representing the rich tapestry of human experience.

Structures Within the Symbolic Order

1. Introduction to Symbolic Structures:

The exploration of symbolic structures forms a cornerstone within the domain of psychoanalytic theory and sociolinguistics. At its essence, symbolic structures constitute the web of significations and signifiers that underpin and organize the fabric of human reality. Grounded in the seminal works of Ferdinand de Saussure and further developed by Jacques Lacan, the framework of symbolic structures fundamentally revolves around the capacity for language and symbols to shape our understanding of the world. This network of linguistic and cultural codes creates a tapestry through which individuals work within their existence, construct their identities, and engage with others.

Central to this discourse is the concept of the signifier—an element within language that conveys meaning through its relation to other signifiers. Within this structure, the dynamic interplay between signifier and signified gives rise to the complex system of meanings and representations that encompass human experience. Furthermore, symbolic structures extend beyond the milieu of language, permeating societal institutions, rituals, and norms. The construction of these symbolic frameworks plays a pivotal role in informing individual subjectivities, social hierarchies, and power dynamics.

The influence of symbolic structures extends into the unconscious, as posited by Lacanian theory. The symbolic order, one of Lacan's three registers, constitutes culture and language, shaping the ways in which individuals both perceive themselves and relate to the external world. Embedded within the symbolic structures are the cultural myths, narratives, and archetypes that imbue significance and meaning into the human experience.

2. The Framework of Structural Linguistics:

Structural linguistics offers a distinctive lens through which to examine the relationship between language and the symbolic order. At its core, this framework delves into the underlying structure of language, emphasizing the pivotal role of signifiers and signifieds in shaping meaning. Developed by prominent linguists such as Ferdinand de Saussure and subsequently adopted and expanded upon by Jacques Lacan, structural linguistics poses fundamental implications for our understanding of communication, culture, and the human psyche.

Central to the framework of structural linguistics is the concept of the linguistic sign, comprising the signifier (the sound image) and the signified (the concept it represents). Saussure's seminal work highlighted the arbitrary nature of the sign, where the connection between the signifier and signified is not based on inherent meaning but rather on convention within a given linguistic community. This insight reverberates deeply into the symbolic order, underlining the constructed nature of meaning and identity.

The framework delineates the notion of langue (language system) and parole (individual speech acts), illuminating the duality of language as both a structured system and a dynamic manifestation in everyday communication. Within this dichotomy lies the tension between the collective and the individual, reflecting the interplay between societal norms and personal expression within the symbolic order. By scrutinizing the rules and patterns governing language usage, structural linguistics unveils the hidden mechanisms that dictate our interactions and cultural discourse.

The structuralist approach extends beyond the confines of syntax and semantics, extending its purview to encompass the broader fabric of society and culture. Through the analysis of myths, rituals, and social institutions, linguistic structures are discerned, unveiling recurring patterns and deep-seated symbolic meanings. This interdisciplinary reach underscores the far-reaching implications of the structuralist perspective, transcending linguistic inquiry to offer profound insights into the symbolic foundations of human experience.

3. Symbolic Networks and Their Implications:

In exploring the symbolic networks and their implications, we delve into the web of interconnected meanings and representations that define the Symbolic Order. Symbolic networks encompass a complex system of signifiers, codes, and symbols that structure our understanding of the world and mediate our interactions within it. These networks are not limited to linguistic communication but extend to various forms of cultural expressions, including rituals, customs, and traditions. Understanding the implications of these networks is crucial for comprehending the profound impact they have on individual identity, societal norms, and collective behaviors. Symbolic networks play a central role in shaping our perceptions, beliefs, and values, influencing not only our conscious thoughts but also our unconscious desires and motivations. Furthermore, these networks contribute to the construction and perpetuation of power dynamics, hierarchies, and social structures. By examining the implications of symbolic networks, we can gain insight into how they influence our experiences, relationships, and sense of belonging within different social contexts. Moreover, the study of symbolic networks allows us to uncover the underlying mechanisms through which meaning is produced, negotiated, and contested in diverse cultural settings. Understanding the implications of symbolic networks also sheds light on the ways in which individuals and communities engage in processes of meaning-making, interpretation, and semiotic negotiations. This awareness is essential for fostering intercultural understanding, addressing conflicts arising from divergent interpretations, and promoting inclusive dialogue across diverse social groups. As we further explore the implications of symbolic networks, we come to appreciate the significant role they play in shaping our realities, constructing our identities, and perpetuating cultural systems. By critically examining these implications, we open up avenues for reimagining and transforming the symbolic landscapes in ways that foster equity, solidarity, and cross-cultural appreciation.

4. Interconnections with Social Constructs:

The interconnections between the symbolic order and social constructs are integral to comprehending the complexities of human interaction and societal functioning. The symbolic order, as expounded by Lacanian theory, is deeply intertwined with social constructs, playing a pivotal role in shaping and regulating human behavior within various cultural contexts.

At the heart of this discussion lies the concept of symbolic norms and rituals, which form the cornerstone of social structures. These norms and rituals are imbued with symbolic meanings that govern interpersonal relationships, collective identities, and societal norms. Considerations of power dynamics, gender roles, class distinctions, and cultural practices are rooted in the symbolic order, permeating every aspect of social life. Moreover, the symbolic order serves as the framework through which individuals orient themselves within and interpret their place within the broader social landscape, influencing their perceptions, aspirations, and interactions.

An exploration of the symbolic underpinnings of language and communication unveils the indispensable link to social constructs. Language, as a primary vehicle of the symbolic order, not only reflects prevailing social values and norms but also actively contributes to their perpetuation and evolution. Through linguistic codes and discursive practices, individuals engage with and reinforce established social constructs, perpetuating or challenging prevailing systems of meaning. The dialectical relationship between language and society thus reveals the symbiotic nature of their interaction, underscoring the inextricable connection between the symbolic order and social constructs.

Additionally, an analysis of how symbolic representations and cultural symbols permeate societal institutions illuminates the pervasive influence of the symbolic order on social constructs. Whether in legal systems, religious institutions, educational frameworks, or artistic expressions, symbolic meanings and representations play a fundamental role in shaping and perpetuating social hierarchies, values, and belief systems. By scrutinizing these symbolic manifestations in different institutional settings, one gains insight into the ways in which social constructs are upheld, contested, and transformed within the symbolic order.

5. The Architecture of Symbolic Relations:

In delving into the intricacies of the symbolic order, it is essential to explore the architecture of symbolic relations. The framework within which symbolic relations are established and maintained plays a pivotal role in shaping the individual's interactions with the external world and with others in society. Symbolic relations can be viewed as the dynamic network of signifiers and symbols through which individuals create meaning and engage with their social reality.

At the heart of symbolic relations lies the concept of language and communication. Language serves as the primary medium through which symbolic relations are constructed and articulated. Within linguistic structures, symbolic relations are manifested through the use of signifiers and the process of signification. This linguistic foundation provides the scaffolding for the construction of symbolic meanings and representations.

The architecture of symbolic relations extends beyond individual interactions to encompass broader social and cultural contexts. Social institutions, such as family units, educational systems, and religious organizations, contribute to the establishment and perpetuation of symbolic relations within society. These institutions serve as the platforms through which individuals acquire and internalize symbolic meanings, norms, and values that shape their understanding of the world.

Cultural codes also play a significant role in shaping the architecture of symbolic relations. Cultural codes encompass the shared systems of meaning and interpretation within a given culture or society. These codes influence the ways in which individuals interpret and respond to symbolic expressions, thereby influencing the dynamics of symbolic relations within a cultural context.

Additionally, the architecture of symbolic relations intersects with power dynamics and social hierarchies. Symbolic relations are not neutral; they are imbued with power dynamics that reflect and perpetuate social inequalities. Certain symbols and signifiers may carry privileged meanings, while others may be marginalized or excluded within the symbolic order, contributing to stratifications and disparities in societal interactions.

6. The Influence of Cultural Codes:

Cultural codes are pivotal in determining how individuals perceive and interact with the world around them. These codes encompass a wide array of societal conventions, norms, traditions, rituals, and belief systems that are transmitted across generations. By examining the influence of cultural codes within the framework of the symbolic order, we gain valuable insights into the mechanisms that govern human cognition, behavior, and social dynamics.

At its core, cultural coding operates as a set of symbolic representations that imbue objects, actions, and phenomena with meaning, creating a shared semiotic landscape within a given community or society. This communal semiotics underpinning cultural codes enables the interpretation of symbols and the construction of collective narratives, fostering a sense of belonging and identity among individuals. Moreover, cultural codes serve as a lens through which individuals make sense of their experiences, guiding their understanding of relationships, customs, and existential questions.

Cultural codes permeate various dimensions of life, from artistic expressions and language to moral frameworks and social hierarchies. They contribute to the formation of structures of power, influence modes of communication, and shape perceptions of reality. Additionally, cultural codes often delineate social roles, behavioral expectations, and standards of morality, engendering a collective consciousness that exerts a profound impact on individual subjectivity and intersubjective interactions.

Understanding the significance of cultural codes is imperative in deciphering the complexities of human existence within the symbolic order. Cultural codes not only facilitate the transmission of knowledge and values but also act as mediators between the individual and the broader social fabric, anchoring individuals within a web of shared meanings and practices. By critically examining the cultural codes prevalent in different societies, we illuminate the ways in which norms, traditions, and rituals intersect with the symbolic order, shedding light on both the stabilizing and transformative forces inherent in cultural coding.

7. Symbolic Order in Familial Dynamics:

The familial structure is a microcosm of the larger societal symbolic order, playing a crucial role in shaping an individual's understanding of language, culture, and social norms. Within familial dynamics, the symbolic order is woven into the fabric of relationships, influencing patterns of communication, power dynamics, and the transmission of cultural codes from one generation to the next. Through interactions within the family unit, individuals are introduced to the symbolic register, where language and signifiers construct meanings and create a framework for understanding the world. This process begins at a young age, as children internalize the linguistic and cultural elements presented within their familial context.

The symbolic order in familial dynamics extends beyond language to encompass a system of values, beliefs, and traditions that are passed down through generations. These symbolic structures shape familial roles and expectations, governing the behavior and interactions of family members. In this context, the symbolic order serves as a mechanism for maintaining continuity and coherence within the family unit, providing a framework for understanding one's place within the familial hierarchy and broader society.

Familial dynamics are influenced by the symbolic representations of gender, authority, and kinship, which are constructed and reinforced through language and cultural practices. The symbolic order within families influences the construction of gender identities, the distribution of power, and the formation of familial bonds. These symbolic dynamics can contribute to the perpetuation of traditional gender roles, hierarchical structures, and cultural paradigms, impacting the experiences and socialization of individuals within the familial context.

The symbolic order within familial dynamics plays a pivotal role in the intergenerational transmission of cultural codes and practices. Family rituals, traditions, and narratives serve as vehicles for the preservation and dissemination of cultural knowledge, shaping the collective identity of the family unit. The symbolic structures embedded within these familial practices reflect and reinforce broader societal values, serving as a link between the private sphere of the family and the public sphere of the broader cultural milieu.

8. Institutions and the Symbolic Structure:

Institutions play a pivotal role in shaping and perpetuating the symbolic structure within society. These organized systems, such as government bodies, educational establishments, religious organizations, and economic entities, wield significant influence over the construction and dissemination of symbolic meanings and values. The structural dynamics within institutions are deeply intertwined with the functioning of the symbolic order, often serving as conduits for the transmission and reinforcement of symbolic representations. As such, it is essential to explore the relationship between institutions and the symbolic structure, shedding light on their mutual impact. In examining the intersection of institutions and the symbolic order, one must consider the ways in which institutional practices and norms contribute to the maintenance of symbolic hierarchies and power dynamics. Additionally, the institutionalization of certain symbols and rituals can solidify their significance within the broader societal framework, consolidating their role as arbiters of meaning and identity. Furthermore, institutions often serve as gatekeepers of knowledge production and dissemination, thereby wielding immense authority in defining and regulating the parameters of the symbolic register. Moreover, the symbolic structure exerts its influence within institutions through the codification of language, disciplinary mechanisms, and normative behaviors, generating a set of rules and norms that govern social interactions and perpetuate the symbolic order. This process not only reinforces existing symbolic hierarchies but also contributes to the reproduction and internalization of dominant symbolic forms. Additionally, institutions act as sites for the negotiation and contestation of symbolic meanings, with various stakeholders seeking to assert their interpretations and values within the institutional context. Consequently, the dialectical interplay between institutions and the symbolic structure gives rise to complex power struggles and ideological conflicts, influencing the trajectory of symbolic evolution within society. Ultimately, unraveling the web of relations between institutions and the symbolic structure is paramount in comprehending the multifaceted ways in which symbolic meanings are constructed, transmitted, and transformed within the fabric of social life.

9. Symbols as Mediators of Reality:

Through the lens of the Symbolic Order, symbols are not mere representations but dynamic entities that shape our perceptions, behaviors, and social interactions. At the core of this exploration is the concept of signification, where symbols act as carriers of meaning. Drawing from semiotics, we examine how symbols function as linguistic signs, conveying cultural, social, and psychological significance. Whether in the form of language, imagery, or rituals, symbols encapsulate rich layers of interpretation, reflecting the complexities of human thought and expression.

Symbols operate within a network of interconnected meanings, forming a web of associations that construct our understanding of the world. The symbolic mediation of reality extends beyond personal experience to encompass broader societal dynamics.

From national flags to religious emblems, symbols serve as conduits for expressing ideologies, values, and collective identities. These symbolic representations not only reflect societal narratives but also influence the construction of social norms and power structures.

Symbols as mediators of reality are embedded within cultural codes and practices, shaping our perceptions of self and others. For instance, the symbolism of gender roles and stereotypes encompasses a wide array of cues and signals that influence interpersonal relationships and societal expectations. By dissecting these symbolic constructs, we gain insights into the mechanisms through which meaning is attributed and negotiated within various cultural contexts.

Additionally, symbolic mediation transcends individual and interpersonal domains to permeate institutional frameworks. Within educational, legal, and political systems, symbols assume significant roles in dictating protocols, hierarchies, and disciplinary measures. Their pervasive influence underscores the impact of symbolic structures on organizational dynamics and power relations, illustrating how symbols sustain and perpetuate societal orders and arrangements.

In conclusion, the exploration of symbols as mediators of reality reaffirms their profound influence on human consciousness, social interactions, and cultural paradigms. Understanding the complex interplay between symbols and reality illuminates the underlying mechanisms of meaning-making and symbolization, offering valuable perspectives for interdisciplinary fields such as psychology, linguistics, anthropology, and sociology.

Individual Identity and Social Structures Influenced by the Symbolic

1. The Concept of Identity in Lacanian Psychoanalysis:

In contrast to traditional psychological perspectives, Jacques Lacan's theory delves into the notion of identity as something constructed and influenced by external forces, particularly through language and social interaction. At the core of Lacanian thought is the understanding that identity is not fixed or inherent but rather constitutes an ongoing process shaped within the Symbolic order. Instead of viewing identity as an individual's internal essence, Lacan posits that it emerges through a complex interplay of linguistic signifiers, cultural norms, and psychic structures.

Central to Lacanian psychoanalysis is the idea of the 'ego' as a product of identification with symbolic representations, which are dictated by the Other and internalized during the formative stages of development. This process of identification underpins the construction of an individual's identity within the symbolic framework. Accordingly, the ego evolves as a reflection of the subject's perception of themselves in relation to societal demands and norms, rather than as an authentic expression of their inner self. Lacan's emphasis on the 'mirror stage' underscores the significance of external images in shaping the individual's sense of self, stressing the impact of the symbolic register on one's self-perception.

Lacanian analysis recognizes the fragmentary nature of identity, wherein the subject's sense of self is riddled with contradictions and inconsistencies. This dissonance arises from the disjunction between the real self and the idealized image constructed within the symbolic order. As individuals strive to conform to societal expectations and establish their identities within the symbolic framework, they encounter inevitable ruptures and disruptions that give rise to feelings of alienation and inadequacy.

From a Lacanian perspective, identity is deeply intertwined with language and the network of symbolic representations. Language serves as the primary medium through which individuals negotiate their identities within the symbolic order, as it provides the framework for signification and meaning-making. The process of subject formation unfolds through linguistic mediation, encompassing the acquisition of symbolic codes, narratives, and cultural discourses that shape an individual's understanding of themselves and their place in society.

In essence, the concept of identity in Lacanian psychoanalysis elucidates the web of influences that mold subjective selfhood within the symbolic order. By examining how individuals engage with the complex interplay of language, cultural dictates, and social constructs, Lacanian theory offers profound insights into the formation, negotiation, and dissonance of identity in contemporary society.

2. Formation of Subjectivity in the Symbolic Order:

The formation of subjectivity in the symbolic order constitutes a central aspect of Lacanian psychoanalysis, delving into the depths of individual identity construction within the framework of language and social structures. This process elucidates the interplay between linguistic signifiers and the establishment of the self within a broader societal context. In this domain, subjectivity is not autonomously generated but is deeply entwined with the symbolic order, which serves as the regulating mechanism shaping an individual's perception of reality. The symbolic order acts as a vast network of signifiers that influence and structure the way individuals engage with the world around them. Through the acquisition of language and entry into the symbolic register, individuals internalize these social, cultural, and linguistic constructs, thereby affecting their subjective experiences and perceptions. Moreover, the symbolic order plays a crucial role in mediating and regulating interpersonal relationships and interactions, further influencing the formation of subjectivity. As individuals engage with the symbolic domain, they become integrated into broader social systems, solidifying their sense of self through the interplay of societal norms, values, and expectations. These external influences are internalized, imprinting themselves onto the individual's subjective reality and contributing to the development of their unique identity. Furthermore, the formation of subjectivity within the symbolic order involves the internalization of linguistic and cultural codes, leading to the adoption of specific roles, behaviors, and belief systems that align with the societal framework. This process shapes the individual's understanding of themselves and their position within the social fabric, ultimately contributing to the ongoing construction of their subjectivity. Consequently, the formation of subjectivity in the symbolic order encompasses a complex interweaving of linguistic, cultural, and social elements that mold and sculpt the individual's sense of self within the broader symbolic landscape, emphasizing the profound influence of the symbolic register on the construction of subjective identity.

3. Role of the 'Other' - Language and Social Interaction:

As previously stated, the 'Other' is not limited to a specific person but signifies the broader social sphere encompassing language, cultural norms, and societal structures. The linguistic interactions within this 'Other' profoundly impact an individual's understanding of self and others. Within the Symbolic Order, language serves as the primary medium through which the 'Other' influences personal identity. Through linguistic exchanges, individuals learn to engage with the socio-cultural landscape, internalizing shared meanings, and integrating them into their self-perception. This process inherently involves a constant negotiation of meanings and identities within the larger social context. Moreover, the 'Other' also embodies the presence of authority figures, institutions, and power dynamics that contribute to the regulation of social behaviors and norms. The influences of the 'Other' through language and social interaction are not merely passive but actively shape the construction of an individual's identity and role in society. Furthermore, the exposure to diverse perspectives and ideologies within the 'Other' fosters a complex interplay of beliefs, values, and social roles. Consequently, individuals engage in various symbolic identifications, positioning themselves in relation to the prevailing discourses and societal expectations. Through this dynamic engagement with the 'Other', individuals forge their subjectivity while simultaneously contributing to the perpetuation and evolution of social structures. It is essential to acknowledge that the impact of the 'Other' is not unidirectional, as individuals also partake in constructing the symbolic register through their linguistic and social expressions. By engaging in conversations, debates, and discourses, individuals actively influence and reshape the symbolic network, perpetuating or challenging existing paradigms. Therefore, the 'Other' functions as a multidimensional force that substantially molds individual identity and social dynamics through the web of language and interaction.

4. Cultural Norms and Their Impact on Personal Identity:

In Lacanian psychoanalysis, cultural norms are viewed as the external influences that contribute to the formation of an individual's subjective identity. These norms encompass a wide range of societal expectations, values, beliefs, and behaviors that are transmitted through socialization processes, language, and symbolic representations within a specific culture or community. The impact of cultural norms on personal identity is multifaceted and may manifest in various aspects of an individual's life, including self-perception, interpersonal relationships, and societal roles. It is essential to recognize the interplay between cultural norms and personal identity within the context of the Symbolic Order. Cultural norms can influence an individual's understanding of themselves and others, as well as their aspirations, expressions, and experiences. Moreover, they can shape the construction of gender, race, ethnicity, sexuality, and other aspects of identity, contributing to the complexities of human subjectivity. Additionally, cultural norms can create expectations and pressures that individuals may internalize, leading to the formation of unconscious desires, anxieties, and conflicts related to conformity and acceptance within their cultural environment. Furthermore, the imposition of cultural norms can affect the symbolic positioning of individuals within social structures, delineating power dynamics, privileges, and inequalities. Understanding the impact of cultural norms on personal identity is crucial for assessing the ways in which individuals negotiate their sense of self within the broader societal context. It also raises important questions about the potential constraints and freedoms that result from cultural norms, as well as the possibilities for agency, resistance, and transformation. Exploring the relationship between cultural norms and personal identity offers valuable insights into the complex dynamics of human subjectivity, social belonging, and the perpetuation or subversion of cultural hegemony.

5. Social Structures - Authority, Hierarchies, and Influence:

Social structures are integral components of the Symbolic order, shaping individuals' experiences and identities. Within these structures, authority, hierarchies, and influence play crucial roles in determining power dynamics and social relationships. Authority, often vested in institutions or individuals, dictates norms, rules, and regulations that govern behavior and interactions within a society. This authoritative influence can stem from various sources, such as governmental bodies, religious organizations, educational systems, or cultural traditions, and it shapes the expectations and boundaries of acceptable conduct. Hierarchies within social structures establish levels of status, privilege, and access to resources, which significantly impact individuals' opportunities and life trajectories. Whether in the workplace, community, or broader societal contexts, hierarchies create stratifications that influence people's sense of belonging and worth. Moreover, influence permeates social structures through persuasive or coercive means, shaping attitudes, beliefs, and collective behaviors. Individuals may wield influence through leadership roles, activism, or advocacy, while media, technology, and economic systems also exert considerable influence on societal values and practices. Understanding the dynamics of authority, hierarchies, and influence within social structures is essential for comprehending the complex interplay between individual identity and the larger socio-cultural milieu. Moreover, it is crucial for psychoanalytic practitioners to explore how these dynamics impact their clients' experiences and perceptions, as well as to critically examine their own positions and responsibilities within these structures. By recognizing and interrogating these dynamics, one can foster a more nuanced understanding of the way social structures shape subjectivity, identity, and interpersonal relations, thereby enriching therapeutic interventions and social discourse. Furthermore, acknowledging the inherent complexities and power differentials within social structures allows for greater insights into the ways in which the Symbolic order intersects with societal forces to mold individual subjectivities and collective identities.

6. Gender Identity and the Symbolic Domain:

Gender identity within the symbolic domain is a complex and multifaceted topic that intersects with various aspects of Lacanian psychoanalysis and social theory. In examining gender identity through the lens of the symbolic order, it becomes evident that language, culture, and societal norms play crucial roles in shaping individuals' understanding and experience of their own gender. One fundamental concept is the idea that gender identity is not solely a product of biological determinants, but rather it is significantly influenced by symbolic representations and linguistic structures. Lacanian theory emphasizes the role of language in constructing subjectivity, and this extends to the formation and expression of gender identity. The symbolic domain provides a framework for understanding how individuals come to identify with and express themselves within culturally defined gender categories. Furthermore, the symbolic order contributes to the establishment of gender norms and expectations, which shape individuals' experiences of their own gender and their interactions within society. It is within this context that the concept of the 'Other' holds particular significance in relation to gender identity. The 'Other' represents the external social forces and expectations that influence an individual's sense of self and identity. This includes societal perceptions of what it means to be masculine or feminine, as well as the internalization of these perceptions within one's psyche. Gender identity within the symbolic domain also encompasses issues of power dynamics, as the symbolic order constructs and perpetuates hierarchies and power differentials between genders. These power dynamics are evident in social institutions, cultural representations, and interpersonal relationships, where gender often intersects with issues of authority and influence. Moreover, the symbolic domain influences the ways in which gender is represented and perceived within cultural discourses, media, and language usage. Understanding the impact of the symbolic order on gender identity opens up avenues for exploring the complexities of symbolic identification. By delving into case studies and applications, we can gain insights into how individuals engage with their gender identities within the broader symbolic framework. Through these investigations, we can analyze the ways in which the symbolic domain shapes individuals' relationships with their own gender identities, as well as the implications for psychological well-being, social integration, and cultural practices. Ultimately, examining gender identity within the symbolic domain expands our understanding of the interplay between language, culture, and individual subjectivity, offering valuable insights for both theoretical developments and practical applications within the field of psychoanalysis and gender studies.

7. Conflict and Resolution - The Interplay with thc Real:

In Lacanian psychoanalysis, the concept of the 'Real' intersects with both the symbolic and imaginary registers, contributing to the formation of individual identity and influencing social structures. At the core of this exploration lies the tension between the unconscious and conscious experience, as well as the manifestation of repressed desires and unresolved traumas in everyday life. The Real disrupts the established symbolic order, introducing elements that resist symbolization and linguistic representation, thereby giving rise to conflicts characterized by dissonance and ambiguity. These conflicts permeate individuals' subjective experiences, leading to internal struggles and external tensions within social frameworks. Furthermore, the Real is linked to trauma, evoking distressing and often unassimilable experiences that challenge an individual's sense of self and their engagement with others. As such, it becomes imperative to investigate the mechanisms of resolution within the interplay with the Real. Overcoming these conflicts demands a complex process of acknowledgment, processing, and integration, which is essential for the restoration of balance and well-being. Additionally, engaging with the Real necessitates a recognition of the limits of language and the inadequacy of symbolic systems in encapsulating certain aspects of human experience. By embracing these limitations, individuals can strive towards genuine introspection and authentic connections, thus fostering personal growth and enriching social interactions. Furthermore, the resolution of conflicts arising from the Real extends beyond the individual, permeating communal and societal dimensions. Addressing collective traumas and acknowledging shared vulnerabilities becomes paramount in building empathetic and inclusive social structures.

Functionality of the Symbolic Order in Psychoanalytic Practice

1. Introduction to the Symbolic's Clinical Relevance

The Symbolic Order's clinical relevance extends far beyond theoretical abstraction; it permeates the very fabric of psychoanalytic practice and shapes the contours of psychological transformation. As the analyst assumes the responsibility of mediating the Symbolic, the interplay between language, signifiers, and cultural frameworks becomes palpably manifest in the therapeutic process. The Symbolic operates as an indispensable lens through which the nuances of human subjectivity are deciphered, rendering it indispensable for understanding the intricacies of unconscious processes and symbolic communication. By delving into the Symbolic, analysts gain insight into the structural underpinnings of their patients' psychic worlds, thereby facilitating an enriched understanding of the individual's narrative and the intersubjective dynamics at play. Furthermore, the Symbolic unfolds as a cornerstone that elucidates the impact of linguistic constructs and socio-cultural contexts on the formation of unconscious desires and the complexities of identity construction. This critical awareness enables the exploration of how language and cultural mores shape the manifestation of symptoms and the articulation of subjective distress within the therapeutic setting. Moreover, by recognizing the pivotal role of the Symbolic in mediating meaning and structuring the terrain of human experience, analysts can skillfully traverse the web of symbolic representations, thereby fostering a deeper engagement with the patient's internal world. Importantly, by integrating the Symbolic framework into the therapeutic process, analysts can illuminate the covert symbolic exchanges underlying unconscious communications, thus enhancing the interpretive acumen necessary for uncovering latent meanings embedded within verbal utterances, dreams, and interpersonal interactions. In doing so, therapy transcends the confines of surface-level manifestations, allowing for a profound exploration of the Symbolic substratum that informs the patient's subjective reality.

2. The Analyst's Role as Mediator of the Symbolic:

In psychoanalytic practice, the analyst acts as the mediator of the symbolic register within the therapeutic setting. Central to this role is the analyst's ability to engage with the patient's unconscious through the language and symbols that permeate the symbolic order. The analyst serves as a translator, deciphering the patient's expressions, dreams, and fantasies to identify the underlying signifiers that manifest within the symbolic framework. By delving into the web of linguistic and cultural constructs, the analyst facilitates the exploration and interpretation of the patient's subjective experiences. Engaging with the symbolic necessitates the analyst's adeptness in maneuvering through the layers of meaning attached to words and symbols, while also recognizing the nuances and ambiguities that characterize these manifestations. Moreover, the analyst must remain attuned to their own countertransference reactions, whereby they may inadvertently project their own symbolic interpretations onto the patient, potentially distorting the therapeutic process. Therefore, the analyst's capacity for self-reflection and introspection is crucial in maintaining the integrity of the symbolic mediation. As a mediator, the analyst endeavors to bridge the gap between the conscious and unconscious registers, providing a safe space for the patient to articulate and explore the symbolic representations that underpin their psychic reality. This involves fostering a collaborative dialogue where the patient feels empowered to articulate their thoughts, allowing the analyst to discern patterns and themes that emerge from within the symbolic fabric. The analyst's role extends beyond mere interpretation; it encompasses creating an environment where the patient feels validated in their symbolic expressions, encouraging deeper exploration and understanding. Through skillful mediation, the analyst aids the patient in unraveling the complexities of their internal world, promoting insight and transformation.

3. Symbolic Transference and Countertransference Dynamics:

The concept of transference, as originally conceptualized by Sigmund Freud and further developed by Jacques Lacan, refers to the unconscious redirection of a patient's feelings, desires, and expectations onto the analyst, often mirroring significant past relationships. Within the symbolic order, this transfer of emotions and attachment can manifest through language and communication, illustrating the connection between linguistic symbols and psychic structure. Consequently, understanding and interpreting transference within the context of the symbolic order is essential for maneuvering through the complexities of the therapeutic process.

Countertransference, on the other hand, encompasses the analyst's emotional reactions and subjective responses to the patient, influenced by their own unresolved conflicts and unconscious processes. In the symbolic, countertransference dynamics can provide valuable insights into the interplay of signifiers and the analyst's subjectivity, offering a deeper comprehension of the symbolic exchanges occurring within the therapeutic relationship.

Lacanian theory emphasizes the significance of the analyst's ability to traverse the symbolic dimension, establishing an intersubjective space where both transference and countertransference can be critically examined. This approach calls for a heightened awareness of the linguistic and symbolic components underlying the patient's narratives and expressions. By recognizing the symbolic structures at play, analysts can orchestrate the transference and countertransference dynamics to uncover latent meanings and unconscious signifiers embedded within the patient's discourse.

The symbolic transference and countertransference dynamics also shed light on the broader societal and cultural influences that shape an individual's symbolic interactions. The collective symbolic representations and shared signifiers present in the cultural milieu contribute to the formation and expression of transference phenomena, enriching the understanding of how cultural frameworks affect psychic development and therapeutic processes.

In analyzing symbolic transference and countertransference dynamics, it becomes evident that the symbolic order serves as a rich tapestry interwoven with linguistic, cultural, and historical threads, fundamentally shaping the psychoanalytic encounter. Successfully engaging with these dynamics empowers analysts to facilitate profound transformations and promote the evolution of individual subjectivity within the context of the symbolic register.

4. Lacanian Techniques for Engaging the Symbolic Order:

In the milieu of psychoanalysis, Lacanian techniques for engaging the symbolic order play a pivotal role in uncovering the unconscious dynamics that govern an individual's psyche. Central to Lacanian theory is the concept of the 'mirror stage,' where an infant begins to form a sense of identity through their reflection in the mirror and subsequently enters the symbolic order through language and social interactions. Building on this foundation, the therapeutic process employs various techniques to engage with the symbolic order.

One significant technique is the use of free association, wherein the patient verbalizes thoughts, feelings, and images without censorship. This unfiltered expression provides access to the patient's unconscious and allows the analyst to discern underlying symbolic patterns and conflicts. Moreover, the therapist may introduce the 'analytic third' as a tool to locate the patient within the broader context of the symbolic order. Through this lens, individual experiences are reframed within the societal and linguistic structures, enabling a deeper understanding of the patient's subjective reality.

Lacanian psychoanalysis further utilizes the interpretation of dreams as a means to decode symbolic content embedded in the unconscious. The dream, viewed as the 'royal road to the unconscious,' serves as a rich source of symbolic material, offering insights into the patient's unconscious desires, conflicts, and anxieties. By decoding the latent content of dreams, the therapist engages with the symbolic manifestations of the patient's inner world, facilitating profound insights and promoting therapeutic growth.

Language itself becomes a crucial tool for engaging with the symbolic order. Lacan emphasizes the significance of speech and its impact on subject formation, positing that language constructs and shapes one's experience of reality. Therapists adept in Lacanian techniques traverse the nuances of language to unveil the symbolic underpinnings of the patient's narratives, shedding light on repressed symbols and cultural significances.

Lastly, Lacanian techniques employ the analysis of resistance as a fruitful avenue for engaging with the symbolic order. Resistance, often manifested in the form of opposition or reluctance, reveals underlying conflicts and defenses entrenched within the symbolic framework. By carefully examining resistance, therapists gain access to the symbolic networks that contribute to psychological impasses, paving the way for transformative interventions and heightened self-awareness.

5. Language as a Tool in Psychoanalytic Intervention:

In the context of the symbolic order, language serves as the primary vehicle through which unconscious desires and conflicts are both expressed and explored. As patients engage in discourse, they provide valuable linguistic clues that shed light on their innermost thoughts and emotions. The analyst, equipped with a deep understanding of linguistic signifiers and their symbolic meanings, is able to decipher these linguistic expressions, unraveling the complex web of meaning woven by the patient's words.

Lacanian theory underscores the significance of language not only as a means of communication but also as a fundamental determinant of subjectivity. Through linguistic analysis, the analyst identifies the patient's use of specific signifiers and considers how these verbal manifestations shape the individual's subjective reality within the symbolic order. Language thus becomes an indispensable tool for delving into the construction of identity, elucidating the unconscious, and traversing the terrain of the human psyche.

The psychoanalyst adept at utilizing language as a tool employs linguistic interventions to disrupt entrenched patterns of thought and behavior. By prompting the patient to examine the underlying meanings of their speech, the analyst facilitates a heightened awareness of the unconscious forces at play. This analytical process fosters a transformative journey, allowing the individual to confront previously unacknowledged aspects of their inner world.

Language operates within the therapeutic setting as a mechanism for fostering catharsis and insight. As the patient articulates their experiences and engages in dialogue, the act of verbalizing deep-seated emotions and memories can lead to profound revelations and emotional release. The carefully guided linguistic exchange becomes a conduit for cathartic expression and introspective exploration, catalyzing the therapeutic process.

Within the framework of the symbolic order, language assumes a multifaceted role, serving as both a medium for communication and a portal to the depths of the unconscious mind. Harnessing the power of language, the psychoanalyst engages in a nuanced dance of interpretation, dialogue, and linguistic exploration, ultimately unveiling the intricacies of the human psyche and laying the groundwork for profound therapeutic transformation.

6. The Interpretations of Dreams Through the Symbolic Lens:

As psychoanalysts, we often turn to dreams as a rich source of material for understanding the unconscious dynamics at play within our patients. Dreams, in their fragmented and often nonsensical nature, provide a direct pathway to the unconscious, representing unfulfilled desires, anxieties, and repressed emotions.

When applying the symbolic lens to dream interpretation, it is crucial to recognize that the manifest content of dreams, or the actual events and images experienced by the dreamer, serves as a disguise for the latent content, which encapsulates the true symbolic meaning. By engaging with patients to explore the latent content of their dreams, analysts gain insight into the unconscious signifiers and structures that shape the psyche.

Lacan's emphasis on language and signifiers underscores the significance of interpreting the symbols present in dreams. Through an analysis of these symbolic elements, such as objects, people, and actions, we can uncover the hidden meanings encoded within the dreamer's unconscious. Furthermore, the use of linguistic tools, such as free association and exploring the multiple possible interpretations of a symbol, allows us to traverse the complex web of associations within the dream.

The act of interpreting dreams through the symbolic lens also necessitates an awareness of the interplay between the various orders—symbolic, imaginary, and real—within the dream landscape. By discerning how these orders intersect and intertwine, analysts can decipher the underlying conflicts and tensions that manifest in the dream narrative. This holistic approach not only enriches the interpretative process but also provides a deeper understanding of the patient's internal world.

7. Resistance and Acceptance within the Symbolic Framework:

When individuals engage in therapy, they often display resistance towards delving into deeper aspects of their unconscious minds. This resistance can manifest as defense mechanisms, such as denial or repression, as they strive to protect themselves from experiencing emotional discomfort or facing unresolved conflicts. It is crucial for psychoanalysts to recognize and explore these resistance patterns to facilitate meaningful breakthroughs in the therapeutic process.

On the other hand, acceptance within the symbolic framework refers to an individual's willingness to acknowledge and confront the unconscious symbols, signifiers, and representations that surface during the therapeutic journey. Embracing these elements allows for a deeper understanding of the self and paves the way for transformative insights and personal growth. Through the acceptance of their inner symbolic realities, individuals can unravel the layers of their psyche and work towards resolving internal conflicts and distress.

Within psychoanalytic practice, managing resistance and fostering acceptance involves a balance of empathy, patience, and skillful interpretation. Analysts must approach resistance with understanding, recognizing it as a natural response to the discomfort associated with unveiling repressed thoughts and emotions.

By creating a safe and non-judgmental space, analysts can help clients gradually overcome their resistance and explore the symbolic landscape of their subconscious without fear of criticism or condemnation.

Cultivating acceptance within the symbolic framework requires fostering an atmosphere of trust and openness. Individuals need to feel validated and supported as they manage the complexities of their inner worlds. By emphasizing the significance of self-discovery and the potential for healing through acceptance, analysts can empower their clients to embrace the symbolic manifestations that emerge, paving the path towards self-realization and insight.

8. Ethical Considerations in Engaging with the Symbolic:

Traversing the complex terrain of the Symbolic Order within psychoanalytic practice necessitates a profound awareness of the ethical considerations that underpin this delicate endeavor. Ethical considerations in psychoanalysis are paramount, given the potential for uncovering deeply personal and sensitive aspects of individuals' inner worlds. Within the context of the Symbolic Order, ethical deliberation becomes even more crucial as analysts engage with the symbolic meanings and cultural constructs that shape an individual's identity and perception of reality.

One prominent ethical consideration when engaging with the Symbolic revolves around the issue of confidentiality. As the exploration of the Symbolic often involves delving into the intimate spheres of a patient's linguistic and cultural framework, maintaining strict confidentiality becomes imperative. Analysts must be vigilant in safeguarding the privacy and dignity of their patients, ensuring that sensitive information remains strictly within the confines of the therapeutic space.

The ethical implications of power dynamics come to the fore when traversing the Symbolic register. Psychoanalysts wield significant influence over the interpretative process of the Symbolic and must conscientiously manage this power dynamic. It is essential for analysts to recognize and address any potential imbalances of power that may arise during the exploration of the Symbolic, ensuring that the therapeutic relationship remains grounded in mutual respect and autonomy. The transparent management of power differentials contributes to the ethical integrity of the therapeutic process and fosters an environment of trust and collaboration.

In addition, ethical considerations extend to the use of language and interpretation within the Symbolic Order. Given the pivotal role of language in shaping the Symbolic, analysts must approach linguistic interpretation with sensitivity and cultural competence. Respectful engagement with diverse linguistic and cultural backgrounds is vital to honor the rich complexities inherent within the Symbolic framework. Moreover, the ethical use of interpretation demands that analysts remain attuned to the potential impact of their interpretations on the patient's self-perception and worldview, prioritizing the preservation of the patient's agency and authenticity.

Lastly, ethical considerations encompass the integration of the Symbolic insights into the broader therapeutic process. Ensuring that the symbolic revelations are ethically integrated into treatment plans requires thoughtful discernment and consideration of the patient's well-being. The ethical application of Symbolic insights seeks to empower individuals to traverse and transcend the symbolic constraints that may have hindered their psychological growth, fostering a sense of self-awareness and agency within the constructed realities of the Symbolic Order. By incorporating the ethical dimensions of the Symbolic into psychoanalytic practice, analysts can strive to create a therapeutic milieu that upholds the principles of beneficence, non-maleficence, and justice, thereby promoting the holistic well-being of their patients.

Interplay with the Imaginary and Real Orders

1. Symbolic and Imaginary - Dynamics and Tensions:

The imaginary order, as previously elucidated, encompasses images and perceptions that contribute to an individual's sense of self and others. Within this framework, the symbolic order operates as a structuring system, employing language and signifiers to organize and make sense of these perceived constructs. This relationship between the symbolic and imaginary orders gives rise to dynamic tensions, as the symbolic imposes its own structures onto the fluid and imaginative aspects of the imaginary.

At the core of the dynamics between these two orders lies the concept of the mirror stage, a pivotal moment in early development posited by Lacanian theory. This phase marks the infant's recognition of its image in the mirror as separate from its actual self, thereby initiating a dual relationship with the external world - one through the symbolism of the image and the other through the bodily experience. This duality sets the stage for ongoing tensions between the symbolic and imaginary, as the individual oscillates between the structured, linguistic representations and the fluid, pre-linguistic dimension of the imaginary.

The tensions arising from this interplay are further compounded by the differing temporalities inherent in each order. While the symbolic order is characterized by linear and sequential temporality, the imaginary order is marked by a timeless, simultaneous quality encapsulated in visual images and fantasies. This incongruity in temporality infuses the relationship with tension, as individuals oscillate between interpreting their experiences within the constraints of language and societal structures, and experiencing the unbounded, non-linear nature of their internal imaginings.

The imagery and representations within the imaginary often serve as a source of resistance to the symbolic imposition. The symbolic order attempts to impose cohesive meanings and categorizations upon the diverse and multifaceted aspects of the imaginary, leading to ongoing tensions and resistances. This resistance plays a crucial role in fostering creativity and divergent thinking, as individuals traverse the interstices between the prescribed symbolic order and the kaleidoscopic terrain of the imaginary.

It is within these tensions and dynamics that the richness of human subjectivity emerges, as individuals grapple with the interweaving influences of the symbolic and imaginary. Understanding and unraveling these complexities furthers our comprehension of the human psyche and the interplays of language, representation, and imagination.

2. Symbolic and Real - Points of Convergence:

While the Symbolic Order operates within the milieu of language, signifiers, and cultural norms, the Real Order is characterized by the raw, unmediated experiences and sensations that resist symbolization. Despite their seemingly disparate natures, these two orders intersect in significant ways that deeply influence the constitution of the human psyche and social reality. The points of convergence between the Symbolic and Real Orders are not only pivotal for understanding the intricacies of individual identity formation but also hold profound implications for psychoanalytic practice and broader sociocultural contexts.

Central to the examination of their convergence is the recognition that both the Symbolic and Real Orders shape and are shaped by the subject's interactions with social structures, linguistic frameworks, and embodied experiences. This interactive process highlights the co-constitutive nature of the orders, wherein the Symbolic not only influences the subject's perception and interpretation of the Real but is also influenced by the non-symbolizable aspects of the Real. Moreover, at the points of convergence, there emerges a tension between the symbolic meanings ascribed to experiences and the ineffable, unmediated quality of the Real, exposing the inherent paradoxes within human subjectivity.

The intersection of the Symbolic and Real Orders engenders moments of disruption and dissonance that prompt crucial transformations in the subject's relationships to self and others. These transitional junctures, marked by ruptures in symbolic coherence and encounters with the real, challenge established subject positions and invite the reconfiguration of subjective understandings. Such instances of convergence and rupture offer fertile ground for clinical exploration within psychoanalytic practice, inviting analysts to engage with the complexities of the human psyche as it grapples with the dialectical tensions between the Symbolic and Real Orders.

Ultimately, the points of convergence between the Symbolic and Real Orders invite an interrogation of the fluid boundaries between language and experience, representation and embodiment, and collective narratives and lived realities. Recognizing and probing these intersections not only enriches our theoretical grasp of Lacanian psychoanalysis but also deepens our appreciation of the tapestry of human subjectivity within the broader fabric of culture and society.

3. Transitional Phases Among the Orders:

Transitional phases among the orders represent pivotal moments in an individual's development and subjectivity formation, as they traverse the complex terrain of symbolic representation, imaginary identifications, and encounters with the raw, unmediated real. The shifts between these orders are not always discrete or linear; they often occur in a fluid and overlapping manner, leading to multilayered psychological processes that shape human experience.

One significant transitional phase is the mirror stage, a concept central to Lacan's understanding of the formation of the ego and the entry into the symbolic order. During the mirror stage, an infant recognizes their own reflection in a mirror and experiences a sense of unity and coherence, marking the emergence of the imaginary order. This moment sets the stage for the ongoing negotiation between the idealized images of the self and the fragmented, alienating aspects of reality. It represents a crucial movement from the pre-linguistic, undifferentiated real to symbolic signification, laying the groundwork for symbolic identity construction.

Another transitional phase occurs in the planes of language acquisition and early socialization. As children begin to interact with others and internalize linguistic structures, they undergo a profound process of entering the symbolic order. This transition involves adapting to the rules and norms governing language use and participating in the construction of shared meanings within a specific cultural context. Simultaneously, they grapple with the impact of the symbolic order on their subjective experience, negotiating the constraints and possibilities it presents in relation to their imaginary identifications and encounters with the real.

Adolescence constitutes a critical transitional phase characterized by intensified conflicts and challenges in reconciling the demands of the symbolic, imaginary, and real dimensions. The adolescent's search for identity and autonomy involves grappling with societal expectations, parental influences, and personal aspirations, further complicating the interplay among the three orders. This phase highlights the ongoing negotiation of symbolic representations, imaginary projections, and encounters with the real, contributing to the complex formation of individual subjectivity.

4. Identity Formation across the Three Orders:

The formation of one's identity occurs within the context of the Symbolic, Imaginary, and Real orders, each exerting its influence on an individual's sense of self. The inherent tensions and interactions among these orders shape the construction of identity in profound ways. In the Symbolic order, identity formation is deeply rooted in language, culture, and societal structures. This order provides individuals with a framework through which they understand and define themselves in relation to others. The acquisition of language, the internalization of societal norms, and the assimilation of cultural values all contribute to the symbolic construction of identity. The Imaginary order plays a significant role in identity formation as well, particularly through the development of the ego and the formation of mental images or idealized representations of the self. This process often involves mirroring and identification with external figures, such as caregivers and peers, which significantly influence the formation of one's self-image. Moreover, the Real order, though inherently elusive and resistant to symbolic representation, also contributes to the formation of identity. The encounter with raw, unfiltered experiences and bodily sensations shapes an individual's subjective sense of self and their understanding of reality. The interplay of these orders during the formative stages of development lays the groundwork for an individual's enduring sense of identity. Furthermore, disruptions or imbalances in the interplay of these orders can create psychological conflicts and challenges in the maintenance of a stable and coherent identity. Understanding the complex dynamics of identity formation across the three orders can offer profound insight into the multifaceted nature of human subjectivity. Moreover, it underscores the ways in which individuals engage with their internal and external worlds, constantly negotiating the competing influences of language, perception, and lived experience.

5. Influence on Subjectivity and Perception:

The interplay of the Symbolic, Imaginary, and Real orders significantly influences an individual's subjectivity and perception. Subjectivity refers to an individual's experience of the world, shaped by their unique perspectives, emotions, and beliefs. Perception encompasses how individuals interpret and make sense of the external world and their internal experiences. The dynamics among the three orders deeply impact these fundamental aspects of human experience.

At the intersection of the Symbolic and Imaginary orders, subjectivity is forged through language, culture, and social norms. Language, as a product of the Symbolic order, not only provides a means of communication but also constructs the framework through which individuals comprehend and articulate their subjective experiences. The Imaginary order contributes to subjectivity by fostering the formation of one's ego and self-image based on early interactions and identifications. These early impressions shape an individual's perception of themselves and influence how they engage with the world around them.

Simultaneously, the Real order disrupts and challenges an individual's subjectivity and perception. Unlike the Symbolic and Imaginary orders, the Real defies symbolization and representation. It introduces elements such as trauma, disorientation, and disruptions in meaning, which profoundly impact an individual's sense of self and their understanding of reality. This disruption can lead to the reevaluation and reconstruction of subjective experience and perception in response to encounters with the inexplicable aspects of the Real.

The interplay of these orders shapes subjective realities, leading individuals to perceive and interpret the world through the lens of their unique experiences and symbolic frameworks. This often results in diverse interpretations of shared experiences, as each person's subjectivity is informed by their distinct history of interactions with the Symbolic, Imaginary, and Real orders. Furthermore, this interplay underscores the fluid nature of subjectivity and perception, emphasizing that these constructs are continuously influenced and reshaped by ongoing interactions with the three orders.

Clinically, understanding the influence of the Symbolic, Imaginary, and Real orders on subjectivity and perception is crucial in psychoanalytic practice. By uncovering the ways in which these orders operate in an individual's psyche, therapists can gain insight into the complex layers of a patient's subjectivity, enhancing their ability to provide effective therapeutic interventions.

Furthermore, recognizing the impact of the interplay among the orders allows for a deeper understanding of the diverse ways in which individuals construct and engage with their subjective and perceptual worlds, ultimately contributing to more nuanced and comprehensive psychoanalytic approaches.

Critiques and Debates Surrounding the Symbolic Order

1. Philosophical Challenges:

Within philosophical discourse, one of the central challenges to Lacanian theory revolves around the nature of language and its relationship to the construction of reality. Critics argue that Lacan's emphasis on language as the primary mediator of human experience overlooks the complexities of embodied existence and the non-linguistic aspects of subjectivity. This critique raises fundamental questions about the limitations of language in representing and shaping lived experience. Additionally, Lacan's symbolic framework has been challenged by post-structuralist and deconstructionist thinkers who question the stability of signifiers and the possibility of a coherent symbolic structure. These philosophical challenges have prompted a reevaluation of Lacan's conceptualization of the Symbolic Order and its relationship to the formation of individual and collective identities. Moreover, critiques from phenomenological and existential perspectives emphasize the importance of subjective experience and lived embodiment, highlighting potential blind spots in Lacanian theory's focus on linguistic and symbolic structures. Such challenges call for a nuanced exploration of the interplay between language, subjectivity, and intersubjectivity within the context of broader philosophical debates. Furthermore, Lacan's borrowing from structuralist linguistics has drawn scrutiny from thinkers critical of structuralist paradigms, who assert that Lacan's reliance on Saussurean linguistics oversimplifies the complexities of meaning-making and communication. These challenges compel scholars and practitioners to engage in interdisciplinary dialogues that integrate psychoanalytic concepts with diverse philosophical frameworks.

2. Empirical and Clinical Objections in Psychoanalysis:

In the milieu of psychoanalysis, critics have raised concerns about the practical application of Lacanian theory in clinical settings, questioning its ability to effectively address the diverse array of psychological disorders and conditions presented by patients. One key objection revolves around the interpretive nature of psychoanalytic practice within the framework of the Symbolic Order, with critics arguing that subjective interpretations may lack empirical evidence and scientific validation. This raises questions about the reliability and validity of clinical outcomes derived from a theoretical framework that places significant emphasis on linguistics, signifiers, and unconscious meaning. Additionally, empirical challenges have emerged regarding the testability and replicability of Lacanian concepts, as the abstract nature of the Symbolic Order makes it difficult to empirically verify or refute. Critics argue that the lack of empirical grounding poses significant limitations to the overall credibility and applicability of Lacanian psychoanalysis in contemporary clinical practice. Furthermore, the clinical implications of the Symbolic Order have sparked contentious debates among practitioners, with some expressing skepticism about its capacity to provide comprehensive understanding and treatment for mental health problems. Opponents question whether the Symbolic Order adequately addresses the complexities of human experience, especially in cases where psychiatric symptoms manifest in ways that diverge from the linguistic and symbolic frameworks proposed by Lacan. This has led to ongoing discussions about the integration of the Symbolic Order with other therapeutic modalities and the need for a more inclusive approach that considers the multifaceted nature of psychological distress. These objections underscore the necessity for rigorous empirical research and critical evaluation of the clinical utility of Lacanian concepts within the broader landscape of psychoanalytic practices.

3. Feminist Perspectives:

In feminist theory, scholars have interrogated the ways in which language, signification, and symbolic structures perpetuate gendered power differentials within society. The patriarchal underpinnings of the Symbolic Order have been a focal point for feminist investigations, highlighting how the construction of male-dominated linguistic and cultural norms contributes to the marginalization of women and non-binary individuals. Feminist perspectives on the Symbolic Order also scrutinize the privileging of phallic symbolism and its implications for the subjugation of femininity.

Additionally, feminist theorists engage with Lacanian psychoanalysis from a critical standpoint, questioning the universality of Lacan's formulations and their applicability to diverse experiences of gender and sexuality. They argue that Lacan's emphasis on the Oedipus complex and the role of the phallus in structuring subjectivity overlooks the complexities of female desire and the impact of intersecting identities such as race, class, and sexual orientation. Furthermore, feminist critiques challenge the notion of a fixed, universal language system, positing instead that language is inherently tied to social and cultural contexts, and thus subject to continual redefinition and transformation.

Feminist perspectives on the Symbolic Order extend beyond theoretical analysis to encompass practical interventions aimed at unsettling and reconstructing existing symbolic hierarchies. These interventions include the deconstruction of gendered language and discourse, the subversion of traditional symbolic representations, and the promotion of alternative modes of signification that validate diverse gender identities and expressions. Moreover, feminist movements have sought to dismantle entrenched patriarchal structures within social institutions and discourse, advocating for the recognition and validation of marginalized voices within the symbolic register.

As feminist scholarship continues to evolve, the exploration of the Symbolic Order remains a central area of inquiry, with contemporary theorists addressing the intersectionality of gender, race, class, and other axes of identity within the symbolic landscape. Intersectional feminist perspectives offer a nuanced understanding of the complex interplay between language, power, and subjectivity, and underscore the imperative of challenging and reconceptualizing the symbolic frameworks that shape our social reality.

4. Cultural and Postmodern Critiques:

Cultural and postmodern critiques of the symbolic order emerge within the broader context of challenging traditional power structures, linguistic paradigms, and socio-cultural norms. Postmodernism's rejection of metanarratives and its emphasis on plurality and fragmentation pose a significant challenge to Lacanian psychoanalytic theory, which is inherently rooted in a structured understanding of subjectivity and language. Critics argue that the symbolic order, as conceived by Lacan, perpetuates particular cultural, gendered, and racial biases, thereby reinforcing existing hierarchies and marginalizing alternative experiences. The privileging of certain signifiers and the construction of a universalizing symbolic framework come under scrutiny for neglecting the diverse expressions of subjectivity and identity present within contemporary cultural landscapes. Additionally, postmodern critics question the assumed stability and coherence of the symbolic order, highlighting the fluid and contingent nature of meaning and representation. This critique challenges the notion of a fixed and authoritative symbolic system, advocating instead for a more dynamic and open-ended understanding of the ways in which individuals traverse complex social realities. Furthermore, cultural critiques of the symbolic order interrogate its interplay with power dynamics, particularly within the context of colonial and postcolonial discourses. These critiques illuminate how the symbolic order is intertwined with systems of oppression and hegemonic control, shedding light on the ways in which language and symbols are mobilized to reinforce dominant narratives and subjugate marginalized voices. Scholars drawing from cultural studies, critical race theory, and postcolonial theory provide invaluable insight into the intersections of language, culture, and power, prompting a reevaluation of the implications of the symbolic order within diverse social contexts. Moreover, the influence of digital technologies and the proliferation of new media platforms have introduced novel challenges to the traditional contours of the symbolic order. Culturally situated critiques interrogate the impact of virtual spaces, hyperreality, and fluid identities on the established symbolic framework, urging a reconceptualization of subjectivity and social meaning-making processes. In traversing these multifaceted critiques, it becomes evident that the symbolic order is entwined with the complexities of cultural production, representation, and resistance within an ever-evolving global landscape.

5. The Role of the Symbolic Order in Identity Politics:

Identity politics has become a crucial focal point in contemporary discourses, with implications that reverberate across various fields, including psychology, sociology, and political theory. In the context of Lacanian psychoanalysis, the concept of the Symbolic Order offers a lens through which to dissect and understand the dynamics at play within identity politics.

One of the fundamental tenets of the Symbolic Order is its role in the formation and negotiation of individual and collective identities. By delving into language, signifiers, and social structures, the Symbolic Order shapes the way in which individuals construct and perceive their identities within societal frameworks. Consequently, this process intersects with identity politics, where marginalized groups seek recognition and representation within dominant power structures.

Critics and proponents engage in ongoing debates about the implications of the Symbolic Order on identity politics. Some argue that the Symbolic Order perpetuates hegemonic power dynamics by imposing normative standards and constricting the agency of marginalized communities. This perspective emphasizes how the Symbolic Order can be wielded as a tool for perpetuating oppression and marginalization.

Conversely, defenders of the Symbolic Order assert that it provides a framework for understanding the complexities of identity politics without reducing them to mere essentialist categories. They argue that the Symbolic Order offers a space for negotiating multiple subjectivities and fostering inclusive dialogues that transcend reductive identity constructs. Proponents advocate for leveraging the Symbolic Order to deconstruct dominant narratives and challenge systemic inequalities entrenched within identity politics.

The intersectional nuances within identity politics intersect with the Symbolic Order's capacity to elucidate the intricacies of multiple, overlapping social identities. The Symbolic Order sheds light on the ways in which language and cultural symbols shape and interconnect various facets of an individual's identity, acknowledging the complex interplay between factors such as race, gender, sexuality, class, and ethnicity.

As scholarship continues to evolve, examining the interwoven dynamics of the Symbolic Order and identity politics remains pivotal for fostering nuanced understandings of power, agency, and representation within diverse social contexts. It prompts scholars and practitioners to critically interrogate the entanglements between language, culture, and social norms in shaping identity while traversing the multifaceted terrain of contemporary identity politics.

6. Defense Strategies from Contemporary Lacanians:

Contemporary Lacanian theorists offer a compelling defense of the Symbolic Order in response to the critiques and debates that have emerged within the field of psychoanalysis. One key defense strategy involves an exploration of the relationship between language, subjectivity, and social structures. By elucidating the ways in which language shapes the individual's entry into the symbolic register, contemporary Lacanians assert the necessity of the Symbolic Order for understanding the construction of human subjectivity. They emphasize that the Symbolic Order is not merely a linguistic construct but a fundamental framework through which individuals engage with their identities and relationships within society. Moreover, proponents argue that the Symbolic Order provides a crucial lens through which to examine power dynamics, ideology, and the perpetuation of societal norms. This defense underscores the Symbolic Order's relevance in illuminating the complex interplay between language, culture, and individual agency. Another pivotal aspect of the defense put forward by contemporary Lacanians involves addressing the criticisms related to gender and sexuality. Scholars within this framework engage with feminist perspectives to underscore how the Symbolic Order can be used to unpack the intricacies of gendered identity formation and the impact of patriarchal norms on subjectivity. By highlighting the Symbolic Order's capacity to reveal the underlying power structures that shape gender dynamics, these defenders seek to demonstrate its continued significance in contemporary discourse. Furthermore, proponents confront the challenges posed by postmodern critiques by advocating for a nuanced understanding of the Symbolic Order's adaptability to fluid and hybrid identities. They assert that rather than being rigid or limiting, the Symbolic Order offers a framework for comprehending the multiplicity and complexity of identity constructions in an ever-changing cultural landscape. Through these diverse strategies, contemporary Lacanian theorists aim to fortify the conceptual integrity and practical applicability of the Symbolic Order within the evolving landscape of psychoanalytic theory and clinical practice.

7. Significance of Current Debates on the Symbolic:

The current debates surrounding the Symbolic Order are of profound significance within the field of psychoanalysis and related disciplines. One crucial dimension of these debates lies in the opportunity they present for critical reflexivity. As scholars engage in dialogues regarding the Symbolic Order, they simultaneously interrogate their own assumptions, biases, and preconceptions. This process of self-examination is essential for cultivating a nuanced and dynamic discourse, capable of integrating diverse viewpoints and methodological approaches. In this way, the debates propel the field towards a richer and more comprehensive understanding of the Symbolic Order.

The current debates serve as a catalyst for innovation and evolution within psychoanalytic practice. By foregrounding areas of contention and divergence, these discussions stimulate the development of new theoretical frameworks, clinical methodologies, and interdisciplinary collaborations. Through this process, the field becomes responsive to the evolving needs and complexities of the individuals and communities it seeks to serve.

The debates also hold significance in terms of their wider cultural and societal ramifications. As concepts related to the Symbolic Order intersect with issues of power, language, and subjectivity, the ongoing conversations reverberate beyond the confines of academic discourse. They inform public discourse on identity, agency, and the nature of human experience, offering valuable insights for traversing the multifaceted challenges of contemporary life.

Finally, the significance of these debates stems from their potential to generate renewed interest in the questions that underpin psychoanalysis and its foundational concepts. By reigniting intellectual curiosity and fostering an environment of rigorous inquiry, the debates invigorate the ongoing quest for deeper comprehension of the human condition and the interplay of psychic and social forces.

THE IMAGINARY ORDER - ILLUSIONS & IDENTIFICATIONS

Core Concepts and Constructs

1. Introduction:

Defined as one of the three crucial orders in Lacan's psychoanalytic framework, the Imaginary pertains to images, representations, and identifications that shape an individual's sense of self and relation to others within their social and cultural milieu. It encompasses visual imagery, mental representations, and the early formation of the ego through symbolic objects, particularly highlighted in the Mirror Stage. The construct of the Imaginary is not confined to literal visual perceptions but extends to include symbolic and imaginary identifications that influence an individual's subjective reality.

The structuring of the Imaginary is intimately linked to the emergence of a unified self-identity, often mediated through idealized images and distorted reflections within the subject's psychic landscape. Through a process of misrecognition and idealization, individuals internalize and project images that generate a sense of wholeness and coherence, thus contributing to the formation of the ego ideal – a central aspect within Lacanian theory.

Crucially, the Imaginary does not operate in isolation but interacts dynamically with the Symbolic and Real orders, leading to multifaceted processes of subjectivation and desire within the individual. By unpacking these interrelated dynamics, we gain insight into the complex interplay between language, representation, and the constitution of subjectivity.

2. The Mirror Stage - The Genesis of Imaginary Identifications:

The Mirror Stage, occurring during early infant development, is characterized by the infant's initial encounter with their own reflection in a mirror. Through this experience, the infant enters into a crucial moment of self-recognition and identification, which subsequently forms the basis for their sense of ego and identity. The Mirror Stage represents the embryonic structure of the Imaginary order, whereby the infant constructs a coherent sense of self through the act of mirroring. In this context, the mirror itself serves as a metaphor for the Other, as the infant's identification with its mirrored image prompts a dual process of fascination and alienation. This dichotomy becomes integral in shaping the child's emerging subjectivity and lays the groundwork for future relationships with both oneself and others. Furthermore, the Mirror Stage transcends mere physical reflection and embodies a symbolic dimension, encapsulating the formation of the ego and its entwinement within imagery. Additionally, the Mirror Stage underscores the inherent illusory nature of ego formation, as the idealized image reflected back to the infant cultivates a foundation of idealization and misrecognition. Lacan emphasizes that the ego rooted in this stage becomes an 'imaginary function' rather than a true representation of the self, thus establishing the notion of a fundamental rift between the ego and the true essence of the subject. Moreover, the Mirror Stage extends beyond its immediate implications, exerting a profound influence on the individual's psychic development and relational dynamics in later life. This is evidenced in the perpetuation of idealized self-images and the pursuit of external validation throughout the stages of maturation.

3. Illusions, Fantasies, and the Imaginary Order:

In Lacanian theory, the concept of the Imaginary Order encompasses a complex tapestry of illusions and fantasies that profoundly shape human subjectivity. Integral to this framework is the role of illusions and fantasies in constructing and perpetuating the Imaginary Order, which plays a pivotal role in the individual's formation and understanding of self and others. At its core, the Imaginary Order is rife with the interplay of deceptive perceptions, idealized images, and distorted realities, all of which intertwine to weave the fabric of human experience. It is within illusions and fantasies that individuals often construct their most enduring and profound identifications, which exert a pervasive influence on their relationships, desires, and sense of self. The allure of the imaginary is irrevocably intertwined with the allure of perfection and the desire for a cohesive, unblemished self-image. In this context, it becomes essential to engage with the intertwined web of illusions and fantasies to comprehend the intricacies of the Imaginary Order. This includes exploring how these illusions and fantasies directly impact individual subjectivity, interpersonal dynamics, and the broader societal fabric. Delving into the diverse manifestations of illusions and fantasies within the Imaginary Order unveils the complexities of human experience and sheds light on the nuanced construction of personal narratives and social identities. Furthermore, examining the interconnectedness of illusion and reality within the Imaginary Order serves to underscore the relationship between truth and fiction in shaping the human psyche.

4. The Role of Images in the Formation of the Subject:

The Imaginary Order, with its foundation in visual imagery and identification, highlights the significance of images in the constitution of subjectivity. The apprehension of one's image in the mirror during the Mirror Stage initiates a foundational identification process, where the subject sees themselves as a unified and coherent entity. This pivotal moment marks the genesis of the ego, as the subject strives to integrate the fragmented perceptions of themselves into a singular, cohesive image. This process underpins the formation of the ego-ideal, representing the idealized image towards which the subject continually aspires. However, alongside this idealized image lies the shadowy dimension of misrecognition, where the subject's relationship with their own image becomes entangled in illusions and distortions. As such, the continuous negotiation between the ideal and the distorted image profoundly influences the subject's self-concept and interpersonal dynamics. Furthermore, the omnipresence of societal and cultural images further complicates the subject's self-formation. From media representations to social expectations, the subject encounters a myriad of external images that interplay with their internal self-images, shaping their perception of self-worth and desirability. The cultivation of these internal and external image representations contributes significantly to the subject's self-identification and the construction of their identity. Moreover, the internalization of such images manifests in the subject's fantasies and desires, further intertwining the imaginative sphere with the formation of the subject. These fantasies serve as a crucial bridge between the inner world of images and the external realities, illustrating the pervasive influence of the Imaginary Order on the subject's psyche.

5. The Imaginary and Its Relation to the Ego:

The Imaginary, as understood in this context, encompasses images, identifications, and visual representations that contribute to an individual's sense of self. Central to this construction is the concept of the mirror stage, where the infant first encounters its own reflection and begins to form a coherent, albeit illusory, sense of identity.

In this context, the Ego emerges as a product of the Imaginary process, representing the individual's idealized self-image and embodied sense of coherence. However, it is crucial to recognize that the Ego, rather than being a stable and unified entity, is inherently linked to the fragmented and often contradictory nature of the Imaginary. This duality presents a fundamental tension in the formation of the self, as the Ego simultaneously strives for wholeness while being inherently entangled with the multiplicity of images and identifications that constitute the Imaginary.

The Imaginary-Ego relationship is not merely confined to the internal psychic dimension; it also encompasses external dynamics and interactions with others. As individuals traverse social landscapes, they engage in a continual process of projecting and receiving images, thereby shaping and reshaping their Ego in relation to others. This dynamic interplay not only influences the individual's self-perception but also determines the manner in which they are perceived by and relate to the external world.

Lacan posits that the Ego is characterized by a fundamental alienation – an inherent discord between the idealized self-image and the lived experience. This dissonance gives rise to a perpetual struggle for authenticity and recognition, as the Ego strives to reconcile its constructed identity with the realities of everyday existence. Through this lens, the Ego can be seen as a site of ongoing conflict and negotiation between the subjective inner world and the external demands of society.

Ultimately, the relationship between the Imaginary and the Ego serves as a cornerstone in understanding the complexities of human subjectivity within Lacanian psychoanalytic framework. It offers profound insights into the persistent tensions, illusions, and aspirations that underpin the construction of selfhood, shedding light on the interplay between internal fantasies, external perceptions, and the elusive quest for coherence and authenticity.

6. Distortions and Misrecognitions

Distortions refer to the ways in which individuals perceive and interpret external reality through the filter of their inner psychological landscape. These distortions are not merely errors in perception but are deeply intertwined with the construction and maintenance of one's ego. In Lacanian theory, misrecognitions, also known as misidentifications, involve the fundamental misunderstanding or misinterpretation of one's own self-image in relation to perceived social ideals or significant others. This process contributes significantly to the formation of identity and subjectivity within the Imaginary order. It is crucial to explore the core mechanisms underlying these processes to comprehend their psychological implications. One of the primary drivers of distortions and misrecognitions is the phenomenon of projection, where individuals unconsciously attribute their own thoughts, desires, or emotions onto others. This projection often shapes how individuals assess and engage with the external world, reinforcing their subjective perceptions and misconceptions. Additionally, the concept of introjection plays a vital role in internalizing external influences, such as societal norms, cultural expectations, and familial dynamics, thereby contributing to the formation of distorted self-perceptions. Moreover, the interplay between idealized self-images and the actual lived experiences further complicates the web of misrecognitions and distortions. These idealized self-images, or ego ideals, often serve as benchmarks against which individuals evaluate their own worth and adequacy, perpetuating an ongoing cycle of misrecognition. Furthermore, Lacan emphasizes the role of language and symbolic representations in fueling distortions and misrecognitions within the Imaginary order. The use of linguistic constructs and societal discourses can create internal conflicts and discrepancies between one's perceived self and the accepted social norms, leading to profound distortions and misidentifications.

7. Lacan's Structural Model - Components of the Imaginary:

In Lacanian theory, the Imaginary occupies a central position within the broader framework of the human psyche. At the heart of this conceptualization lies Lacan's structural model, which delineates the components that constitute the Imaginary order. To grasp the essence of this structural model, one must first acknowledge the pivotal role of the mirror stage in the formation of the Imaginary. This critical phase, occurring in early infancy, establishes the dyadic relationship between the infant and its own reflected image, thereby inaugurating the construction of the ego as a unified and coherent entity.

Beyond the mirror stage, Lacan's structural model further unfolds to encompass key elements such as the specular image, the ideal ego, and the dual relationship. The specular image, often perceived as an illusory counterpart to reality, holds profound implications for the subject's self-identity and perception of others. Concurrently, the ideal ego emerges as a regulatory construct, stemming from the individual's inclination towards perfection and unitary wholeness. This idealized projection shapes the way individuals aspire to be perceived and acknowledged by external entities.

The structural model unveils the notion of the dual relationship, elucidating the dynamic interplay between the ego and its mirrored reflection. Within this framework, the ego seeks validation and coherence through the reflected image, engendering a continuous dialectic of identification and disidentification. As a result, the process of identifying with the specular image becomes integral to the subject's quest for self-affirmation and confirmation of identity.

Emanating from Lacan's structural model is the concept of the imago, encapsulating the manifest attributes and traits that populate the imaginary register. The imago represents a vestige of past experiences and collective representations, intertwined with the individual's subjective interpretation and internalization. This amalgamation gives rise to a network of images and symbols that configure the foundation of the Imaginary, shaping the individual's perceptions and self-constructions within the psychic landscape.

8. Psychodynamic Implications of the Imaginary:

By delving into the Imaginary, we explore the complexities of subject formation and the dynamics of psychological processes. One of the key psychodynamic implications of the Imaginary lies in its role in shaping an individual's internal world. Through the interplay of images, identifications, and illusions, the Imaginary becomes a foundational aspect in understanding the formation and functioning of the ego. The mirror stage, a pivotal concept within the Imaginary, illuminates how early experiences of self-recognition and mirroring contribute to the construction of identity and psychic structures. The manner in which these processes unfold has far-reaching implications for an individual's psychological development and overall mental well-being. Furthermore, the Imaginary plays a crucial part in the formation of fantasies and desires, offering insights into the inner workings of unconscious processes and the ways in which individuals create and relate to their own realities. Understanding the psychodynamic implications of the Imaginary provides clinicians with valuable tools for therapeutic intervention. By recognizing the influence of the Imaginary on subjective experience, psychotherapists can offer more insightful and effective interventions that address underlying issues related to identity, emotional disturbances, and self-perception. Moreover, exploring the psychodynamic implications of the Imaginary opens up avenues for deeper understanding of human behavior and interpersonal dynamics. This conceptual framework enables professionals in various fields to gain a nuanced understanding of the ways in which individuals construct and maintain their sense of self and engage in relationships.

The Interplay between the Imaginary and the Symbolic Orders

1. Intersecting Modalities of Operations:

The interplay between the Imaginary and the Symbolic Orders gives rise to intersecting modalities of operations that deeply influence human subjectivity and social formations. Within this interweaving, the Imaginary Order fosters the construction of subjective experiences based on images, perceptions, and identifications rooted in early developmental stages. Conversely, the Symbolic Order operates through linguistic systems, cultural norms, and social structures that shape individuals' understanding of themselves and their place within the broader societal framework. These modalities intersect in profound ways, exerting simultaneous influences on an individual's self-perception and interactions with the external world. The intersection of these modalities occurs at multiple levels, from personal identity to collective cultural practices, and understanding these intersections is vital to unveiling the complexities of human experience. At the individual level, this intersection manifests in the mechanisms through which images and symbols intertwine to shape one's sense of self and relationship with others. It is crucial to examine how the images and symbols internalized through the Imaginary and Symbolic Orders inform an individual's worldview, values, and behaviors. Moreover, the intersecting modalities reveal the dynamic nature of subject formation, shedding light on the continuous negotiation between personal imagery and social symbols. Furthermore, at the social level, the interplay between the Imaginary and the Symbolic contributes to the construction of intersubjective relationships and the formation of collective identities. Through the mediation of symbolic systems, shared cultural narratives, and collective imaginaries, communities develop unique modes of interacting and understanding one another. Understanding the converging effects of these modalities becomes pivotal for comprehending the complexities of social dynamics and cultural phenomena.

2. Characterization of Intersubjective Relationships:

Within the psychoanalytic framework, intersubjective relationships are essential to understanding the dynamic interplay between the imaginary and the symbolic orders. Characterizing intersubjective relationships involves delving into the web of shared meanings, emotions, and experiences that shape human connections. These relationships encompass a range of interactions, from intimate dyadic exchanges to broader social dynamics, all of which contribute to the construction and negotiation of subjective realities. Understanding the nature of intersubjectivity requires an exploration of how individuals perceive and relate to one another within the context of larger cultural and societal systems. Such analysis involves examining the influence of historical, cultural, and familial contexts on the formation of intersubjective ties, as well as the impact of power differentials, social norms, and collective beliefs on these relationships. Furthermore, the lens of intersubjectivity provides insight into the ways in which individuals come to identify with certain social groups, engage with conflicts, and negotiate their sense of self within the framework of relational dynamics. From a clinical perspective, an understanding of intersubjective relationships informs therapeutic interventions, as it sheds light on the complexity of transference, countertransference, and the therapeutic alliance. By delineating the contours of intersubjective dynamics, clinicians can more effectively manage the complexities of the therapeutic relationship, honing their ability to attune to and comprehend the subjective experiences of their clients. The study of intersubjective relationships also extends beyond clinical practice, offering valuable insights for fields such as sociology, anthropology, and cultural studies. It provides a lens through which to examine social phenomena, conflict resolution, and identity formation within diverse cultural contexts, illuminating the nuanced ways in which individuals construct shared realities.

3. Psychological Dynamics and Their Manifestations:

In the context of the interplay between the Imaginary and the Symbolic Orders, psychological dynamics bear significant relevance as they influence how individuals perceive themselves and others within their social and cultural contexts. Central to this exploration is the notion of internalized representations, which inform an individual's self-concept and relational patterns. The Imaginary order, with its emphasis on visual imagery and identifications, plays a pivotal role in the formation of these internal representations. Through the lens of the Imaginary, individuals construct idealized images of themselves and others, which serve as benchmarks for comparison and evaluation. Simultaneously, the Symbolic order, with its system of language and shared cultural symbols, mediates the internalization of societal norms and values, contributing to the formation of one's sense of self and interpersonal conduct.

The manifestations of psychological dynamics extend to desire and lack. Within the Lacanian framework, desire is linked to the Imaginary's mirroring mechanisms and the Symbolic's structuring function. Individuals engage with their desires through interactions with others, engaging in a continual pursuit of recognition and validation while grappling with the inherent lack that underpins human subjectivity. These dynamics manifest in diverse ways, from the quest for symbolic accolades to the cultivation of imaginary ideals, all of which reverberate in the construction of personal narratives and relational schemas.

The interplay between the Imaginary and the Symbolic influences the manifestation of defense mechanisms and coping strategies. Individuals deploy a myriad of defense mechanisms to manage the tensions arising from the dissonance between their subjective experiences and external reality. These mechanisms, ranging from projection and repression to identification and sublimation, reflect the dance between the individual's internal world and the external demands imposed by the Symbolic order. Understanding these manifestations offers critical insights into the complexities of human behavior and the underlying mechanisms at play in the negotiation of psychic conflicts.

4. Symbolic Structure's Influence on the Imaginary:

At its core, the symbolic order encompasses the milieu of language, cultural norms, societal institutions, and the myriad of symbolic representations that shape the human experience. These symbolic constructs not only provide the scaffolding for meaning-making but also play a pivotal role in constructing and shaping the imaginary dimension of human subjectivity. It is within this framework that individuals negotiate their identities, desires, and understanding of reality.

The symbolic structure exerts a profound influence on the imaginary through its regulatory function. As symbolic representations permeate various aspects of an individual's life, they become internalized and integrated into the fabric of the imaginary. This internalization process shapes the construction of the imaginary world, impacting an individual's self-perception, relationships, and existential orientation. Moreover, the symbolic order sets the parameters within which the imaginary can manifest, leading to the formation of socially mediated fantasies, aspirations, and ideals.

The symbolic order not only shapes the content of the imaginary but also mediates its expression and reception. Language, as a primary component of the symbolic order, serves as a vehicle for articulating and communicating imaginary phenomena. Through linguistic expressions, individuals engage with and communicate their subjective experiences, imbuing their imaginary constructions with symbolic meaning and significance.

The dynamic interplay between the symbolic and imaginary extends beyond individual subjectivities, permeating collective and cultural dimensions. Symbolic systems and cultural discourses influence the collective imaginary, molding shared representations, myths, and narratives that contribute to the construction of collective identities. This interaction underscores the relationship between cultural symbolism and the shared imaginary frameworks within society.

5. Imaginary Distortions within Symbolic Frameworks:

In the web of human cognition, the interplay between the imaginary and the symbolic orders manifests through a complex array of cognitive processes and psychological phenomena. Central to this dynamic is the manifestation of imaginary distortions within symbolic frameworks, which warrants careful examination. An individual's construction of identity, perception of reality, and understanding of self and others can become entangled within the symbolic structures, often giving rise to distortions that profoundly impact interpersonal relationships and internal psychic landscapes. These distortions may lead to misinterpretations, misconceptions, and illusions that influence an individual's thoughts, emotions, and behaviors. Understanding these distortions necessitates delving deep into the layers of symbolic structures and their interaction with the imaginary order. Symbolic frameworks, characterized by language, culture, and social norms, provide the contextual backdrop against which the imaginary takes shape. However, it is within these very frameworks that distortions can emerge, significantly impacting an individual's subjective experiences and relational dynamics. The influence of language as a symbolic system on the construction of meaning and the formation of imaginary representations cannot be underestimated. Language not only shapes our perceptions but also acts as a conduit for symbolic distortions to permeate our imaginary constructions. Additionally, cultural and societal norms serve as pervasive symbolic frameworks that strongly mold the imaginary register. Consequently, the distortions that arise within these contexts influence the way individuals perceive themselves and others, often leading to misunderstandings and conflicts. It is essential to explore these distortions through various clinical and real-world vignettes to comprehend their multifaceted nature.

Images, Identity Formation, and the Role of the Mirror Stage

1. Theoretical Foundations:

Lacan's concept of the Mirror Stage elucidates the pivotal role of visual perception and the psyche in shaping an individual's sense of self. The Mirror Stage represents a critical juncture in human development, typically occurring between 6 to 18 months of age, where a child first encounters their mirrored image. This encounter triggers a series of complex psychological processes that form the foundation of their ego and contribute to their evolving self-identity. Lacan posits that during the Mirror Stage, the child experiences a dual recognition - firstly, there is a fascination with the external image reflecting back at them, and secondly, an internal identification with the idealized, unified image. This process engenders a sense of wholeness and cohesiveness within the child's psyche. Moreover, Lacan asserts that this moment also inaugurates a lifelong pursuit of seeking unity and mastery, often leading individuals to further engage with reflective entities and representations as they manage the complexities of their social environments. Furthermore, the Mirror Stage illustrates Lacan's departure from traditional psychoanalytic perspectives, such as those of Freud, by emphasizing the visual dimension in the formation of subjectivity. This emphasis on the visual component repositions the gaze and visual representation as pivotal forces that shape interpersonal relations and the construction of the self. Importantly, Lacan's Mirror Stage sheds light on the influential role of the image and the ego ideal, offering profound insights into the mechanisms that underpin human cognition and selfhood. Thus, comprehending the theoretical foundations of the Mirror Stage is essential for grasping the interplay between visual stimuli, psychological construction, and the emergence of identity, offering a compelling lens through which to appreciate human subjectivity.

2. Visual Perception and the Psyche:

Visual perception plays a fundamental role in shaping an individual's psyche, serving as a crucial channel through which they perceive the external world and construct their internal mental representations. The interplay between visual stimuli and cognitive processing gives rise to a complex web of associations, emotions, and self-perceptions. At the heart of this process lies the concept of visual schema, wherein individuals build cognitive frameworks based on their experiences, encounters, and interpretations of visual information. These schemas profoundly shape their understanding of themselves and their place in the world. Moreover, these frameworks are inherently intertwined with the development and construction of identity. Through visual perception, individuals not only observe external objects and events but also internalize and reflect upon them, thereby influencing their sense of self. The significance of visual perception in relation to the psyche becomes particularly pronounced during formative stages of development, as children engage in a process of active exploration and learning through their visual experiences. This period is pivotal in laying the groundwork for later identity formation, as it marks the genesis of self-recognition and the understanding of one's own physicality. Additionally, visual cues from caregivers and the surrounding environment significantly impact the construction of a child's burgeoning self-concept. Furthermore, the profound influence of visual perception on the psyche extends into adulthood, encompassing the continual assimilation and interpretation of visual stimuli in relation to one's evolving identity. This ongoing interaction shapes individuals' perceptions of themselves, others, and the world, contributing to the tapestry of their psychological makeup.

3. Developmental Milestones in the Mirror Stage:

The mirror stage typically occurs during the early years of a child's life, primarily between six and eighteen months. At this juncture, the child undergoes a significant psychological recognition when encountering their reflection in a mirror or other reflective surfaces. This momentous encounter is not merely an act of perceiving oneself but rather marks the genesis of the individuation process.

During the mirror stage, the child experiences a profound interaction with their own mirrored image, leading to a sense of unity and coherence between the self-perception and the external visual representation. This newfound realization catalyzes a fundamental shift in the child's cognitive and psychological development, laying the groundwork for a more complex understanding of themselves within the world. The identification with the reflected image triggers a surge of narcissistic pleasure and serves as the initial step in forming a stable, albeit illusory, egoic identity.

As the child progresses through the mirror stage, they exhibit observable behaviors that denote their growing cognizance of their own image. These behaviors can include actions such as smiling or making gestures towards their reflection, indicating a burgeoning awareness of self-recognition. Furthermore, the child may display signs of fascination and curiosity with the mirror, demonstrating an emerging understanding of the correlation between their physical movements and the corresponding reflections.

A noteworthy aspect of the mirror stage is the dichotomy between the wholeness of the reflected image and the actual fragmented nature of the child's body and self-perception. This disjuncture gives rise to a dualistic experience, where the child oscillates between a cohesive, idealized mirroring and the stark reality of their incomplete bodily control and self-awareness. This divergence confers a sense of alienation and discrepancy, fueling Lacan's assertion that the construction of ego is inherently founded on misrecognition.

4. Fragmentation and Wholeness:

In the mirror stage, the infant first encounters its mirror image and undergoes a dual process of fragmentation and integration that profoundly shapes its psychological constitution. This duality encompasses the fragmentation of the self, as the infant perceives a disjointed and incomplete reflection, alongside the aspiration towards wholeness, the quest for a coherent and idealized self-image.

The fragmented nature of the mirror reflection serves as a metaphor for the inherent vulnerability and disarray that characterize the early stages of identity formation. The infant's initial encounter with its mirror image introduces a schism between its subjective experience and the external perception of itself, leading to an internal sense of incompleteness and discordance. This stage marks the genesis of a fragmented self-identity, wherein the ego is yet to be fully realized, and the symbolic order is not yet internalized.

Conversely, the pursuit of wholeness represents the innate human inclination towards unity and integration. As the infant strives to reconcile the disparity between its self-perception and the reflected image, an idealized sense of coherence and completeness gradually emerges. Through this process, the ego begins to crystallize, forming the foundation of the individual's self-concept and their relationships with the external world. Thus, the duality of fragmentation and wholeness encapsulates the complex interplay between disintegration and unification that underpins the formative stages of human subjectivity.

This duality in the Mirror Stage holds profound implications for understanding the nuanced dynamics of human identity and the complexities of the ego. It illuminates the balance between the fragmented aspects of the self, characterized by internal inconsistencies and incongruities, and the unifying tendency towards a cohesive and integrated self-perception. Moreover, it underscores the dialectical nature of identity formation, highlighting the ongoing negotiation between disparate fragments and the aspirational drive towards a unified and harmonious self-representation.

In essence, the duality of fragmentation and wholeness embodies a fundamental paradox in the construction of human subjectivity, offering invaluable insights into the processes of self-discovery, self-representation, and interpersonal relationships. It is through this duality that the Mirror Stage transcends mere visual perception, becoming a profound metaphor for the profound complexities that underlie the formation of identity and the evolution of the ego.

5. The 'I' - Emergence of the Ego:

The emergence of the ego, a pivotal aspect in identity formation, occurs through the complex interplay between the individual and their perceptions of their surroundings. As a central component of the psyche, the ego serves as the mediator between the internal desires and external reality, thus playing a crucial role in the construction of one's sense of self. This process involves the assimilation of experiences, impressions, and interactions with others, leading to the development of a distinct self-image. Furthermore, the ego's formation is deeply intertwined with the individual's encounter with the mirror stage, where they are confronted with their own reflection as a separate entity. Lacan posits that this initial encounter with the mirror plays a significant role in the formation of the ego, as the individual begins to identify with their mirror image, thereby initiating the construction of their 'I'. The duality inherent in this process lies in the simultaneous fragmentation and cohesion of the ego. On one hand, the ego strives for unity and coherence, seeking to integrate the myriad facets of the self into a cohesive whole. On the other hand, the ego also grapples with the fragmented nature of human experience, encountering internal and external contradictions that challenge its quest for wholeness. This tension between fragmentation and wholeness deeply influences the individual's ongoing struggle to reconcile diverse aspects of their identity. Additionally, the emergence of the ego involves a negotiation of the symbolic representation versus the reflective image. The individual confronts the symbolic representations provided by language, culture, and societal norms, which shape their understanding of themselves, juxtaposed with the reflection presented in the mirror, representing a physical embodiment of their self-perception. This interplay introduces complexities and conflicts, as the ego attempts to negotiate between the internally constructed self and the external reflections and projections placed upon it. In understanding the emergence of the ego, we gain valuable insights into the intricacies of identity formation, shedding light on the multifaceted processes that contribute to the construction of the 'I'.

6. Symbolic Representation versus Image Reflection:

While symbolic representation pertains to the linguistic and culturally mediated aspects of identity, image reflection encapsulates the visual and perceptual dimensions that contribute to self-recognition. Understanding the distinction between these two concepts is integral to comprehending the intricacies of human subjectivity. Symbolic representation encompasses the use of language, symbols, and cultural norms to assign meaning and construct narratives about one's identity. This involves the internalization of societal values, beliefs, and norms, which inform an individual's understanding of themselves within the broader social context. It is through this symbolic framework that individuals interpret and communicate their experiences, emotions, and aspirations, thereby contributing to the complex tapestry of their identity. On the other hand, image reflection delves into the visual and perceptual aspects of identity formation, particularly elucidated by Lacan's Mirror Stage. This stage marks the pivotal moment when an infant first identifies with their own mirror image, thus initiating the process of self-recognition and the gradual construction of the 'I'. The mirror simultaneously serves as a metaphorical reflection of societal ideals and standards, which the individual strives to embody. However, it is essential to recognize that the image reflected in the mirror constitutes an idealized and fragmented version of the self, often leading to discrepancies between the perceived image and the internalized symbolic representation. These incongruities can give rise to inner conflicts and struggles in reconciling the idealized self with the reality of one's existence, subsequently influencing the individual's self-esteem and emotional well-being. Moreover, the inherent tension between symbolic representation and image reflection underscores the complex negotiation of identity within both personal and societal contexts. This interplay implicates the fluid nature of identity, emphasizing the dynamic process of self-construction as individuals engage with the myriad influences that shape their sense of self.

7. Psychological Impacts of Misrecognition:

Misrecognition, as proposed by Lacanian theory, is a crucial concept that contributes significantly to our understanding of psychological development and its complex impact on individual subjectivity. Within the Lacanian framework, misrecognition refers to the misperception or misunderstanding of one's own identity or image, often stemming from the flawed perceptions imposed by the external world, particularly through societal expectations and cultural norms.

This misalignment between one's self-perceived identity and the projected societal norms can lead to profound psychological consequences. The individual, plagued by an ever-expanding chasm between the 'real' self and the idealized persona created through misrecognition, experiences deep-seated feelings of inadequacy, alienation, and internal conflict. This inner turmoil can manifest in various forms, such as anxiety, depression, or an overwhelming sense of dissonance with one's surroundings.

The psychological impacts of misrecognition extend beyond an individual's emotional state and permeate various aspects of their interpersonal relationships and social interactions. The inability to reconcile one's authentic self with the distorted reflection perpetuated through misrecognition may lead to difficulties in forming genuine connections with others, fostering a sense of isolation and detachment from the broader social fabric.

Misrecognition can exert a notable influence on an individual's cognitive processes, potentially distorting their perception of reality and impeding their capacity for sound decision-making. This cognitive dissonance may contribute to a cycle of self-doubt and perpetuate a pervasive sense of impostor syndrome, wherein individuals constantly question their competence and accomplishments, attributing their successes to external factors rather than acknowledging their inherent abilities.

In clinical practice, traversing the psychological terrain wrought by misrecognition demands a nuanced approach that entails empowering individuals to embark on a journey of self-discovery and self-acceptance, untangling the web of misperceptions that hinder their emotional well-being. By unraveling the layers of misrecognition through therapeutic techniques and introspective exploration, individuals can strive toward reconstituting a more harmonious relationship with themselves, ultimately fostering a greater sense of authenticity and resilience in the face of societal pressures and expectations.

Conclusively, comprehending the profound psychological impacts of misrecognition within the Lacanian framework illuminates the interplay between societal constructs and individual subjectivity, unveiling the tapestry of human experience and cognitive processes in the context of existence.

Mechanisms of Illusions and Misrecognitions

1. The Formation of the Imaginary - Historical Underpinnings:

The concept of the imaginary has deep historical roots that extend beyond Lacanian theory, dating back to ancient philosophical inquiries into the nature of perception and reality. Early Greek philosophers such as Plato and Aristotle contemplated the relationship between the perceived world and the world of ideas, which laid the groundwork for later explorations of the imaginary within the context of human consciousness and cognition.

During the Renaissance period, advancements in art, literature, and philosophy brought forth a renewed interest in the nature of representation and the construction of reality. Artists and thinkers grappled with the idea of mimesis—the imitation or representation of the external world—prompting reflections on the subjective nature of perception and the role of the imagination in shaping individual perspectives.

The Enlightenment era marked a pivotal juncture in the understanding of the imaginary, as thinkers like René Descartes and Immanuel Kant delved into questions of subjectivity, cognition, and the formation of mental representations. Descartes' exploration of the mind-body duality and the notion of an 'evil demon' deceiving perceptions underscored the pervasive influence of illusions and misrecognitions in human consciousness, while Kant's transcendental idealism emphasized the constructive role of the mind in shaping sensory experiences through categories of understanding.

The emergence of psychoanalysis in the late 19th and early 20th centuries further propelled the exploration of the imaginary within a clinical context. Sigmund Freud's pioneering work on the unconscious mind and dreams paved the way for Lacan's conceptualization of the three psychoanalytic registers—the symbolic, the imaginary, and the real. Drawing from Freudian theory and structuralist linguistics, Lacan positioned the imaginary as a fundamental dimension of human subjectivity, contributing to a richer understanding of the complexities inherent in our perceptual processes and self-identification.

In contemporary discourse, the study of the imaginary continues to intersect with diverse fields such as cognitive psychology, cultural studies, and media theory, fostering interdisciplinary dialogues on the nature of representation, cognition, and mediated realities.

2. Lacan's Mirror Stage as a Precursor:

Lacan's Mirror Stage serves as a pivotal concept in understanding the formation of the imaginary. Lacan posited that the child's encounter with their mirror image initiates a dual process: the transformation of one's visual perception and the emergence of an idealized, unified self. This idealized self is inherently illusory, serving as the foundational basis for the formation of the imaginary. One key aspect lies in recognizing the significant psychological impact of this initial identification. Consequently, the mirror stage lays the groundwork for the individual's perpetual engagement with images and surfaces in the construction of their self-identity. Moreover, Lacan emphasized that the mirrored reflection symbolizes a gestalt of wholeness and coherence that transcends the child's fragmented self-experience. As such, this symbolic unity within the mirror fosters an illusory sense of completion, contrasting the actual psychological disarray inherent in infancy. The mirror stage also introduces the element of misrecognition, where the child mistakes their idealized mirror image for their true self, thus perpetuating the illusion of a unified, autonomous identity. Furthermore, the mirror stage acts as a precursor to the formation of the ego, which becomes intertwined with the images and ideals projected within the imaginary order.

3. Mechanisms of Imaginary Construction and Distortion:

The construction of the imaginary involves the formation of mental images, representations, and identifications that contribute to an individual's sense of self and reality. However, these constructions are susceptible to distortion, influenced by internal and external factors. It is essential to delve into the underlying mechanisms driving this process to grasp the complexities of human consciousness and behavior.

Within the framework of Lacanian theory, the imaginary operates as a fundamental component of the psychic apparatus, intertwining with the symbolic and real orders. This integration is characterized by the interplay between the ego and the idealized images created through identification processes. Individuals engage in self-representations and projections onto others, constructing mental images that serve as the bedrock for their perceptions and interactions.

The distortion within the imaginary stems from the inherent gap between the idealized self-images and the actual lived experiences. This dissonance leads to disruptions in perception, contributing to the formation of illusions and misrecognition. Furthermore, cultural and societal influences shape the construction of the imaginary, often imposing normative ideals and values that may conflict with personal experiences, leading to further distortions.

As individuals engage with their social environments, the process of introjection and projection plays a critical role in the construction of their perceived realities. Introjection involves the internalization of external experiences, beliefs, and attitudes, contributing to the formation of the individual's self-image. On the other hand, projection entails the externalization of internal conflicts, allowing individuals to attribute certain qualities or traits to others that they may struggle to acknowledge within themselves. These mechanisms significantly impact how individuals perceive themselves and others, influencing their interpersonal dynamics and emotional responses.

Lacan's insights into language and its role in sustaining the imaginary further elucidate the intricacies of construction and distortion. Language serves as a medium for signification and representation, influencing the way individuals articulate and interpret their experiences. Within the imaginary, language contributes to the perpetuation of certain illusions and misrecognitions through symbolic expressions and communication. The linguistic construction of narratives and discourses shapes individuals' understanding of themselves and their relationships with others, reinforcing or challenging the existing imaginary frameworks.

4. Projection, Introjection, and their Role in Perception:

Projection and introjection elucidate the processes through which individuals perceive and interact with the external world. Projection involves attributing one's own unconscious desires, feelings, or thoughts onto others, thus making them external to oneself and ascribing them to others. Conversely, introjection occurs when an individual internalizes external stimuli or qualities of others into their own psyche, leading to the assimilation of external thoughts or attributes. Both projection and introjection play pivotal roles in shaping an individual's perception of reality and self-identity within the framework of the Imaginary Order. As individuals manage the complexities of human relationships and societal interactions, the mechanisms of projection and introjection significantly influence their interpretative frameworks and emotional responses. Through the process of projection, individuals often externalize unresolved inner conflicts, fears, or desires onto others, thereby altering their perception of those around them. This mechanism can lead to the misrecognition of others and contribute to the perpetuation of illusions within the Imaginary register. Conversely, introjection contributes to the internalization of external norms, beliefs, and ideals, shaping an individual's self-concept and influencing their behaviors and attitudes. The interplay between projection, introjection, and perception is deeply intertwined with Lacanian theory, as it unveils the dynamics between the subject and the external world. Understanding these mechanisms not only sheds light on the construction of the Imaginary but also provides insights into the complexities of human subjectivity and interpersonal relationships. Moreover, recognizing the impact of projection and introjection enables clinicians and practitioners to uncover underlying psychosocial issues and guide individuals towards a more comprehensive understanding of their subjective experiences.

5. Symbolic Interaction and Imaginary Discrepancies:

In the context of Lacanian theory, the domain of the Symbolic is essential in understanding the complexities that arise from interactions within the Imaginary Order. The Symbolic register encompasses language, culture, societal norms, and the overarching systems of meaning that influence human subjectivity. An exploration of symbolic interaction within the framework of the Imaginary reveals subtle discrepancies and tensions that shape individual identity and perception. Within the symbolic register, language acts as a primary mediator, encoding and organizing experiences and perceptions, thus shaping the formation of the Imaginary. This interplay between the Symbolic and the Imaginary underscores the nuanced ways in which individuals engage with reality and construct their sense of self. Drawing from sociolinguistic theories, the symbolic dimension unveils the implications of cultural and linguistic influences on the construction of the Imaginary. Furthermore, the discrepancies that arise between the Symbolic and the Imaginary registers highlight the inherent conflicts and misalignments embedded within human subjectivity. These discrepancies often manifest as internal struggles, external social discord, and incongruities in communication, contributing to a myriad of psychological and interpersonal challenges. Understanding the symbolic interaction within the context of the Imaginary is vital in recognizing the complexities that underpin human cognition, communication, and behavior. It offers valuable insights into the construction of identities, the perpetuation of illusions, and the propagation of misrecognitions. Unraveling the intricacies of symbolic interaction and its impact on the Imaginary enables practitioners and scholars to comprehend the multifaceted nature of human experience and provides a foundation for intervention and critical analysis. Lastly, acknowledging the dynamic interplay between the Symbolic and the Imaginary invites a deeper examination of the socio-cultural, linguistic, and contextual determinants that underpin human subjectivity, paving the way for a more comprehensive understanding of the complex mechanisms at play within the psyche.

6. The Role of Language in Sustaining the Imaginary Fallacy:

Language plays a pivotal role in perpetuating the fallacies within the imaginary domain. The symbolic nature of language allows individuals to convey meanings and construct representations of reality. However, in the context of the imaginary, language can also serve as a mechanism for sustaining and reinforcing misconceptions and illusions. Through linguistic expressions, individuals may inadvertently contribute to the construction of distorted perceptions and misrecognition patterns.

One of the ways in which language sustains the imaginary fallacy is through the use of symbolic signifiers that are inherently tied to subjective interpretations. Words and phrases, while carrying shared cultural meanings, are subject to individual interpretation and projection within the imaginary register. This subjective filtering of linguistic symbols contributes to the formation of illusory representations, leading individuals to misconstrue their own identities and relational dynamics. Moreover, the symbolic nature of language enables the proliferation of societal expectations, norms, and stereotypes, which further solidify the imaginary constructs that individuals internalize.

The role of language in sustaining the imaginary fallacy extends to the spheres of narrative and discourse. Through storytelling and the reinforcement of societal narratives, language becomes a vehicle for perpetuating idealized self-images and stifling authentic self-expression. Individuals may find themselves conforming to socially constructed scripts and linguistic tropes that align with the illusions propagated by the imaginary order, thereby perpetuating misrecognition patterns and hindering self-realization.

The complexities of language within the imaginary are linked to Lacan's concept of the 'big Other' – the symbolic order that represents the overarching system of social norms and language. The 'big Other' exerts influence over individuals' constructions of self and reality, enmeshing them within linguistic frameworks that sustain imaginary fallacies. This perpetuation occurs through the internalization of societal expectations and the incorporation of societal norms into individuals' self-concepts.

7. Clinical Revelations:

In the clinical sphere, identifying and understanding misrecognition patterns within the imaginary holds paramount significance for psychoanalytic practitioners. First and foremost, psychoanalysts must be attuned to the subtle manifestations of misrecognition, which often transcend overt behavioral cues. By meticulously analyzing verbal expressions, non-verbal cues, and affective responses, clinicians can discern the underlying misalignments between the symbolic meaning and the imaginary representation within an individual's psyche.

On the other hand, drawing on Lacanian theory, practitioners must unravel the interplay between the signifier and the signified, highlighting how misrecognition distorts the subjective understanding of self and others. Unraveling this distortion requires a balance of empathy, introspection, and theoretical acumen.

Additionally, exploring the role of early childhood experiences in shaping misrecognition patterns proves instrumental in clinical practice. Examining the dynamics of familial relationships, societal influences, and cultural conditioning enables clinicians to trace the roots of misrecognition and unveil its pervasive impact on an individual's psychosocial development.

Clinicians employ a multi-modal approach in uncovering misrecognition patterns, integrating methods such as free association, dream analysis, and transference-countertransference dynamics. These techniques facilitate the exploration of subconscious registers, paving the way for a comprehensive understanding of the web of misrecognition within the patient's psyche.

Case conceptualization stands as a pivotal phase where clinicians synthesize their observations and interpretations, discerning overarching themes and recurrent motifs that underpin the patient's misrecognition patterns. Through this process, clinicians construct a cohesive narrative that delineates the nuances of the patient's misrecognition, providing a solid foundation for intervention strategies.

Ultimately, the ability to identify and unravel misrecognition patterns within the imaginary enriches the therapeutic process, fostering profound insights and transformative breakthroughs for individuals grappling with the tapestry of their subjective reality.

Implications of the Imaginary on Human Subjectivity

1. The Interrelationship between Self-Perception and the Imaginary Order:

Self-perception is entwined with the Lacanian concept of the Imaginary Order, which serves as a crucial lens through which individuals construct their identities and engage with their subjective realities. The formation of self-perception involves a complex interplay between the internal image of oneself and the external mirroring provided by others and social contexts. In the context of the Imaginary Order, this process takes on added significance, as it is within this domain that individuals engage in constant negotiations between their idealized self-image and their actual sense of self. This negotiation is influenced by the early experiences of the mirror stage, where individuals encounter their reflected image and begin the lifelong journey of constructing their subjective identities. Central to this interrelationship is the notion of the 'ideal-I', a projected image of perfection and completeness that individuals seek to embody. This ideal-I, rooted in the imaginary, becomes a point of reference against which individuals measure and shape their self-perceptions, often leading to a perpetual quest for an unattainable ideal. The Imaginary Order further impacts self-perception by shaping the individuation process, influencing the development of personal narratives, and sculpting the emotional responses evoked by interactions with one's mirrored and constructed self. Moreover, the sustained operation of the Imaginary Order perpetuates the dichotomy between a surface-level idealized self and the deeper, less favorable perceptions that lay beneath, generating ongoing tension and conflict within an individual's self-concept. As a result, individuals are frequently confronted with a divergence between their conscious self-presentation and their underlying, less polished self-image, leading to internal dissonance and feelings of disconnection. Within the psychoanalytic framework, understanding this interrelationship offers valuable insights into the profound impact of the Imaginary Order on human subjectivity, shedding light on the mechanisms by which self-perception is molded, maintained, and perpetually negotiated.

2. Exploration of the Mirror Stage's Role in Subject Formation:

The Mirror Stage occurs during early infancy when a child first recognizes their reflection in a mirror and begins to develop a sense of self. At this juncture, the infant's uncoordinated sense of self becomes temporarily aligned with the unified and whole image reflected back, engendering a profound moment of misrecognition, wherein the ideal-I (the coherent self-image) is initially formed.

The experience of the Mirror Stage sets the foundation for an individual's ongoing relationship with their own image, as well as their perception of others' images. The gestation of the ego-ideal is catalyzed through this visual identification process, establishing a standard against which the individual will measure themselves throughout their life. This process lays the groundwork for desires and aspirations, while also nurturing a cognitive dissonance between the idealized self and the actual self, perpetuating an enduring quest for fulfillment and coherence.

The Mirror Stage plays a seminal role in the construction of subjectivity by initiating the differentiation between the subject and the external world. As the child identifies with the specular image, notions of separateness and distinctness from the external environment emerge. This pivotal delineation is the precursor to the subject's entry into the symbolic register, where linguistic and cultural systems further mold subjectivity.

It is important to note that the Mirror Stage's influence on subject formation extends beyond individual psychology to intersect with sociocultural dynamics. The intersubjective nature of the mirrored self-image perpetuates a societal culture of comparison, competition, and validation-seeking behaviors. These cultural dimensions warp the individual's self-perception and contribute to the perpetuation of normative ideals, evoking feelings of insufficiency or achievement based on perceived alignment or divergence from these standards.

3. Dynamics of Desire and Identification within the Imaginary:

During the formative stages of human development, the Imaginary Order manifests a profound influence on the dynamics of desire and processes of identification. In this context, desire is intertwined with the individual's fragmented self-image, shaped by the mirroring process that occurs during the Mirror Stage. Lacanian theory posits that desire stems from lack, inscribed through the alienating experience of self-recognition. The subject's idealized image, constructed within the imaginary register, becomes the object of desire, leading to a perpetual quest for wholeness and validation.

Within the Imaginary, identification plays a pivotal role in shaping subjectivity. Individuals engage in a continuous process of identifying with images, representations, and idealized constructs propagated by societal norms, cultural paradigms, and interpersonal interactions. This constant identification contributes to the creation and maintenance of the ego, intertwining the individual's self-perception with external references, perpetuating a cycle of desire and recognition.

The interplay between desire and identification within the Imaginary Order extends beyond the individual level and permeates collective experiences, shaping shared notions of identity and fulfillment. The cultural and societal constructs projected within the imaginary domain often become the focal points for collective desires and identifications, influencing the formation of social norms, aspirations, and behavioral patterns. These dynamics underscore the pervasive impact of the Imaginary Order on both individual and communal subjectivities.

Within the psychoanalytic framework, the exploration of desire and identification within the Imaginary introduces profound implications for clinical practice and socio-cultural analysis. Understanding the mechanisms through which desire and identification unfold within the imaginary register provides insights into the complexities of human subjectivity, offering a lens through which to interpret and intervene in myriad psychological phenomena and social dynamics.

Through a nuanced examination of desire and identification within the Imaginary Order, practitioners can gain valuable perspectives on the determinants of individual behavior, the roots of psychological conflicts, and the intricacies of societal structures. Moreover, this exploration invites critical reflections on the construction of personal and collective narratives, shedding light on the underlying motivations driving human actions, aspirations, and interpersonal dynamics.

4. The Influence of Imaginary Constructs on Reality Perception:

The Imaginary Order, as postulated by Jacques Lacan, plays a pivotal role in shaping individuals' perceptions of reality. At its core, the Imaginary encompasses not only visible images but also a complex web of symbolic representations and idealized conceptions that inform an individual's understanding of the world. It is through this framework that individuals construct their realities, perceiving and interpreting the external world according to internalized imaginary templates. These constructs are not merely passive reflections but active filters through which individuals process and make sense of their experiences. From the mirroring process that begins in the early stages of development to the ongoing formation of identity, the Imaginary exerts a profound influence on how individuals perceive their surroundings and their place within them. Moreover, the imposition of societal norms and ideals as perpetuated by the Imaginary further distorts the authentic experience of reality, leading to a skewed and subjective perspective. Through a Lacanian lens, the nuanced relationship between the Imaginary and reality perception underscores the significance of exploring the ways in which internalized constructs alter one's understanding of the world. This investigation challenges conventional notions of objectivity and highlights the subjective nature of reality construction. Indeed, the influence of imaginary constructs on reality perception shapes not only an individual's worldview but also influences social dynamics, belief systems, and behavioral patterns. By unraveling the intricacies of this influence, we gain insight into the profound impact of the Imaginary on human subjectivity and the collective psyche. Investigating these complexities opens avenues for critical reflection, deepening our comprehension of the interconnections between the internal and external spheres.

5. Subjectivity at the Crossroads - The Impact of Symbolic Mediation:

Subjectivity is a complex web of internalized perceptions, desires, and identifications that shape an individual's experience of self and interaction with the external world. At the nexus of this structure lies the concept of symbolic mediation, which plays a profound role in influencing and delineating human subjectivity. The symbolic register, as posited by Lacanian theory, encompasses language, culture, and socially constructed meanings that can both elucidate and obscure the true nature of subjective experience. In understanding the impact of symbolic mediation on subjectivity, it becomes imperative to recognize its function as both a facilitator and a constrainer of individual identity.

Symbolic mediation functions as a double-edged sword in shaping subjectivity. On one hand, it provides the framework through which individuals interpret their experiences and construct meaning within social and cultural contexts. Language, narratives, and shared symbols form the bedrock upon which subjective reality is built, allowing individuals to comprehend their place within the broader sociocultural landscape. Conversely, the symbolic also imposes limitations and constraints on subjectivity, as it imposes normative frameworks and societal expectations that may restrict the full expression of individual desires and identities. This tension between the liberating and confining aspects of symbolic mediation underscores its pivotal role in shaping human subjectivity.

The influence of symbolic mediation on subjectivity extends beyond individual cognition and behavior, permeating interpersonal relationships, societal structures, and collective ideologies. The symbolic domain engenders shared systems of meanings, roles, and norms that generate a nuanced interplay between personal subjectivity and the broader socio-cultural milieu. As a result, individuals constantly negotiate their subjective experiences within the larger symbolic order, grappling with the tension between conforming to established symbolic dictates and asserting their unique subjective vision. This negotiation fundamentally shapes the contours of subjectivity, revealing how deeply entrenched symbolic mediation is in the fabric of human experience.

Consequently, the impact of symbolic mediation calls for a reevaluation of how we understand and engage with human subjectivity. By interrogating the ways in which symbolic structures both enable and constrain subjective experience, we can unearth the complexities underpinning individual identity formation and interpersonal dynamics. This necessitates a deeper exploration of how individuals contest the symbolic strictures that inform their subjectivity, opening avenues for more nuanced and inclusive conceptions of human identity and agency.

6. Psychological Implications of Misrecognition and its Consequences:

At its core, misrecognition pertains to the misalignment between one's self-perception and external reality, often fueled by the projections of the Imaginary onto the Symbolic register. This process engenders a multitude of consequences, each leaving an indelible mark on an individual's psyche. From an emotional standpoint, misrecognition can sow seeds of inner discord, leading to a dissonance between the constructed self and the disconcerting real. This disharmony may manifest as heightened anxiety, diminished self-worth, or the pervasive sense of being fundamentally misunderstood. These emotional repercussions can significantly influence interpersonal dynamics, engendering strains within relationships and fostering a proclivity towards maladaptive coping mechanisms. Cognitively, consistently engaging in misrecognition may culminate in a distorted perception of the world, wherein one's understanding of the external environment becomes clouded by the idiosyncratic lens of the Imaginary. This cognitive bias can impact decision-making processes, leading to choices that are rooted in the maintenance of illusory constructs rather than responding to the genuine exigencies of actuality. Moreover, the cumulative effect of protracted misrecognition extends into identity formation, introducing complexities that permeate the very fabric of an individual's sense of self. There exists a palpable tension between the projected idealized self and the stark realities of lived experiences, precipitating an existential quandary that necessitates a recalibration of one's existential bearings. Such disenchantment may not only impede personal growth but also render one susceptible to existential crises, fostering a perpetual struggle to reconcile the disjunction between the imagined and the authentic. Harnessing these insights is pivotal in fostering therapeutic interventions equipped to ameliorate the psychological wounds inflicted by the chasms wrought by misrecognition.

7. Real-Life Manifestations of Imaginary-Driven Subjectivity:

The concept of imaginary-driven subjectivity manifests in numerous real-life scenarios, influencing individuals' perceptions and experiences through the lens of the Lacanian framework. One prominent manifestation occurs in interpersonal relationships. The imagined idealized self, constructed within the Imaginary, often shapes how individuals perceive themselves in relation to others. This can lead to a discrepancy between the actual self and the idealized self, resulting in feelings of inadequacy, insecurity, or the pursuit of unattainable perfection. Furthermore, the influence of the Imaginary becomes evident in social media platforms, where curated images and narratives contribute to the construction of idealized identities, perpetuating the cycle of misrecognition and psychological implications. Additionally, in professional settings, individuals may harbor imaginary-driven subjectivities that affect their career choices, aspirations, and perceptions of success. The pursuit of an idealized image of success, power, or status, often rooted in the Imaginary, can impact decision-making processes and overall satisfaction in one's professional trajectory. Moreover, within the context of body image and self-esteem, the Imaginary order significantly influences subjective experiences. Unrealistic beauty standards and societal constructs contribute to the formation of self-perception, impacting individuals' confidence, emotional well-being, and behaviors. Through the lens of Lacanian theory, these manifestations provide valuable insights into the interplay between the Imaginary and human subjectivity. By unraveling these real-life occurrences, practitioners gain a deeper understanding of the multifaceted ways in which the Imaginary order shapes individuals' perceptions, emotions, and behavior. This awareness facilitates more effective interventions and therapeutic approaches that address the complexities of imaginary-driven subjectivity, fostering healthier self-perception, improved interpersonal relationships, and enhanced overall well-being.

8. Interventions and Transformations from a Lacanian Perspective:

Interventions and transformations from a Lacanian perspective invite a profound reevaluation of traditional approaches to psychotherapy. In the context of the Imaginary Order, intervention strategies must grapple with the intricacies of human subjectivity as shaped by internalized images and illusions. The Lacanian framework underscores the significance of recognizing and disrupting these constructed narratives to facilitate authentic transformation. Rather than solely focusing on conscious thoughts or overt behaviors, Lacanian interventions delve into the underlying symbolic associations, desires, and identifications that operate within the Imaginary domain. This approach necessitates a departure from conventional therapeutic methods, calling for an engagement with the unconscious formations that hold sway over an individual's subjective experience. Lacanian practitioners are tasked with deciphering the web of interpersonal relations and cultural influences that contribute to the construction of the self within the Imaginary register. Through this lens, interventions become a process of unraveling the tangled threads of misrecognition and fostering moments of destabilization that can herald meaningful shifts in subjectivity. By disrupting the fixed and illusory self-images propagated by the Imaginary Order, Lacanian interventions pave the way for transformative encounters with the Symbolic and the Real. These interventions may take various forms, including language-based interventions that challenge entrenched patterns of discourse, encouraging the deconstruction of dominant narratives and opening avenues for new signification. Additionally, the exploration of fragmented and disjointed aspects of the self through the use of metaphors, analogies, and interpretations serves as a means to unsettle established notions of selfhood rooted in the Imaginary. Furthermore, Lacanian interventions may entail an interrogation of recurring symbolic motifs present in the client's narrative, inviting a reevaluation of their underlying significations and implications for subjective experience. Central to the Lacanian approach is the notion that genuine transformation occurs through the recognition and renegotiation of unconscious belief systems and fantasies perpetuated within the Imaginary Order. Accordingly, these interventions strive not only to decode maladaptive patterns but also to engender creative possibilities for restructuring subjectivity amidst the interplay of the three orders proposed by Lacan. Through a commitment to forging new signifiers and cultivating a more limpid encounter with the 'Other', Lacanian interventions envisage the cultivation of a subject capable of traversing the complex terrain of subjective existence beyond the confines of illusory self-imageries.

Clinical Applications of the Imaginary

1. The Therapist's Role within the Imaginary Framework:

The therapist, positioned as the orchestrator of the therapeutic setting, becomes an essential agent in facilitating the exploration and deconstruction of patients' constructed realities embedded within the imaginary dimension. A crucial aspect of the therapist's role lies in fostering a safe and reflective space, allowing clients to engage in meaningful dialogues to reveal their deeply entrenched misperceptions and illusions stemming from the imaginary register. Furthermore, the therapist must harness a profound comprehension of how the clients' identifications with idealized images and their interplay with self-perceptions influence the therapeutic process. This requires a balance between empathy and analytical insight to discern the underlying dynamics at play.

Stepping into the therapist's role within the imaginary framework involves an active traversal of mirroring processes without succumbing to reinforcing clients' distorted self-images. As such, the therapist assumes the responsibility of providing a corrective, yet empathetic, reflective surface for the clients to confront their misconceived reflections while unwinding the entangled web of the imaginary signifiers. Additionally, the therapist's ability to negotiate the tension between acknowledging the validity of clients' experiences within the imaginary and challenging the limiting impact of these manifestations is essential for facilitating constructive therapeutic outcomes.

Practitioners operating within the imaginary framework are tasked with fostering an acute awareness of the power dynamics inherent within the therapeutic relationship, especially as they pertain to the cultivation of alternative meanings and the deconstruction of clients' entrenched symbolic representations. This necessitates cultivating a proactive reflexivity that enables the therapist to transcend personal biases and prejudices, promoting an environment where clients feel empowered to challenge their illusions and reassess their interpretations of reality within the clinic's confines. Therefore, the therapist's role involves embracing a nuanced understanding of the dance between the imagined and the authentic while fostering an environment conducive to uncovering the uncharted territories residing within the clients' imaginary registers.

2. Client Presentations through the Lens of the Imaginary:

When analyzing client presentations through the lens of the imaginary, therapists must manage the complex interplay between an individual's self-image and their perceived reality. The client's presentation often reveals key indicators of their engagement with the imaginary order, as articulated by Lacanian theory. One crucial aspect involves understanding how the client's self-perception intersects with the external world and social dynamics, which are heavily influenced by the imaginary's constructs. As therapists delve into the analysis, they must carefully observe discrepancies between the client's idealized self-image and their actual experiences, unveiling underlying tensions and conflicts within the imaginary framework.

The examination of client presentations from the standpoint of the imaginary necessitates a keen awareness of the role of images and representations in shaping the client's subjective experience. Therapists examine not only what clients express verbally but also their non-verbal cues, including body language, gestures, and affective responses. These manifestations often provide valuable insights into the client's internal struggles and interactions with the imaginary constructs. Furthermore, the therapist's task is to decipher how these visual and emotional cues connect with the client's projections and identifications within the imaginary register, thereby illuminating the web of illusions and misrecognitions that shape their sense of self.

As therapists engage in the process of analyzing client presentations through the lens of the imaginary, they encounter diverse manifestations of identification and alienation within the client's narratives. This calls for a meticulous exploration of the client's relational patterns, desires, and anxieties, all of which are deeply intertwined with the imaginary's influence. By recognizing the ways in which the client's narratives reflect their entanglement with imaginary ideals and societal norms, therapists gain deeper insights into the complex mechanisms at play. This thorough assessment informs the therapeutic strategies aimed at fostering the client's self-awareness and facilitating a fundamental reconfiguration of their relationship with the imaginary in pursuit of positive psychological change.

Unpacking the nuances of client presentations through the imaginary lens demands that therapists remain attuned to the broader sociocultural context that informs the construction of the individual's imaginary landscape. This entails identifying societal norms, values, and standards that contribute to the client's internalization of idealized images and their resulting disillusionments when these images fail to align with lived experiences. Through this process, therapists construct a comprehensive understanding of the interplay between the individual, their imaginary identifications, and the broader cultural forces, laying the groundwork for empathetic and transformative therapeutic interventions.

3. Techniques for Addressing Misrecognitions and Illusions:

Misrecognitions and illusions within the context of the Imaginary framework can present significant challenges in the therapeutic process. It is imperative for clinicians to equip themselves with a repertoire of techniques aimed at addressing and deconstructing these phenomena in order to foster meaningful progress for their clients.

One foundational technique involves creating a safe and reflective space for clients to explore and articulate their subjective experiences. This may entail utilizing open-ended questioning, active listening, and non-judgmental validation to encourage clients to express their inner conflicts and confront their distorted perceptions. It is through this process that misrecognitions and illusions can gradually come to light, allowing for collaborative exploration and reinterpretation.

Integrating psychoeducation into the therapeutic endeavor can be instrumental in helping clients comprehend the nature of misrecognitions and illusions. By offering accessible explanations of how these phenomena manifest within the Imaginary framework, therapists can empower their clients to develop a more critical and self-aware perspective towards their own cognitive processes. Delving into the ways in which social and cultural influences contribute to the formation of misrecognitions and illusions can also aid in enriching clients' understanding of their experiences.

Cognitive restructuring techniques serve as another valuable tool in addressing misrecognitions and illusions. By guiding clients through the identification and re-evaluation of distorted thought patterns, therapists can assist in dismantling harmful cognitive frameworks and nurturing more adaptive modes of perception. Through targeted interventions, such as cognitive-behavioral exercises and mindfulness practices, clients can begin to challenge and recalibrate their entrenched misperceptions, leading to enhanced emotional regulation and cognitive flexibility.

Strategic utilization of metaphor and storytelling within therapy offers an innovative approach to traverse misrecognitions and illusions. Metaphors have the capacity to bypass cognitive resistance and directly engage the client's imagination, allowing for the exploration of preconscious and unconscious dynamics. By co-creating narratives that symbolically encapsulate the client's experiential reality, therapists can elucidate complex psychological processes and facilitate transformative insight.

Lastly, fostering a collaborative and supportive therapeutic relationship is fundamental in addressing misrecognitions and illusions. Therapists must cultivate an empathetic and validating environment where clients feel empowered to actively confront and deconstruct their misperceptions. This may involve nurturing resilience, emphasizing self-compassion, and affirming the client's agency in reconstructing their sense of self within the Imaginary framework.

4. Integration of Symbolic and Imaginary in Therapeutic Practice:

The symbolic order, characterized by language, culture, and social norms, influences an individual's perception of reality and identity construction. Conversely, the imaginary domain encompasses images, fantasies, and misrecognitions that shape an individual's self-image and interpersonal relationships. Integrating these two orders allows therapists to access a deeper understanding of the client's unconscious processes and facilitates meaningful therapeutic interventions.

One approach to integrating the symbolic and imaginary in therapeutic practice is through the exploration of linguistic and visual symbols. By engaging clients in verbal dialogue and examining their narratives, therapists can uncover the embedded symbolic constructs that contribute to their lived experiences. Simultaneously, exploring the client's internal visualizations and representations, such as dreams or daydreams, provides insight into the imaginary aspects influencing their emotions and behaviors. This dual approach fosters a holistic understanding of the client's psychological dynamics and enhances the therapeutic process.

The integration of the symbolic and imaginary can be leveraged in techniques such as transference and countertransference analysis. Therapists attuned to the symbolic dimensions of transference can decode the client's projections and unconscious associations, shedding light on their inner conflicts and relational patterns. Concurrently, recognizing and interpreting the imaginary aspects within countertransference phenomena enables therapists to manage their emotional responses and maintain empathic attunement to the client's subjective world. This symbiotic utilization of symbolic and imaginary insights fortifies the therapeutic alliance and nurtures a safe space for transformative healing.

Moreover, applying Lacanian concepts of the symbolic and imaginary in therapeutic practice involves demystifying preconceived notions of reality and identity. Through deconstruction and reconstruction processes, clients are invited to question the illusory aspects of their self-perception and societal roles, fostering a reimagining of their subjective truth. Engaging in this dialectical journey between the symbolic and imaginary not only elucidates the depths of human subjectivity but also empowers clients to transcend constraining narratives and cultivate new meanings in their lives.

5. Common Clinician Pitfalls:

Clinicians operating within the framework of the Imaginary order often encounter various challenges that can significantly affect the therapeutic process. Understanding and addressing these common pitfalls is crucial for enhancing the efficacy of clinical practice and ensuring optimal outcomes for clients. One prevalent challenge faced by clinicians is the potential for overreliance on the Imaginary constructs to the neglect of other essential dimensions of the therapeutic relationship. While the Imaginary offers valuable insights into the formation of subjectivity and identity, an exclusive focus on this dimension may inhibit the exploration of broader symbolic and real aspects that are integral to comprehensive psychotherapeutic work. This imbalance can limit the depth of understanding and hamper the therapeutic progress. Furthermore, clinicians may encounter challenges related to the balance between encouraging client autonomy and challenging misrecognitions or illusions. Striking the right equilibrium between fostering independence and intervening to address detrimental patterns rooted in the Imaginary register demands a nuanced approach. Guiding through this balance entails remaining attuned to the client's developmental needs while guiding them towards a more accurate understanding of their experiences. Additionally, clinicians must remain vigilant against the risk of perpetuating or reinforcing harmful misperceptions during the therapeutic process. Another frequently encountered pitfall involves the potential for misinterpretation or misapplication of Lacanian principles within the Imaginary framework. Misunderstandings or misrepresentations of key concepts, such as the mirror stage or the nature of imaginary identifications, can lead to ineffective interventions and erroneous conclusions about the client's experiences. Therefore, it is imperative for clinicians to engage in ongoing education, supervision, and self-reflection to ensure their grasp of Lacanian theory remains accurate and enhances rather than hinders the therapeutic alliance. Moreover, the inherent complexity of the Imaginary domain can present challenges in effectively integrating theoretical knowledge with clinical practice. Clinicians may struggle with translating abstract concepts into tangible interventions and working through the dynamic interplay between the symbolic and imaginary registers in therapy. Successfully overcoming this challenge requires a dedication to continued learning, peer collaboration, and a willingness to adapt therapeutic approaches according to individual client needs. Lastly, ethical considerations loom large as clinicians operate within the landscape of the Imaginary. Ensuring that interventions uphold principles of beneficence, non-maleficence, autonomy, and justice while ethically traversing the terrain of illusion and misrecognition presents a formidable challenge. Clinicians must constantly evaluate their practices to ascertain that they adhere to ethical guidelines and prioritize the well-being of their clients above all else.

6. Ethical Considerations in Applying Imaginary Constructs:

As practitioners delve into the Imaginary, they must manage a complex landscape of ethical considerations to ensure the well-being of their clients and uphold professional standards. One primary ethical concern lies in the potential for power differentials to manifest within the therapeutic relationship. The inherent authority held by the therapist may intersect with the vulnerable state of the client, especially when discussing deeply personal constructs such as identity and misrecognitions embedded within the Imaginary. It is imperative for clinicians to acknowledge and address the power dynamics at play, ensuring that the therapeutic space remains conducive to the client's empowerment and self-actualization while utilizing Lacanian concepts. Moreover, maintaining confidentiality and privacy becomes increasingly fraught when delving into the depths of the Imaginary. The disclosure and interpretation of a client's imaginary constructs require a balance between exploration and safeguarding their private mental landscapes. Practitioners must engage in ongoing reflection and consultation to ethically manage these sensitive territories. Additionally, ethical considerations extend to the theoretical lens through which therapists frame a client's experiences. While the Imaginary offers valuable insights, it is crucial to approach its interpretations with a nuanced understanding, avoiding pathologization or reductionism. By grounding clinical applications within an ethical framework, practitioners can conscientiously leverage Lacanian theory to enhance their therapeutic interventions, promoting the holistic well-being of their clients. Furthermore, ethical engagement within the Imaginary framework calls for a continual commitment to self-awareness and reflexivity on the part of the clinician. This introspective stance allows therapists to critically evaluate their own biases, assumptions, and limitations when employing Lacanian constructs, thereby preserving the integrity and ethical depth of the therapeutic process.

7. Training and Development for Practitioners Utilizing Lacanian Theory:

Practitioners seeking to integrate Lacanian theory into their clinical practice must undergo comprehensive training and professional development. Embracing the complexities of Lacanian thought and its application within therapy requires a deep understanding of psychoanalytic principles and the unique nuances of the Imaginary Order.

Firstly, individuals aspiring to apply Lacanian theory in clinical settings should seek formal education and specialized training programs that delve into the intricacies of Jacques Lacan's theoretical framework. These programs typically cover the historical evolution of Lacanian theory, the key concepts of the Imaginary,

Symbolic, and Real Orders, and practical methods for integrating these constructs into therapy.

Mentorship and supervision play a critical role in the development of practitioners utilizing Lacanian theory. Aspiring clinicians benefit significantly from engaging with experienced mentors who can provide guidance, support, and opportunities for reflective practice. Additionally, peer consultation and participation in professional communities focused on Lacanian theory contribute to ongoing learning and growth in this specific area of psychoanalysis.

In parallel, developing proficiency in applying Lacanian theory necessitates ongoing self-reflection and personal analysis. Practitioners are encouraged to engage in their own psychotherapy to gain insight into their unconscious processes, thereby enhancing their capacity to work effectively within the Imaginary Order. This introspective journey fosters self-awareness, empathy, and an appreciation of the complexities inherent in psychoanalytic work.

Continuous professional development activities such as attending conferences, workshops, and seminars dedicated to Lacanian thought enrich practitioners' knowledge and skill set. Engaging with contemporary research and case studies allows for the integration of evolving perspectives and insights into clinical practice, promoting adaptability and relevance in therapeutic engagements.

Critiques and Debates

1. Historical Critiques of the Imaginary Order

Throughout history, the concept of the Imaginary Order has been met with a wide range of critiques, offering valuable insights into its implications and limitations. One prominent historical critique originates from metaphysics, where scholars and philosophers have questioned the ontological status of the imaginary register and its impact on human consciousness. This line of critique delves into existential inquiries about the nature of reality and the challenges posed by the construction of subjective perceptions. Furthermore, during the Enlightenment era, the Cartesian skepticism regarding the reliability of sensory perceptions and the possibility of self-deception contributed to a critical discourse on the validity of the imaginary constructs. These historical perspectives offer a rich tapestry of intellectual debate that continues to inform contemporary discourses on the Imaginary Order. Moving into the 20th century, critical theorists such as Theodor Adorno and Max Horkheimer introduced a scathing critique of the mass media's role in perpetuating illusory images that shape individual and collective identities. Their seminal work on the 'Culture Industry' challenged the notion of agency within the Imaginary Order and highlighted the manipulative forces that foster false consciousness. This critique extends to the present day, with modern scholars examining the pervasive influence of social media and advertising in constructing idealized images that perpetuate dissatisfaction and alienation. Additionally, feminist scholars have offered insightful historical critiques, unraveling the gendered dimensions of the Imaginary Order and its complicity in perpetuating stereotypical norms and ideals. By scrutinizing historical texts, artworks, and cultural practices, these critiques underscore the intersectionality of power dynamics within the imaginary representations, shedding light on the socio-political implications of these constructions. Moreover, psychoanalytic critics such as Sigmund Freud and Carl Jung have engaged in rigorous debates revolving around the perceived objectivity of the Imaginary Order. Freud's interpretation of the ego's formation through identification processes and the conflicts arising from ego-ideal discrepancies has spurred critical examinations of the psychic mechanisms underpinning the imaginary manifestations. Jung's archetypal theory, while providing a unique lens to explore the collective unconscious, has also invited critiques questioning the potential essentialism inherent in his conceptualization of the imaginary symbols.

2. Philosophical Debates - Interpretation and Misinterpretation:

Philosophical debates surrounding the interpretation of the Imaginary Order have been the subject of intense scrutiny within theoretical frameworks, particularly in the milieu of psychoanalysis. The complexities inherent in Lacanian theory have sparked countless discussions on the nature of interpretation and misinterpretation. At the heart of these debates lies the challenge of adequately grasping the concept of the imaginary and its implications for understanding human subjectivity. Philosophers, psychologists, and scholars from various disciplines have engaged in critical dialogue to unpack the nuances of interpretation and the potential missteps that can occur in comprehending the fabric of the Imaginary Order.

From a philosophical standpoint, the debate often centers on the hermeneutic approaches to Lacanian theory, wherein scholars delve into questions pertaining to the correct interpretation of key concepts such as the mirror stage, narcissism, and the formation of the ego. This has given rise to a wide spectrum of perspectives, ranging from those who advocate for a strict adherence to Lacan's original formulations to others who propose innovative interpretations that adapt his ideas to contemporary intellectual landscapes.

The notion of misinterpretation looms large in these debates, as scholars grapple with the possibility of misunderstanding or distorting Lacanian concepts when integrating them into broader philosophical frameworks. The risk of overlooking the subtleties embedded in the Imaginary Order, thereby leading to erroneous conclusions, forms a central concern in these discussions. Critics argue that misinterpretation can stem from oversimplifying Lacan's theories or approaching them with preconceived notions that may not align with the nuanced nature of the imaginary dimension.

At the intersection of philosophy and psychoanalysis, questions emerge regarding the legitimacy of diverse interpretative lenses through which the Imaginary Order is scrutinized. Should Lacanian concepts be exclusively analyzed within the confines of psychoanalytic discourse, or do they warrant exploration through multidisciplinary philosophical lenses? These queries prompt extensive deliberation over the epistemological foundations that underpin interpretations of the Imaginary Order, underscoring the complexity of reconciling divergent viewpoints within this rich intellectual terrain.

3. Controversies in Identity Construction Theories:

Identity construction theories have long been a subject of intense debate within the field of psychology and psychoanalysis. At the heart of these controversies lies the question of whether identity is primarily shaped by internal psychological processes or external social and cultural factors. Proponents of the former viewpoint argue that identity formation is predominantly influenced by innate psychological mechanisms, such as those delineated in Freudian and Lacanian frameworks. They emphasize the role of unconscious desires, ego development, and the mirror stage in shaping an individual's sense of self. On the other hand, advocates of the latter perspective contend that identity is deeply intertwined with cultural norms, societal expectations, and interpersonal relationships. They assert that one's identity is linked to the social milieu in which they are situated, and that cultural narratives play a fundamental role in shaping one's understanding of themselves. These differing viewpoints have given rise to heated debates regarding the relative significance of internal psychological processes versus external socio-cultural influences in the construction of identity. Furthermore, the implications of these controversies extend beyond theoretical frameworks and have practical repercussions in clinical and therapeutic settings. Understanding the controversies surrounding identity construction theories is pivotal for practitioners working in various fields, as it impacts how individuals are assessed, understood, and supported. Moreover, these debates serve as a catalyst for ongoing research and critical inquiry, leading to the development of more nuanced and integrated perspectives on the complex interplay between internal psychic forces and external cultural influences in the construction of identity.

4. The Role of Culture in Shaping Imaginary Constructs:

The intersection of culture and the imaginary order offers insights into how societal norms, beliefs, and values impact an individual's construction of self-identity and perception of reality. In diverse cultural contexts, the imaginary is entwined with collective representations, rituals, and symbolic practices that contribute to the formation of identity.

One significant aspect is the influence of cultural narratives and mythologies on the imaginary. Cultural storytelling, folklore, and oral traditions embed archetypal images and symbols into the collective unconscious, thereby affecting personal imaginaries. For instance, the hero's journey in various cultures shapes individuals' aspirations, self-concept, and ideals of achievement. Moreover, cultural art forms such as literature, visual arts, and performing arts serve as reservoirs of imagined worlds and idealized representations, fostering the internalization of cultural imaginaries.

The cultural regulation of social behaviors, gender roles, and familial structures exerts profound effects on individuals' imaginations. Gendered imaginary constructs are socially constructed through cultural norms and expectations, delineating perceptions of masculinity, femininity, and gender fluidity. Additionally, cultural heritage and traditions dictate the collective imaginary, influencing concepts of belonging, heritage, and legacy. Norms surrounding beauty standards, body image, and physical appearance are ingrained in cultural imaginaries, impacting individuals' self-esteem and body perceptions.

The interplay between culture and the imaginary also extends to rituals and ceremonies. Rites of passage, religious ceremonies, and communal celebrations infuse symbolic meaning and significance into individuals' lifeworlds, contributing to the construction of personal imaginaries. The ceremonial aspect of cultural practices reinforces a sense of shared imaginary experiences and communal identity, emphasizing the interconnectedness of individuals within their cultural milieu.

Understanding the role of culture in shaping imaginary constructs is essential for comprehending the nuanced dynamics of identity formation and subjective experiences. By acknowledging the cultural influences embedded in the imaginary, practitioners and scholars can adopt more culturally sensitive approaches in psychoanalytic and therapeutic interventions. This recognition fosters an appreciation for the diversity of human imaginaries and the contextual underpinnings that contribute to their complexities.

5. Critiques from Psychoanalytic Practitioners:

Through their clinical experiences, psychoanalytic practitioners have raised thought-provoking critiques that enrich the discourse surrounding the Imaginary. One significant critique revolves around the potential oversimplification of human subjectivity within the Imaginary framework. Practitioners argue that while the Imaginary provides a compelling model for understanding identity formation, it may overlook the complexities and variations within individual subjective experiences. Additionally, psychoanalytic practitioners have highlighted the challenges of applying the concept of the Imaginary in therapeutic settings. They emphasize the need to manage the balance between acknowledging the significance of imaginary constructs in shaping patients' psyches while also avoiding reductionist interpretations. Furthermore, these practitioners have engaged in lively debates regarding the interplay between the Imaginary and the Symbolic orders, underscoring the dynamic and often convoluted interactions between these two registers. Their critical reflections prompt a reconsideration of the intricacies involved in the co-constitution of the Imaginary and the Symbolic within the psychoanalytic context. Moreover, psychoanalytic practitioners draw attention to the evolving nature of the Imaginary in contemporary society. They articulate concerns about the impact of digital culture, social media, and virtual realities on the construction of imaginary representations and the subsequent effects on individuals' self-perceptions.

6. Challenges from Cognitive Psychology:

Cognitive psychology presents a unique set of challenges and critiques when juxtaposed with the concepts and constructs of the Imaginary Order within Lacanian theory. This intersection prompts a deeper exploration into the cognitive processes underlying human perception, reasoning, and decision-making, and their potential impact on the formation and functioning of the imaginary domain. One of the primary challenges arises from the emphasis placed by cognitive psychology on the role of information processing, mental representations, and cognitive biases in shaping human behavior and experiences. This focus often diverges from the psychoanalytic perspective, which centers on unconscious drives, desires, and the influence of early childhood experiences. By delving into these differing paradigms, we can gain invaluable insights into the complexities that emerge when attempting to reconcile the cognitive understanding of the mind with Lacan's conceptualization of the Imaginary Order. Furthermore, examining the phenomenon of cognitive dissonance and its implications provides a lens through which to scrutinize the tensions arising from conflicting mental representations and the discrepancies between idealized self-images and actual experiences. This calls for a nuanced analysis of how individuals manage and mitigate cognitive dissonance within the framework of the imaginary, shedding light on the intricacies of identity negotiation and self-illusion within this theoretical context. Additionally, scrutinizing the cognitive mechanisms behind perception and memory unveils fundamental questions about the authenticity and stability of the imagery constructed within the imaginary register. Understanding the limits and fallibility of human cognition in the construction and retention of mental images and self-representations injects a layer of skepticism and critical inquiry into the very foundation of the Lacanian imaginary. Moreover, the application of cognitive psychology principles, such as concept formation and categorization, exposes the multifaceted nature of the imaginary constructions and their interplay with symbolic representations and social schemas. This integration elucidates the complex web of influences and processes that contribute to the shaping of the imaginary register, transcending the purely psychoanalytic domain and inviting interdisciplinary dialogue and examination. Furthermore, exploring the cognitive underpinnings of emotion regulation and affective processes offers a fresh perspective on the dynamics of the imaginary, prompting an exploration of how individuals manage and negotiate the emotional landscape within this theoretical framework. Unpacking the ways in which cognitive psychology illuminates the dance between cognition and affectivity within the imaginary attests to the enriching potential of interdisciplinary encounters, expanding our comprehension of the human psyche and its multifaceted operations.

7. Ethical Considerations and Implications:

As we delve into the ethical implications of the Imaginary Order, it is imperative to explore how this construct intersects with individual autonomy, identity formation, and societal norms. One of the key ethical considerations pertains to the potential impact of the Imaginary on an individual's agency and self-determination. The nature of the Imaginary, as a sphere of illusions and misrecognitions, raises questions about the extent to which individuals can exercise free will and make autonomous choices. Furthermore, the process of identifications and idealizations within the Imaginary implicates ethical dilemmas concerning cultural influences, stereotypes, and power dynamics. Such considerations are particularly pertinent in diverse and multicultural societies where the construction of identities is linked to social, racial, and gendered norms. Additionally, examining the ethical implications of the Imaginary Order necessitates a critical engagement with the therapeutic practices and interventions employed within clinical settings. Psychoanalysts and mental health practitioners must ethically manage the complexities of working with clients' imaginary constructs, ensuring that interventions do not perpetuate harmful narratives or reinforce oppressive ideologies. Moreover, ethical concerns also arise in the context of research involving the Imaginary Order, prompting scholars to reflect on the potential impact of their work on participants and wider society. This ethical reflection extends to the dissemination of knowledge and ideas related to the Imaginary, emphasizing the responsibility to present these concepts in a manner that respects the dignity and diversity of human experiences. As we draw this discussion to a conclusion, it is evident that grappling with the ethical considerations and implications of the Imaginary Order demands a nuanced understanding of power dynamics, cultural sensitivities, and the complexity of human subjectivity.

THE REAL ORDER - BEYOND PERCEPTION

Historical Context and Philosophical Grounding

1. Origins of the Real in Classical Philosophy:

Classical philosophy, originating in ancient Greece with influential thinkers such as Plato and Aristotle, laid the groundwork for our understanding of the concept of the real. Within this philosophical tradition, the notion of 'the real' was intertwined with the quest for ultimate truth and knowledge. Plato, in his famous Allegory of the Cave, presented a compelling allegory that delved into the nature of reality and perception, setting the stage for future explorations of the real. Furthermore, Aristotle's metaphysical inquiries into the nature of being and existence deeply influenced subsequent discussions on the real. The works of these ancient philosophers marked a significant starting point in the intellectual journey towards grasping the enigmatic concept of the real.

Central to the classical understanding of the real was the idea that reality existed beyond sensory perception – an enduring essence that transcended mere appearances. Philosophers of this era grappled with distinguishing between the material world and the true nature of reality. Questions regarding the existence of a separate, immutable reality independent of human cognition became focal points of inquiry. Formulating a coherent understanding of the real required wrestling with fundamental philosophical questions about the nature of existence, consciousness, and the relationship between the observer and the observed.

The pivotal contributions of pre-Socratic philosophers, including Parmenides and Heraclitus, enriched the dialogue on the real within classical thought. Parmenides, known for his exploration of the concept of 'being,' posited ideas about the immutable and unchanging nature of reality. In contrast, Heraclitus emphasized the ever-changing and dynamic character of the world. The juxtaposition of these perspectives spurred profound reflections on the complexities of defining what constitutes the real, heralding a longstanding discourse on the nature of reality.

Additionally, the influence of Hellenistic philosophy further shaped the evolving understanding of the real, particularly through the works of Stoic and Epicurean philosophers. These philosophical schools delved into concepts of perception, knowledge, and the nature of the cosmos, contributing to an increasingly nuanced comprehension of the real.

2. The Influence of Enlightenment Thinking

During the Enlightenment era, a pivotal shift occurred in the philosophical and intellectual landscape of Western thought. This period, spanning from the late 17th to the 18th century, witnessed the rise of rationalism, empirical science, and a profound emphasis on the power of human reason. The influence of Enlightenment thinking on the concept of the Real is both intriguing and significant, as it shaped our understanding of reality, truth, and human existence.

Enlightenment philosophers such as René Descartes, Immanuel Kant, and John Locke set the stage for redefining how we perceive the world and our place within it. Descartes's dualistic approach, which separated the mind and body, had far-reaching implications for the understanding of the Real. His famous assertion, 'Cogito, ergo sum' (I think, therefore I am), underscored the supremacy of individual consciousness and laid the groundwork for exploring the nature of reality from a subjective standpoint.

Kant's transcendental idealism revolutionized philosophical discourse by challenging the traditional dichotomy between appearances and things-in-themselves. His concept of the noumenal plane, inaccessible to human perception, introduced a new dimension to the notion of the Real. Kantian philosophy compelled contemporaries and subsequent generations to grapple with the limitations of human cognition and the elusive nature of objective reality.

Furthermore, Locke's empiricism posited that all knowledge originates from sensory experience, fundamentally shaping the understanding of what constitutes the Real. His advocacy for the tabula rasa (blank slate) theory implied that human beings are born devoid of innate ideas, thereby emphasizing the role of environmental stimuli in constructing our perceptions of reality.

The Enlightenment's emphasis on reason, skepticism, and empirical inquiry permeated the intellectual climate, fostering critical examination of longstanding doctrines and institutional authority. It engendered a spirit of inquiry that sought to scrutinize established dogmas, including those pertaining to the nature of the Real. The legacy of Enlightenment thinking continues to resonate in contemporary philosophical discourse, as scholars engage in ongoing dialogues about the nature of truth, objectivity, and the parameters of human comprehension.

3. 19th-Century Philosophical Developments:

The 19th century, marked by a departure from traditional rationalist and empiricist viewpoints, witnessed the rise of existentialism, idealism, and phenomenology, each of which contributed to a reevaluation of human existence, consciousness, and the nature of reality itself. Existentialist philosophy, exemplified by the works of Søren Kierkegaard and Friedrich Nietzsche, emphasized individual freedom, choice, and the overarching concerns of human existence. Their revolutionary ideas challenged existing conceptions of morality, truth, and the role of the individual in society. Concurrently, idealist philosophers such as Georg Wilhelm Friedrich Hegel and Arthur Schopenhauer sought to understand the nature of reality through the lens of the mind, positing that ultimate reality is a product of the human intellect and its constructs. These divergent philosophical movements set the stage for the 20th-century paradigm shifts that would redefine the boundaries of knowledge and understanding. The 19th century also witnessed the emergence of phenomenology, championed by Edmund Husserl and later refined by Martin Heidegger. This approach aimed to uncover the structures of conscious experience and perception, delving into the essence of being and the phenomena that constitute our understanding of the world. As such, the 19th century can be regarded as a crucible of diverse and often conflicting philosophical developments, laying the groundwork for the radical transformations that would unfold in subsequent decades. The interplay between existentialism, idealism, and phenomenology not only reshaped fundamental questions about reality and human consciousness but also provided fertile ground for the exploration of the concept of the real, with far-reaching implications for both philosophy and other intellectual disciplines.

4. 20th-Century Paradigm Shifts:

The 20th century witnessed unprecedented shifts in thought, leading to a reevaluation of established paradigms and the emergence of novel conceptual frameworks that sought to decode the complexities of human existence. One of the most notable developments was the advent of existentialism, a philosophical movement that grappled with the fundamental nature of human existence and the inherent meaninglessness of the universe. Spearheaded by luminaries such as Jean-Paul Sartre and Albert Camus, existentialism posed probing questions about individual agency, free will, and the nature of authentic existence.

Simultaneously, the 20th century also bore witness to the rise of phenomenology, a school of thought that prioritized the subjective experience of consciousness as the primary source of philosophical inquiry. Through the pioneering work of Edmund Husserl and later proponents such as Martin Heidegger and Maurice Merleau-Ponty, phenomenology sought to elucidate the essential structures of human consciousness and perception, fundamentally reshaping traditional understandings of reality and truth.

The 20th century engendered a radical departure from the Cartesian dualism of mind and body, with advancements in psychology and cognitive science fostering a deeper understanding of the interconnectedness between mental phenomena and corporeal embodiment. This holistic perspective, encapsulated in the burgeoning field of embodied cognition, challenged entrenched dichotomies and underscored the inseparability of cognition from the physical and environmental contexts within which it operates.

Additionally, the tumultuous geopolitical events of the 20th century, including two world wars and the Cold War, precipitated intellectual introspection on the nature of power, violence, and ethics. Philosophers such as Hannah Arendt and Michel Foucault probed the complex intersections of politics, power structures, and the nature of human freedom, laying bare the dynamics that underpin societal order and control.

5. The Intersection of Philosophy and Psychoanalysis:

Philosophical inquiry offers a framework for conceptualizing the nature of reality, truth, and existence, while psychoanalysis delves into the depths of the unconscious, examining the complexities of human behavior and psychopathology. As we traverse this terrain, we encounter pivotal moments where these disciplines converge and diverge, offering unique insights into the nature of the Real. At the heart of this intersection is the exploration of the unconscious, a concept central to both philosophical and psychoanalytic thought. While philosophers such as Sigmund Freud and Jacques Lacan have drawn from philosophical traditions in formulating their ideas, they have also challenged and extended the boundaries of traditional philosophical discourse. The integration of psychoanalytic theory into philosophical discourse has sparked debates about subjectivity, language, and the construction of reality. Conversely, philosophy has influenced psychoanalysis by providing a conceptual framework for understanding the nature of being, knowledge, and ethics. This reciprocal relationship has fostered a dynamic inquiry into the nature of the human psyche and its engagement with the perceived and the Real.

Lacanian Concept of the Real

1. The Real within Lacanian Framework:

Within Jacques Lacan's framework, the Real is not synonymous with empirical reality, nor can it be confined to sensory perception or rational understanding. Instead, the Real occupies a unique and enigmatic position as that which transcends symbolic and imaginary constructions. It is crucial to recognize that while reality pertains to the observable and tangible world, the Real encompasses the subconscious, unutterable, and unsettling aspects that elude linguistic representation. Such distinction epitomizes the intricacy of Lacan's construction of the human subject, underscoring the foundation of psychic life in the impenetrable domain of the Real. Moreover, this perspective underscores the dialectical tension between the symbolically mediated ego and the raw, unassimilable experiences constitutive of the Real. Crucially, the Real is characterized by a lack or void, manifesting in disruptive and traumatic encounters that defy symbolic coherence. This radical disjuncture propels individuals into a confrontation with the limits of language and meaning, unraveling the veneer of reality and plunging them into a destabilizing encounter with the Real. As such, the Real emerges as a constant source of disruption and contradiction, resisting attempts at conceptual capture and linguistic containment. Furthermore, Lacan posits that access to the Real is fraught with difficulty, as it is apprehended only tangentially through fissures and ruptures in the fabric of symbolic order. Consequently, the Real assumes an elusive and paradoxical nature, often surfacing in moments of crisis or interstices of psychic breakdown. In essence, the Real operates as a disruptive force that fractures the coherence of the symbolic order, compelling subjects to confront the underlying structures of fantasy and illusion that govern their existence. By grounding psychoanalysis in the enigmatic terrain of the Real, Lacan enables a profound reconfiguration of the traditional understanding of identity, desire, and subjective experience, offering invaluable insights into the workings of the human psyche.

2. The Real versus Reality:

Often used interchangeably, the terms 'Real' and 'reality' actually inhabit disparate spheres within philosophical, psychoanalytic, and cultural discourses. While 'reality' pertains to the everyday, tangible world and experiences that are collectively perceived and shared, the 'Real' transcends this and delves into the underlying, fundamental truths that defy conventional notions of existence. As such, delineating between the Real and reality is imperative. In Lacanian theory, the Real encompasses the ungraspable, unsymbolizable aspects of existence that elude linguistic representation, whereas reality is constituted by the visible, material world subject to interpretation and cultural constructions. Furthermore, the Real operates beyond the confines of language and perception, emphasizing its inherent enigmatic and ineffable nature. This differentiation aligns with the Lacanian notion that the Real remains primordial and pre-linguistic, anchored in the authentic, unmediated experiences that evade symbolic appropriation. Moreover, it is essential to appreciate that reality is contingent upon social, historical, and linguistic contexts, while the Real persists as an immutable force that resists assimilation into the symbolic order. Contrasting reality's malleability and susceptibility to interpretation, the Real signifies an enduring, unalterable truth regardless of individual or societal lenses. This disparity illuminates the foundational chasm between these concepts and underscores the pivotal significance of recognizing their contrasting domains in comprehending the complexities of human existence.

3. Core Principles and Characteristics:

Within Lacanian psychoanalysis, the Real is defined by its resistance to symbolization and linguistic capture, making it inherently elusive and challenging to grasp. This opacity is further compounded by the absence of a conceptual representation, rendering the Real an enigmatic construct that defies traditional modes of comprehension. It is crucial to recognize that the Real does not conform to conventional notions of reality; instead, it constitutes a dimension that exists beyond symbolic and imaginary constructs.

One fundamental principle of the Real is its manifestation as traumatic events or experiences that resist assimilation into the symbolic order. These manifestations often arise from encounters with the inherently disruptive nature of the Real, which disrupts established symbolic systems and engenders dissonance within the individual's psyche. Such disturbances serve as reminders of the insurmountable gap between linguistic representation and the ineffable essence of the Real.

The Real is inherently intertwined with the human subject's existential constitution, shaping and influencing subjective experience in profound ways. It permeates through moments of profound emotional intensity, where the boundaries delineating the self and external reality blur, and the unmediated confrontation with the raw, unfiltered aspects of existence becomes palpable. This experiential quality of the Real underscores its pervasive influence on the fabric of human consciousness, laying bare the intrinsic vulnerability and precariousness inherent in our lived realities.

The Real operates as a disruptive force that defies attempts to systematize or rationalize its essence. Its disruptive potential is evinced in instances of radical alterity, where encounters with the unassimilable aspects of existence highlight the fundamental disjuncture between the symbolic order and the ineffable core of the Real. Consequently, the Real persists as an unyielding presence, resisting all forms of reductive categorizations or conceptual encapsulations.

4. The Elusiveness of the Real:

The Real, inherently resistant to categorization and linguistic representation, continually evades straightforward definition or depiction. Intangible and beyond sensory perception, the Real remains enigmatic, defying conventional modes of understanding. Its resistance to symbolization renders it profoundly elusive, leading to ongoing debates and explorations within philosophical and psychoanalytic circles. Furthermore, the notion of elusiveness is embedded within the core principles of the Real, playing a pivotal role in shaping its indescribable and unattainable nature. The very act of attempting to encapsulate the Real paradoxically reinforces its elusiveness, thereby perpetuating the cycle of intellectual pursuit. In this regard, the enigmatic quality of the Real serves as a constant reminder of the limitations inherent in human comprehension and representation. Moreover, the elusiveness of the Real intersects with its relationship to the Symbolic and Imaginary Orders, further compounding its opacity. As such, delving into the intricacies of the Real necessitates an acknowledgment of the futility of apprehending it through conventional means. Consequently, traversing the terrain of the Real demands a nuanced understanding of its enigmatic character and the ways in which it resists conventional methods of inquiry. Despite the inherent challenges posed by its elusive nature, the pursuit of comprehending the Real remains an intellectually stimulating and enriching endeavor.

5. Interactions with the Symbolic and Imaginary Orders:

As previously posited, the Symbolic Order represents the milieu of language, law, and culture, which mediates our understanding of the world and structures our social interactions. Language, as a symbolic system, not only facilitates communication but also shapes our perceptions and constrains our thoughts within a web of signifiers and signifieds. This order plays a crucial role in the formation of subjectivity and the construction of meaning within society.

Conversely, the Imaginary Order encompasses the domain of images, identification, and imaginary identifications. It is characterized by the mirror stage, wherein an individual forms a cohesive sense of self through identification with the reflected image. This stage engenders a dualistic relationship with one's idealized ego and perpetuates the quest for unity and completeness. The potent influence of visual imagery and the desire for wholeness underscore the significance of the Imaginary Order in shaping subjective experiences.

In the interplay of these orders, the Real emerges as that which eludes symbolization and resists integration into the symbolic and imaginary registers. It disrupts the coherence of the symbolic order and shatters the illusory unity of the imaginary, introducing elements of instability and unassimilable experiences into the individual's subjective reality. The Real operates as a disruptive force that breaches the established symbolic and imaginary frameworks, confronting individuals with the limitations of their perceptual and conceptual schemas.

The Symbolic and Imaginary Orders do not exist in isolation but continually intersect and collide with the Real, engendering moments of rupture and dissonance in the subject's psychic landscape. These encounters with the Real manifest in traumatic experiences, disruptions of cultural norms, and encounters with the ineffable aspects of existence that defy symbolic representation.

6. Phenomenological Perspectives on the Real

Rooted in the works of phenomenologists such as Edmund Husserl and Martin Heidegger, phenomenology delves into the fundamental structures of consciousness and the ways in which individuals perceive and engage with the world. Within the Real, phenomenology provides a framework to examine how the Real manifests itself in the lived experiences of individuals, offering a nuanced understanding that transcends traditional empirical observations. Phenomenological inquiry situates the Real as an integral aspect of human existence, shaping our subjective realities and deeply influencing our perceptions of self and others. Through this lens, the Real is not merely an external construct but is intimately linked to the essence of being-in-the-world. Phenomenological explorations further highlight the interplay between the subject and the Real, emphasizing the ways in which the Real permeates consciousness, evoking profound affective and existential responses. Furthermore, phenomenology unveils the intrinsic enigma of the Real, confronting the inherent paradoxes and ambiguities that defy reduction to mere conceptual or linguistic formulations. The Real's enigmatic nature becomes apparent through phenomenological phenomenological reflections, inviting a deeper contemplation of its unfathomable depths and its capacity to disrupt conventional modes of understanding. Moreover, phenomenological phenomenological analyses shed light on the temporal dimension of the Real, illuminating its dynamic and elusive character. As individuals traverse their lived experiences, the Real emerges as a force both constraining and liberating, challenging preconceived notions and compelling continual reevaluation of the nature of existence. Phenomenological engagements with the Real provide a rich tapestry of insights, uncovering the interwoven threads of subjectivity, temporality, and ontological significance.

7. The Real's Influence in Psychoanalysis:

In the milieu of psychoanalysis, the concept of the Real holds profound significance as it intersects with the core principles of human consciousness and subjective experiences. Within the framework established by Freud and subsequently expanded upon by Lacan, the presence of the Real is acknowledged as an essential element in the analytical process. Exploration of the Real within psychoanalysis delves into the depths of human subjectivity, unraveling repressed desires, traumatic experiences, and the fundamental alienation inherent in the human condition. It serves as a lens through which to understand the unconscious forces that shape behavior and mental well-being.

Psychoanalytic practice frequently encounters manifestations of the Real in the form of traumatic memories, irrational fears, and enigmatic dreams that resist easy interpretation. These manifestations challenge analysts to traverse the nebulous terrain of the Real, pushing them to confront the inherent limitations of language and rational understanding. The influence of the Real in psychoanalysis necessitates a dynamic approach to grappling with deep-seated psychological complexities, transcending conventional modes of comprehension and analysis.

Throughout the history of psychoanalysis, clinicians have grappled with the enigma of the Real, endeavoring to integrate its disruptive force within the therapeutic process. The Real's influence permeates the therapeutic relationship, often manifesting in moments of rupture, resistance, and unpredictability. These instances serve to underscore the inescapable confrontation with the Real, compelling analysts to engage with the unfiltered, raw aspects of human experience that defy symbolic representation and linguistic articulation.

The Real's influence extends to the foundational concepts of transference and countertransference, illuminating the dynamics of projection, identification, and emotional resonance within the therapeutic dyad. Its pervasive impact challenges the analyst to manage the boundary between empathic engagement and the unyielding presence of the Real, fostering a nuanced understanding of the complex interplay between conscious and unconscious forces in the analytical encounter.

The interplay between the Real and psychoanalytic praxis extends beyond the confines of the consulting room, permeating cultural discourses and social phenomena. It underscores the relevance and utility of psychoanalysis in elucidating the multifaceted dimensions of human subjectivity and the interplay of internal and external realities.

8. Challenges in Grappling with the Real:

The pursuit of comprehending the concept of the Real is laden with multifaceted challenges that entice scholars, researchers, and practitioners alike. At the core of these challenges lies the intrinsic nature of the Real as posited within the Lacanian framework, which defies straightforward comprehension and assimilation. One of the foremost hurdles encountered in grappling with the Real is its ethereal and enigmatic essence, rendering it resistant to conceptualization within conventional paradigms. This very resistance trenchantly opposes attempts at corraling the Real into established linguistic or symbolic frameworks, thereby complicating endeavors to articulate and grasp its true nature. Moreover, the intertwining of the Real with the Symbolic and Imaginary Orders further complicates its isolation for study and analysis, necessitating nuanced discernment and untangling of their interrelations. In addition to theoretical challenges, practitioners in the field of psychoanalysis often encounter significant impediments when attempting to apply the concept of the Real to clinical scenarios. The elusive and unsettling nature of the Real poses considerable difficulties in transliterating its theoretical underpinnings into practical therapeutic strategies. Furthermore, the hesitance of individuals to confront the Real within themselves and within the therapeutic setting presents substantial barriers to its effective utilization in therapeutic interventions. Another critical challenge arises from the dearth of empirical methodologies and data collection approaches tailored to capture the dynamic intricacies of the Real. The inherently subjective and experiential nature of the Real resists conventional quantitative measures and demands innovative research methodologies capable of encapsulating its complexities. Alongside these intricacies, ethical considerations surrounding the confrontation of the Real in clinical and non-clinical settings necessitate meticulous negotiation. Striking a balance between honoring individuals' autonomy and fostering beneficial engagement with the Real presents an enduring ethical dilemma in the arenas of research and practice. Successfully addressing these challenges requires a concerted interdisciplinary effort, fostering dialogue across fields such as philosophy, psychology, sociology, and literature. Consolidating existing knowledge, probing the frontiers of inquiry, and refining methodological approaches are vital for surmounting these challenges in the ongoing quest to grapple with the enigmatic terrain of the Real.

Barriers to Comprehending the Real

1. Cognitive Limitations and Awareness:

Human cognition plays a pivotal role in shaping our understanding of the world. However, cognitive limitations can significantly hinder our capacity to comprehend the elusive nature of the Real order. These limitations, rooted in the inherent constraints of human cognition, manifest in various ways, impacting our awareness and interpretation of the Real.

One significant cognitive limitation is the tendency for individuals to rely on mental schemas and preconceived notions when processing new information. This cognitive shortcut, while efficient in operating within daily life, can lead to oversimplification and distortion when confronting the enigmatic aspects of the Real. Furthermore, the phenomenon of cognitive dissonance, wherein individuals struggle to reconcile conflicting beliefs or experiences, creates internal barriers that impede genuine engagement with the Real.

The human mind's limited capacity to perceive and retain vast amounts of information poses a formidable barrier to comprehending the Real. Our selective attention and cognitive overload contribute to filtering out elements of reality, potentially causing us to overlook or misinterpret crucial facets of the Real. Additionally, the pervasive influence of confirmation bias, the inclination to favor information that aligns with our existing beliefs, impedes our ability to approach the Real with open-mindedness and objectivity.

Awareness of these cognitive limitations is crucial in engaging with the complexities of the Real. Implementing practices that encourage mindfulness, critical thinking, and intellectual humility can mitigate the impact of these barriers. By fostering an acute awareness of the limitations inherent in human cognition, individuals can cultivate a more nuanced and expansive comprehension of the Real.

2. Cultural Influences on Interpretation:

The customs, beliefs, and practices of a society can imbue individuals with specific lenses through which they view reality. These cultural filters often dictate what is considered acceptable or taboo, influencing how individuals perceive and process the Real. Moreover, cultural norms can lead individuals to adopt particular attitudes towards certain concepts, rendering them more or less open to engaging with the Real. For example, in some cultures, the notion of confronting the unknown and unknowable may be embraced and celebrated, while in others, it may be viewed with suspicion and apprehension.

Language within a culture can profoundly shape its members' understanding of the Real. Different languages may have varying capacities for expressing or even conceptualizing the Real, leading to disparities in comprehension across different linguistic communities. This linguistic influence extends beyond basic vo cabulary to encompass subtleties such as idioms, metaphors, and nuances that color our perception of the Real. Additionally, cultural narratives and storytelling traditions can frame and contextualize experiences of the Real, affecting how individuals interpret and relate to the ineffable aspects of existence.

Another vital aspect of cultural influence on interpretation relates to the social construction of reality. Cultural values and societal structures mold the collective understanding of what is real or unreal, shaping the boundaries of acceptability and believability. In societies where communal consensus holds substantial sway, the prevailing cultural interpretations and constructions of reality are deemed authoritative, potentially stifling alternative perspectives on the Real.

3. Language as an Obstacle:

Language, despite being a fundamental tool for communication and cognitive expression, presents a significant obstacle when attempting to comprehend the concept of the Real. Words and symbols, by their very nature, are inherently limited in their capacity to encapsulate the full depth and complexity of the Real. This limitation arises from the inherent subjectivity and contextual dependency of language, as well as its inability to capture the essence of experiences that transcend linguistic representation. The inadequacy of language becomes particularly evident when grappling with the ineffable nature of the Real, as it defies easy categorization or verbal articulation.

The structure and semantics of language can inadvertently impose constraints on our understanding of the Real. Language relies on dichotomous distinctions and categorical delineations, which may not align with the fluid and indeterminate nature of the Real. As a result, attempts to articulate the Real often lead to a reductionist portrayal that fails to capture the nuances and intricacies inherent in the concept. This reductionism can contribute to the distortion or oversimplification of the Real, hindering genuine comprehension.

The influence of cultural and societal norms on language further exacerbates its role as an obstacle to comprehending the Real. Linguistic conventions are shaped by societal frameworks and collective interpretations, which can subtly mold the boundaries of acceptable discourse and constrain the exploration of concepts that challenge prevailing paradigms. This ingrained influence of cultural language norms can subtly steer individuals away from engaging with the ambiguous and enigmatic aspects of the Real, reinforcing preconceived linguistic structures that may be ill-suited to grapple with the ineffable.

Despite these challenges, acknowledging the limitations of language in approaching the Real opens avenues for alternative modes of expression and interpretation. Embracing metaphor, allegory, and non-verbal forms of communication offers a pathway to transcend the confines of language and access more nuanced insights into the Real. Additionally, fostering a multidisciplinary approach that integrates linguistic perspectives from diverse cultural and historical contexts can enrich and expand the linguistic framework through which the Real is contemplated, striving toward a more comprehensive and inclusive engagement with this profound philosophical concept.

4. Emotional Responses to the Unknowable:

The contemplation of the unknowable, particularly within the framework of the Real Order, often evokes a myriad of emotional responses that can both perplex and intrigue. When individuals are confronted with the limits of their understanding or the existence of phenomena that defy categorization or rational explanation, they may experience a tumultuous range of emotions. One such response is a sense of disorientation and unease, stemming from the inherent human desire for comprehension and control. The realization that certain aspects of reality may forever elude grasp can invoke feelings of vulnerability and insecurity, challenging deeply ingrained beliefs about the nature of existence. Furthermore, encountering the unknowable may provoke a profound sense of awe and wonder, as individuals come face-to-face with the boundless mysteries that permeate the fabric of reality. This awe can lead to a deepened sense of existential humility and reverence for the enigmatic grandeur of the world. Additionally, emotional responses to the unknowable can encompass a spectrum of fear and fascination, with individuals oscillating between apprehension at the unknown and an insatiable curiosity to probe its depths. It is within this emotional tapestry that the contours of the Real Order interweave, inviting introspection and exploration of the fundamental facets of human experience. As we delve into the complexities of emotional responses to the unknowable, we are prompted to unravel the relationship between cognition, affect, and the ineffable mysteries that dwell beyond the boundaries of comprehension.

5. The Role of Denial in Avoidance:

Denial, as a coping mechanism, plays a significant role in avoiding the realization and acceptance of the inaccessible aspects of the Real. When faced with events, ideas, or emotions that challenge our understanding or threaten our sense of security, denial allows individuals to reject or negate these difficult truths. Freudian psychoanalysis contends that denial is a defense mechanism employed by the ego to shield the individual from anxiety or distress. It may manifest as outright refusal to acknowledge evidence, minimization of the significance of information, or the rationalization of uncomfortable realities.

In the context of comprehending the Real, denial can obstruct our ability to confront the inherent limitations of our perceptions and knowledge. By denying the existence of the unknowable, individuals create a psychological barrier that shields them from the discomfort that accompanies the recognition of their cognitive boundaries. This defensive manoeuver impedes the exploration and acknowledgment of the complexities and uncertainties intertwined with the Real. Moreover, denial can contribute to the perpetuation of misconceptions and illusions that distort our understanding of reality.

Social and cultural factors also influence the propensity for denial in grappling with the inaccessibility of the Real. Collective denial may occur within cultures, groups, or societies when faced with confronting inconvenient or unsettling truths. The phenomenon of groupthink, in which a desire for conformity and cohesion leads to the suppression of dissenting viewpoints, can reinforce denial on a larger scale. Additionally, societal taboos and norms may implicitly discourage the exploration of challenging, elusive concepts, further promoting a state of collective denial.

6. Philosophical Perspectives on the Inaccessible:

Within the framework of phenomenology, thinkers such as Edmund Husserl and Martin Heidegger explored the nature of human consciousness and its intrinsic connection to the world around us. They posited that our engagement with reality is characterized by intentional acts of perception, through which we shape and interpret the objects of our experience. However, this inherently subjective process also introduces potential barriers to apprehending the real. Phenomenological analysis invites us to consider how our preconceptions and biases may hinder our grasp of the authentic, unmediated aspects of existence.

Within existentialism, luminaries like Jean-Paul Sartre and Simone de Beauvoir addressed the limitations imposed by consciousness on our ability to comprehend the absolute aspects of reality. Their works assert that the human condition is fraught with anxiety stemming from an awareness of our fundamental finitude and the bounds of our knowledge. This existential angst, they argue, stands as a barrier to penetrating the depths of the real, relegating certain dimensions of existence to the status of the inaccessible. The existential outlook therefore alerts us to the inherent obstacles posed by our subjective position in the world.

Turning to epistemology, the study of knowledge, we encounter critical examinations of the conditions under which genuine understanding can be attained. Philosophers such as Immanuel Kant emphasized the role of human cognitive faculties and their limitations in shaping our comprehension of reality. Kant's insights prompt us to contemplate the constraints imposed by the structure of human cognition, underscoring how these innate frameworks may render certain facets of the real elusive or unfathomable. Additionally, contemporary philosophers grapple with the implications of postmodern thought, which challenges traditional notions of truth, aiming to reveal the constructed and contingent nature of knowledge. Postmodern critiques inject a further layer of complexity into our quest to traverse the terrain of the real, echoing the contention that some aspects of reality may perpetually elude our grasp.

7. Societal Norms and the Resistance to the Real:

Throughout history, societal beliefs and values have influenced how people understand and interact with the world around them. These norms often create a framework within which individuals interpret their experiences, and as a result, they can act as both facilitators and barriers to comprehending the real.

One important aspect to consider is the impact of social conditioning on an individual's perception of reality. Society often imposes certain expectations and standards that mold individuals into conforming to prevailing norms, which can hinder their ability to engage with the real in an unfiltered manner. Furthermore, the fear of deviating from these established norms can lead to an aversion towards confronting the unknown or unfathomable aspects of existence.

Additionally, the societal emphasis on rationality and empiricism may inadvertently restrict individuals from acknowledging the more enigmatic dimensions of the real. This bias towards measurable and quantifiable phenomena may discourage exploration of the mysterious and ineffable elements of human experience. As a result, individuals may struggle to grapple with the existential uncertainties and complexities that lie beyond the confines of traditional scientific comprehension.

Societal pressures and expectations can contribute to the construction of collective illusions that obscure the real. By adhering to societal narratives and ideals, individuals may become entrenched in fabricated realities that shield them from confronting the inherent disquietude of the real. These illusions serve as buffers against existential discomfort, thereby perpetuating a sense of detachment from the genuine, unadulterated aspects of existence.

The resistance to the real within societal structures also extends to the domain of interpersonal relationships. Social conventions and etiquettes often govern interactions, sometimes impeding genuine and authentic exchanges. This veneer of social conformity may hinder individuals from engaging in honest and vulnerable dialogues, inhibiting their ability to confront and embrace the rawness of truth.

8. Pathways to Overcoming Barriers:

One significant pathway to overcome common barriers that impede individuals from comprehending the 'Real' involves developing heightened awareness of perceptual limitations and understanding how these limitations shape our interpretations of reality. This calls for acknowledging the subjective influences on perception and striving to adopt a more objective viewpoint. Additionally, cognitive strategies can be implemented to enhance awareness and discernment. This may involve practices such as mindfulness meditation or cognitive-behavioral therapy, which aim to cultivate present moment awareness and address distorted thought patterns. Furthermore, cultural influences play a pivotal role in shaping our understanding of the world. By embracing cultural diversity and seeking exposure to varied perspectives, individuals can expand their cognitive frameworks and develop a more comprehensive apprehension of the 'Real.' Language, being a tool for communication and interpretation, can also serve as a barrier to perceiving the 'Real.' Overcoming this requires critical reflection on language's inherent limitations and exploring alternative modes of expression that transcend linguistic boundaries. Embracing emotional intelligence is another essential component in engaging with the enigmatic dimension of the 'Real.' Understanding and processing emotions allows individuals to confront the discomfort and uncertainty that often accompany encounters with the 'Real.' Additionally, recognizing psychological defense mechanisms, such as denial and repression, enables individuals to address these barriers and gradually assimilate the elusive aspects of reality. Philosophical perspectives provide an avenue for contemplating the nature of existence and truth. Engaging with philosophical inquiry encourages individuals to question preconceived notions and venture beyond the constraints of societal norms. Furthermore, social conformities can impede our ability to engage with the 'Real.' Thus, fostering critical thinking skills and challenging societal constructs are essential in transcending these barriers.

The Real in Psychoanalytic Practice

1. The Function of the Real in Therapeutic Settings:

In therapeutic settings, the concept of the Real plays a pivotal role in understanding and addressing the deep-seated issues that individuals grapple with. The Real represents the unfiltered, raw experience that often eludes language and conscious comprehension. Therapists manage the complexities of the Real to delve into the authentic core of their patients' struggles, as well as to facilitate profound transformations. It is essential to recognize that the Real operates beyond mere surface manifestations or symptoms, and instead resides in the unarticulated feelings, fears, and desires that underpin an individual's psyche. Understanding the function of the Real in therapeutic settings necessitates an exploration of its impact on the therapeutic process. When patients confront the Real in therapy, it often triggers deep emotional upheaval, pushing them to grapple with their most fundamental anxieties and existential dilemmas. The therapist's role in this context is to provide a safe and supportive environment for the patient to engage with the Real, fostering a space where vulnerability can be explored without judgment. This enables patients to confront buried truths about themselves, leading to the potential for profound insight and personal growth. Furthermore, the function of the Real extends to the therapeutic relationship itself. Therapists must manage the complexities of transference and countertransference, recognizing that these phenomena are deeply entwined with the patient's encounter with the Real. The therapist's attunement to the patient's experience of the Real is crucial in guiding the therapeutic journey towards greater self-awareness and healing. As therapists engage with the Real, they themselves undergo a transformative process, evolving in their capacity to hold and work through the complexities of human existence.

2. Transference and Encountering the Real:

Transference, within the milieu of psychoanalysis, refers to the redirection of a patient's feelings and desires toward the therapist. In the context of the Real, transference takes on added significance as it illuminates the patient's attempts to grapple with the unmediated truth that the Real represents. As patients traverse the unconscious, they often transfer unresolved emotions, notably linked to early experiences, onto the therapist, creating a potent fusion of past and present realities. This phenomenon enables a direct encounter with the Real, serving as a crucible for the emergence of suppressed truths and repressed memories.

The therapist's role in managing transference within the framework of the Real is multifaceted. They must sensitively negotiate the patient's projections while maintaining boundaries to ensure that the therapeutic space remains conducive to genuine exploration. By fostering an environment where the patient feels safe to confront the raw and unfiltered truths embedded within the Real, the therapist can guide the individual toward transformative insights and profound psychological growth.

In this delicate dance between the patient's transference and the therapist's response, techniques such as interpretation, reflection, and clarification serve as instruments for the traversal of the Real. By gently steering the patient's attention toward the underlying emotions and meanings embedded within the transference, the therapist facilitates a conscious reckoning with the Real, thus catalyzing the potential for authentic self-discovery and emotional integration.

However, traversing transference within the terrain of the Real is not without its challenges. The intensity and volatility of the emotions evoked can test the therapist's own engagement with the Real, necessitating self-awareness, emotional resilience, and a deep understanding of one's countertransference reactions. Furthermore, ethical considerations loom large, underscoring the responsibility to uphold professional integrity and prioritize the well-being of the patient amidst the turbulent currents of the Real's revelations.

Despite these complexities, the encounter with the Real through the vehicle of transference holds immense therapeutic promise, offering individuals a profound opportunity to engage authentically with their innermost selves and embark on a journey of profound personal transformation.

3. Techniques for Engaging with the Real:

Working through the Real within the context of psychoanalytic practice requires a nuanced understanding and a diverse set of techniques. The therapist must skillfully guide the patient towards confronting their own truth and experiences, often in the face of resistance or discomfort. One fundamental technique involves creating a safe and supportive environment where the patient feels secure enough to explore previously hidden or repressed aspects of their reality. This can be achieved through empathetic listening, non-judgmental validation, and an unwavering commitment to confidentiality.

Additionally, therapists may employ interpretative strategies to help patients recognize and process the Real. By exploring unconscious thoughts and feelings, the therapist helps the patient gain insight into underlying realities that may have been influencing their conscious behaviors and decisions. This process often entails the examination of dreams, fantasies, and slips of the tongue, all of which can offer valuable glimpses into the patient's authentic experience of the Real.

The use of transference as a tool for traversing the Real is crucial. Therapists must delicately negotiate the complex interplay between their own presence and the patient's perceptions and projections, all while fostering an environment conducive to uncovering the truth. Understanding and addressing transference dynamics allows for a deeper exploration of the patient's genuine reality and lived experiences.

A holistic approach also involves integrating contemporary theories of self-psychology and object relations to comprehend how the patient internally constructs and represents their reality. By recognizing and supporting the patient's evolving self-object relationships, therapists can assist in processing and validating their real experiences in ways that promote self-awareness and healing.

4. Challenges in Addressing the Real with Patients:

Traversing the concept of the Real within psychoanalytic practice poses a multitude of challenges, particularly when directly engaging with patients. One of the primary obstacles is the inherent resistance that individuals may present when confronted with aspects of reality that are discomforting or disruptive to their existing perceptions and defenses. The very nature of the Real, as something that shatters illusions and disrupts the symbolic order, can provoke intense anxiety and defensiveness in patients. Additionally, the Real often encompasses traumatic experiences and repressed material, making it an emotionally charged and vulnerable territory for individuals to explore. Another challenge lies in the balance between gently guiding patients toward encounters with the Real and respecting their psychological boundaries and capacities for processing such encounters. Too forceful an approach can incite resistance, while too passive an approach may result in ineffective therapeutic progress. Furthermore, language and communication barriers can impede the effective addressing of the Real with patients, especially when attempting to verbalize experiences that surpass linguistic and rational understanding. It is crucial for psychoanalysts to develop nuanced and sensitive approaches to engage with the Real, acknowledging the unique vulnerabilities and complexities of each patient's psyche. Additionally, the dynamic interplay between the therapist's countertransference and the patient's transference further complicates the management of the Real in therapeutic settings, as it demands constant self-reflection and attunement to relational dynamics. The ethical considerations surrounding the introduction of the Real into the therapeutic space cannot be overlooked, as therapists must continually assess the potential impact on the patient's well-being and ensure the maintenance of a safe and supportive environment.

5. Integration of the Real into Treatment Plans:

As psychoanalytic practice continues to evolve, the incorporation of the concept of the Real into treatment plans is becoming increasingly relevant. Understanding the Real and its potential impact on a patient's psychological well-being is essential for creating effective treatment strategies. Integration of the Real involves careful consideration of how unconscious beliefs, desires, and fears manifest in the therapeutic process. This integration requires therapists to negotiate the balance between acknowledging the Real and maintaining the boundaries necessary for healthy therapeutic relationships.

Incorporating the Real into treatment plans often begins with an in-depth assessment of the patient's subjective experience and their perception of reality. This may involve exploring their early experiences, traumas, and deep-seated anxieties that have contributed to the construction of their psychic reality. By uncovering the patient's relationship with the Real, therapists can devise interventions tailored to address the core issues that underlie their distress.

Integrating the Real into treatment plans necessitates a nuanced understanding of transference and countertransference dynamics. Therapists must critically examine their own responses to the patient's expressions of the Real, while simultaneously assisting the patient in making sense of their own encounters with the Real within the therapeutic space. This dual focus demands a high level of self-awareness and clinical acumen to manage the complexities inherent in the therapeutic encounter.

Effective integration of the Real into treatment plans also involves considering the broader sociocultural context in which the patient exists. Societal norms and expectations can significantly influence an individual's perception of the Real, and addressing these external influences is crucial for a comprehensive therapeutic approach. Acknowledging the impact of cultural and social factors allows therapists to develop interventions that are sensitive to the patient's unique lived experiences.

The integration of the Real into treatment plans necessitates ongoing collaboration with the patient. It is imperative to engage the patient in dialogue about their own experiences of the Real and to empower them in exploring the implications of these encounters. Encouraging the patient's active engagement facilitates a deeper exploration of their internal world and supports the development of a more authentic sense of self.

6. The Real's Influence on Therapist-Patient Dynamics:

The Real, with its inherent unattainability and disruption of symbolic order, has far-reaching implications for the therapeutic relationship. It is crucial for therapists to recognize that the Real can manifest in unexpected ways during sessions, impacting the dynamics between themselves and their patients.

One significant impact of the Real on therapist-patient dynamics is the potential for destabilization of the traditional power dynamic. As therapists grapple with their own encounters with the Real, they may find themselves vulnerable and disoriented, which can challenge the typical authority associated with the therapeutic role. This displacement of authority can cause both confusion and growth within the therapeutic relationship, as it encourages a more egalitarian dialogue and mutual exploration of underlying truths.

The Real can catalyze intense emotional reactions within both therapists and patients, disrupting the usual patterns of interaction. Moments of shared Realness can evoke deep empathy and understanding, forging genuine connections that transcend the boundaries of traditional therapeutic roles. These moments also hold the potential for re-traumatization and emotional overwhelm, necessitating profound sensitivity and attunement from the therapist.

The Real influences the communication styles between therapist and patient. Unspoken tensions, unspeakable traumas, and submerged fears inhabit the space between them, demanding acknowledgment and management. The language becomes laden with unspoken meanings, requiring a heightened awareness of non-verbal cues and implicit messages. The therapist must contend with the challenge of uncovering these hidden aspects while maintaining a secure and containing presence for the patient.

7. Ethical Considerations in Engaging with the Real:

Engaging with the concept of the Real in psychoanalytic practice necessitates a careful examination of the ethical implications involved. This is particularly crucial as the nature of the Real can evoke profound emotional responses and deeply-rooted vulnerabilities in patients, thereby demanding a high level of ethical responsibility from practitioners.

One of the foremost ethical considerations pertains to the potential impact of delving into the Real on the well-being and stability of the patient. The unveiling of repressed truths or encounters with the unsettling aspects of reality can engender intense distress and psychological upheaval. As such, therapists must judiciously weigh the therapeutic benefits against the potential risks, ensuring that the pursuit of truth does not exacerbate existing trauma or create new sources of anguish for the individual in treatment.

Additionally, the duty of confidentiality takes on heightened significance in the context of exploring the Real. Patients may share deeply personal and sensitive experiences during this process, and it is imperative that therapists maintain the utmost discretion and protect the privacy of their patients. Ensuring that the revelations stemming from engaging with the Real do not compromise the patient's autonomy or rights is fundamental to upholding ethical standards within psychoanalytic practice.

The power dynamic inherent in therapist-patient relationships becomes especially pertinent when dealing with the Real. Given the therapist's role as a guide through the complexities of the patient's subconscious, it is essential to manage this power differential with utmost care, avoiding any transgressions that could lead to exploitation or harm. Ethical conduct demands that therapists cultivate an environment of trust, respect, and empowerment, allowing patients to engage with the Real at their own pace and according to their own needs and boundaries.

The ethical dimensions extend to the interpretations and interventions employed by therapists in response to the Real. It is imperative for practitioners to continually examine their own motivations, biases, and prejudices to ensure that their interventions stem from a place of genuine concern for the well-being of the patient, rather than being influenced by personal agendas or desires. Taking into account the diverse cultural, social, and individual backgrounds of patients is crucial in mitigating the potential imposition of value systems or beliefs onto the patient's experience of the Real.

8. Success and Progress - Metrics of the Real:

Traditional metrics, such as observable behavior changes or self-reported improvements, may not fully capture the impact of engaging with the Real. The Real often operates at a subconscious level, influencing thoughts, emotions, and perceptions without conscious awareness. Consequently, evaluating success in addressing the Real requires a more nuanced approach.

One crucial metric is the integration of the Real into the patient's narrative and understanding of self. Progress can be observed through the patient's willingness and ability to confront the discomfort and disruptions caused by encounters with the Real. This may manifest as an increased capacity for introspection and self-reflection, as well as a greater tolerance for ambiguity and emotional intensity. Furthermore, the reconfiguration of defense mechanisms and coping strategies to accommodate the Real can indicate significant progress in therapeutic work.

Another essential metric involves the impact of the Real on the therapeutic relationship. As patients grapple with the disorienting nature of the Real, the dynamics between therapist and patient are inevitably influenced. Evaluating shifts in these dynamics, such as increased trust, communication, and openness, provides insights into the patient's engagement with the Real and the efficacy of the therapeutic process.

The emergence of new themes and concerns in the patient's discourse can serve as indicators of progress in engaging with the Real. An expanded range of topics, particularly those that evoke vulnerability and existential dilemmas, suggests that the patient is delving deeper into their authentic experience and confronting the Real in meaningful ways.

It is important to note that setbacks and moments of resistance should also be considered within the evaluation process. These instances offer opportunities for further exploration and understanding of the patient's relationship with the Real, contributing to the overall trajectory of therapeutic progress. Additionally, the ethical dimensions of evaluating success in this context necessitate a comprehensive consideration of potential harm, boundaries, and the preservation of the patient's autonomy and agency.

Manifestations of the Real in Literature and Culture

1. The Intersection of the Real and Fictional Narratives:

The interplay between the real and fictional narratives serves as a dynamic reflection of the human experience, compelling us to confront truths about ourselves and the world around us. As readers immerse themselves in fictional worlds, they often encounter characters and situations that resonate deeply with their own lived experiences, blurring the line between reality and fiction. This blurring is where the essence of the real emerges, creating a space for introspection and exploration. Fictional narratives provide a mirror through which the real is refracted, offering insights into our collective consciousness and individual psyches. Through potent storytelling, authors craft narratives that seamlessly weave elements of the real into the fabric of imagination, evoking emotional responses and prompting profound contemplation. The power of fiction lies in its ability to encapsulate universal truths within the framework of invented worlds, inviting readers to engage with the complexities and nuances of the human condition. Furthermore, the intersection of the real and fictional narratives fosters a deep understanding of societal dilemmas, cultural dynamics, and historical perspectives. By delving into these narratives, individuals gain valuable insight into the multifaceted nature of reality and are challenged to question their preconceived notions about the world. The dialogue between the real and fiction spurs critical discourse, intellectual curiosity, and empathetic understanding, thereby enriching our appreciation of diverse narratives. Moreover, this intersection presents an opportunity to explore the boundaries of truth and fabrication, serving as a catalyst for philosophical inquiry and literary analysis. Through the lens of fictional narratives, we are encouraged to contemplate the fluid nature of reality and the impact of storytelling on human consciousness. In essence, the intersection of the real and fictional narratives encapsulates the timeless pursuit of meaning and understanding, transcending the confines of genre or medium. It stands as a testament to the relevance of narrative art forms in illuminating the enigmatic landscapes of human experience.

2. Symbolism and the Reflection of the Real:

By using symbols to represent abstract ideas or concepts, authors and artists can imbue their works with layers of meaning that resonate with the human experience. Through the careful selection and placement of symbols, creators are able to evoke emotions, provoke thoughts, and convey profound truths related to the nature of reality.

In literature, symbolism frequently serves as a bridge between the tangible and intangible aspects of existence. The use of symbolic elements allows readers to delve beneath the surface of a narrative and unearth deeper significance. Whether it's a recurring motif, an object loaded with metaphorical weight, or an allegorical character, symbolism invites readers to contemplate the larger themes and forces at play within a story.

The reflection of the real through symbolism extends beyond the confines of written works. Visual arts, such as paintings and sculptures, harness the power of symbols to express fundamental truths about the human condition and the world at large. From ancient cave paintings to modern installations, artists have utilized symbols as a means of confronting and interpreting reality in all its complexities.

A particularly intriguing aspect of symbolism is its essential connectivity to cultural and societal contexts. Symbols often carry cultural significance, drawing from shared mythologies, historical events, religious beliefs, and social norms. As such, the interpretation of symbols can vary greatly depending on the audience and the cultural milieu in which they are situated. This dynamic interaction between symbols and culture underscores their role in reflecting the multi-faceted nature of the real within diverse human experiences.

When exploring the reflection of the real through symbolism, it becomes evident that these symbolic expressions serve as conduits for universal truths, transcending individual perspectives and tapping into collective consciousness. The language of symbolism enables creators to address existential questions, grapple with the enigma of being, and offer insight into the mysteries of life. Through its interwoven web of signification, symbolism acts as a mirror that illuminates facets of the real that might otherwise remain elusive.

3. Modern Literature - Evolving Perceptions of the Real:

Modern authors have ventured into uncharted territories by challenging traditional perceptions and redefining the boundaries of reality within literary works. This evolution is linked to societal changes, technological advancements, and the dynamic nature of human experiences. As the world underwent profound transformations, so did the depiction of the 'Real' in literature, reflecting the shifting paradigms of existence. Modern authors have skillfully interwoven aspects of the real with the imagined, blurring the dichotomy and inviting readers to ponder upon the essence of truth and authenticity. The themes explored in modern literature often delve into the complexities of identity, existential crises, and the impact of external influences on individual realities. The fluidity of perspectives in modern literature presents a rich tapestry of the 'Real,' portraying diverse and often conflicting interpretations that resonate with contemporary audiences. Furthermore, the advent of postmodernism has dismantled conventional narratives, paving the way for nonlinear storytelling and fragmented representations of reality. This departure from traditional forms has encouraged a more nuanced exploration of the 'Real,' embracing ambiguity and disillusionment as integral elements of the human experience. Authors have harnessed the power of language and narrative structure to capture the elusive nature of the 'Real,' transcending the constraints of linear storytelling to evoke a sense of disorientation and surrealism. As such, modern literature continues to push the boundaries of what constitutes the 'Real,' offering a kaleidoscopic view of existence that challenges preconceived notions and invites introspection. By engaging with the spheres of uncertainty and skepticism, modern authors have illuminated the multifaceted nature of the 'Real,' reshaping its perception as an enigmatic, ever-evolving entity that defies definitive categorization. Through their literary endeavors, these writers have fostered a deeper understanding of reality as a construct influenced by subjective experiences, cultural dynamics, and the perpetual quest for meaning amidst an increasingly complex world.

4. Cinematic Representations:

Cinema has been instrumental in portraying the manifestations of the Real in ways that challenge our perceptual boundaries. The utilization of cinematic techniques, such as cinematography, sound design, and narrative structure, allows filmmakers to create immersive experiences that confront audiences with the raw essence of the Real.

In cinema, the portrayal of the Real often transcends the confines of traditional realism, delving into surrealism, magical realism, and other avant-garde approaches. Directors and screenwriters harness the medium to explore themes of existentialism, alienation, and the enigma of human consciousness, offering audiences an introspective journey into the depths of the psyche.

One prevalent method of visualizing the unimaginable is through the depiction of dream sequences, hallucinations, and altered states of consciousness. These cinematic devices serve as conduits for representing the unfiltered perceptions of reality, blurring the lines between the subjective and objective. Through the evocative power of imagery and symbolism, filmmakers manifest the ineffable aspects of the Real, inviting viewers to grapple with the complexities of human experience.

The use of allegory and metaphor in cinema enables the exploration of existential truths and the confrontation of universal dilemmas. By weaving complex narratives that resonate with profound philosophical inquiries, filmmakers confront audiences with the paradoxes of existence, igniting contemplation on the nature of truth, perception, and the inherent chaos of life.

It is crucial to recognize that the representation of the Real in cinema extends beyond mere allegory; it serves as a vessel for societal critique and cultural reflection. Many filmmakers employ the medium to address pressing sociopolitical issues, employing the Real as a mirror to expose the intricacies of collective consciousness and the pervasive impact of societal constructs on individual lives.

5. The Real in Music and Performative Arts:

Music, with its amalgamation of melody, rhythm, and lyrics, has the capacity to evoke emotions and touch upon the ineffable aspects of human experience. Whether it is the haunting melodies of a requiem or the foot-stomping beats of a protest song, music brings to life the unadorned essence of our existence. Similarly, the world of performative arts— encompassing theater, dance, and visual arts— serves as a canvas for portraying the complexities of the Real. From the emotive movements of contemporary dance to the stark poignancy of abstract art, these forms reflect the profundity of existence through their unfiltered portrayal of human emotions and societal truths. The interplay between the artist's interpretation of the Real and the audience's reception creates a dynamic exchange that shapes cultural understandings of reality.

6. Cross-Cultural Interpretations of the Real:

Each culture possesses its own unique framework for understanding reality, shaped by historical, philosophical, and societal factors. Through the lens of cross-cultural interpretations, we gain a profound appreciation for the multifaceted nature of the Real.

One of the most compelling aspects of cross-cultural interpretations is the examination of indigenous belief systems and mythologies. These narratives often embody rich depictions of the Real, blurring the boundaries between the tangible and the mythic. In many indigenous cultures, the Real is not confined to the material world but extends into spirit, folklore, and ancestral knowledge. This holistic view offers a stark contrast to the Western rationalistic understanding of reality, inviting us to reconsider our perception of the Real.

Cross-cultural interpretations shed light on the role of ritual and tradition in shaping perceptions of the Real. Practices such as ceremonies, dances, and storytelling rituals serve as conduits for connecting with and embodying the Real within various cultural contexts. These rituals not only reflect a society's interpretation of reality but also underscore the inherent interconnectedness between the individual, community, and the transcendent.

Examining cross-cultural interpretations unveils the impact of globalization and interconnectedness on altering perceptions of the Real. As traditional boundaries dissolve and cultures converge, diverse interpretations of the Real encounter one another, giving rise to hybridized understandings that challenge pre-existing paradigms. This phenomenon necessitates a nuanced understanding of how cross-cultural interactions shape and reframe our comprehension of the Real, underscoring the dynamic nature of reality in a globalized world.

7. The Influence of Media on Perceptions of the Real:

Media plays a pivotal role in shaping perceptions of the real in contemporary society. Through various forms such as television, film, social media, and news outlets, the portrayal of reality is subject to interpretation and manipulation.

In the digital era, the pervasive reach of media platforms has enabled the rapid distribution of information and imagery, blurring the lines between truth and fiction. The rise of fake news, photo manipulation, and viral hoaxes has heightened skepticism and confusion regarding what constitutes the real. Consequently, individuals are constantly challenged to discern authentic representations from fabricated content.

The visual power of media significantly influences societal perceptions of reality. The visual language employed in advertisements, films, and social media posts often constructs idealized or hyper-realistic representations that influence individual and collective understandings of the world. Furthermore, the capability of media to disseminate images and narratives across diverse cultures and demographics necessitates an examination of how these representations intersect with varying cultural contexts.

Media's portrayal of events and phenomena also influences public perception of the real. News coverage, documentary filmmaking, and historical dramatizations serve as lenses through which audiences interpret and comprehend critical real-world occurrences. However, biases, agenda-setting, and editorial decisions within media entities can shape narratives in ways that may deviate from objective reality.

This influence extends beyond traditional forms of media, as the advent of virtual reality (VR) and augmented reality (AR) introduces entirely new dimensions of immersive storytelling. These technologies introduce the potential for users to construct personal realities, posing fundamental questions about the nature of the real and the boundaries between physical and simulated experiences.

The convergence of media and technology continues to redefine the parameters of reality, prompting scholars, creators, and consumers to critically evaluate the implications of these developments. As media becomes increasingly intertwined with daily life, understanding its multifaceted relationship with the concept of the real is essential for traversing an ever-evolving information landscape.

8. Conclusion - The Ever-Present Influence of the Real:

Through the lens of media, our perceptions of reality are continuously mediated and constructed. Whether through news outlets, social media, film, advertising, or virtual platforms, the depiction of events, people, and experiences significantly impacts our comprehension of what is real and what is fabricated. The power of visual imagery and storytelling in modern media has the ability to mold and manipulate our perception of the real, often blurring the line between fact and fiction.

The pervasive nature of media means that these constructed realities have the potential to influence societal attitudes, behaviors, and even political ideologies. The constant barrage of information and depictions of reality can create a collective consciousness that may not accurately reflect the unadulterated truth, leading to widespread misconceptions and misunderstandings. This phenomenon underscores the profound impact of media on the construction and interpretation of the real, emphasizing the need for critical consumption and analysis of the media we encounter.

Beyond media, the influence of the real extends into literature, art, and cultural expression. These forms of creative representation serve as mirrors of society, reflecting the complexities and nuances of the human experience. By delving deep into the psyche and emotions of characters and narratives, literature and art offer profound insights into what constitutes the real in various contexts. From classic literary works to modern cinematic masterpieces, the portrayal of the real not only captivates audiences but also challenges them to confront uncomfortable truths and grapple with existential questions.

The proliferation of cross-cultural interpretations and representations enforces the idea that the real is a dynamic, multifaceted concept that evolves across different societies and historical epochs. This diversity of perspectives enriches our understanding of the real, highlighting its adaptability and universality. It is important to recognize that the real is not static; rather, it is subject to reinterpretation and reimagining through the diverse lenses of culture, tradition, and global experiences.

In closing, the ever-present influence of the real in media, literature, and culture reaffirms its significance in shaping our collective consciousness and individual perceptions. To traverse this landscape of constructed realities, one must remain vigilant and discerning, embracing a critical lens in the consumption and interpretation of information. Only then can we begin to unravel the complexities of the real and its profound impact on the human psyche and society as a whole.

The Real's Role in Identity Formation

1. Developmental Perspectives on the Real in Identity:

In the early stages of life, individuals are shaped by experiences that influence their perception of self and reality. During infancy and early childhood, the Real begins to exert its influence as a child's cognitive and emotional capacities develop. The process of forming a cohesive identity is linked to the negotiation between the external world and internal reality. As children encounter moments of unfiltered authenticity, they are confronted with the unyielding nature of the Real. These early encounters play a pivotal role in shaping the individual's understanding of self and the world. Furthermore, the transition into adolescence marks a critical juncture in identity development, as adolescents grapple with the complexities of the Real in relation to societal expectations, peer influences, and self-discovery. This period is characterized by a heightened sensitivity to discrepancies between one's ideal self and the perceived reality, often leading to identity crises and existential introspection. Additionally, the impact of the Real continues to unfold throughout adulthood, as individuals traverse relationships, career pursuits, and personal growth. The developmental trajectory of identity is not only influenced by internal psychological processes but is also shaped by external factors such as cultural norms, familial dynamics, and societal constructs. It is within this interplay that the Real exerts its influence, underscoring the complexity of identity formation. Recognizing these developmental perspectives on the Real in identity provides a nuanced framework for understanding the multifaceted nature of human existence and the ongoing negotiation between the authentic self and societal influences.

2. Identity Fractures - When the Real Intrudes:

In the tapestry of identity formation, the intrusion of the Real can lead to fundamental fractures in the individual's sense of self. This phenomenon is particularly pronounced during key developmental stages, where the conflict between internalized fantasies and the external reality becomes starkly apparent. Identity fractures occur when the individual's constructed self-image is shattered by encounters with the unadulterated Real. These fractures manifest as profound disruptions in cognition, emotional stability, and relational dynamics, often resulting in a pervasive sense of disorientation and alienation. Scholars and practitioners have long grappled with elucidating the complex interplay between the Real and fractured identities, seeking to develop nuanced understandings of this pivotal intersection. Understanding the decisive impact of the Real on identity fractures necessitates an exploration of its manifestations across diverse cultural and socio-economic contexts. The reintegration and healing of fractured identities demand sensitive and empathetic approaches that honor the individual's lived experiences while facilitating a gradual renegotiation of their relationship with the Real. It is imperative for clinicians and scholars alike to consider the potential implications of identity fractures, not only on individual well-being but also on broader societal structures and norms. By engaging with the mechanisms through which the Real intrudes upon identity formation, practitioners and theorists are positioned to deepen their comprehension of human subjectivity and promote more holistic approaches to psychological well-being.

3. The Real in Cultural Contexts:

The manner in which the Real manifests within cultural frameworks often dictates the coping mechanisms and resilience strategies adopted by individuals. Moreover, cultural norms and values heavily influence the interpretation and significance attributed to experiences of the Real.

Within diverse cultural settings, the negotiation of the Real takes on unique nuances. In some cultures, the presence of the Real may be acknowledged and even integrated into everyday life, while in others, it might be suppressed or relegated to taboo. These variations give rise to distinct approaches to negotiating the impact of the Real on identity formation and psychological well-being.

One area of particular importance is the influence of collectivist versus individualistic cultural orientations on the negotiation of the Real. Collectivist societies often emphasize interconnectedness and group harmony, which can lead individuals to downplay personal experiences of the Real in favor of maintaining social cohesion. Conversely, in individualistic cultures, there may be an increased emphasis on personal agency and self-expression, potentially leading to a more pronounced engagement with the Real and its implications for identity.

Cultural narratives and belief systems significantly shape how the Real is understood and engaged with. For instance, in cultures with rich mythological traditions, encounters with the Real may be couched in mythic language, offering a framework for integrating these experiences into a broader cosmological understanding. On the other hand, in secular cultures, the negotiation of the Real may unfold within psychological or existential frameworks, impacting the construction of personal and collective identities.

The interplay between the Real and cultural contexts also underscores the importance of considering power dynamics and social structures. Marginalized communities may confront the Real through the lens of systemic oppression, while dominant cultural narratives may impose their own interpretations of what constitutes reality and legitimate experiences.

4. Psychological Mechanisms of Coping with the Real:

Coping with the profound impact of the Real on identity is a complex and multifaceted process that necessitates the engagement of various psychological mechanisms. One such mechanism is the process of sublimation, where individuals unconsciously redirect the intense discomfort arising from clashes with the Real into creative or productive outlets, thereby finding a way to give shape and form to the ineffable aspects of their experiences. This enables them to transcend the overwhelming nature of the Real and find meaning in their struggles. Similarly, repression emerges as a prominent coping mechanism, as individuals attempt to bury aspects of their experiences that threaten their established sense of self. Yet, this often leads to unconscious simmering tensions and eventual eruptions that disrupt the cohesive narrative of one's identity. Furthermore, the concept of identification comes to the fore, as individuals seek to align themselves with symbols or figures that offer a semblance of coherence and stability amidst the chaotic encounter with the Real. These forms of identification can provide temporary respite, yet may also contribute to a dilution of authenticity in the individual's self-formation. Additionally, through rationalization, individuals endeavor to impose logic and reason onto the tumultuous encounters with the Real, striving to make coherent sense of their experiences. Nevertheless, this cognitive maneuvering often presents a fragile facade that leaves deeper existential quandaries unaddressed. At the heart of coping with the Real lies the interplay between these psychological mechanisms, each offering its unique mode of negotiation and adaptation.

5. Intersections with the Symbolic Order in Identity:

The Symbolic Order, as posited by psychoanalytic theory, represents the milieu of language, culture, and societal norms that shape individuals' perceptions of themselves and others. When exploring the interactions between the Real and the Symbolic Order in the context of identity formation, it becomes evident that these two forces are intertwined. The symbolic representations and societal constructions of identity often act as the intermediary through which the impact of the Real is filtered and interpreted.

One key aspect of this intersection lies in the negotiation of social expectations and individual experiences. The Symbolic Order dictates norms, values, and roles that individuals are expected to fulfill within their respective communities. However, the intrusion of the Real disrupts these expectations, challenging preconceived notions of identity and forcing individuals to confront the raw, unadulterated aspects of their existence. This collision between societal constructs and authentic lived experiences can lead to profound existential crises and internal conflicts, as individuals grapple with the dissonance between their perceived identities and the disruptive force of the Real.

The symbolic representations of identity serve as a framework through which individuals interpret and make sense of their transformative encounters with the Real. As individuals engage with moments of crisis, trauma, or profound self-discovery, they often rely on symbolic references embedded within the cultural and linguistic fabric of their society to articulate and contextualize their experiences. These symbols, whether in the form of narratives, archetypes, or collective myths, provide a template for integrating the disruptive force of the Real into their evolving sense of self.

The Symbolic Order acts as a mechanism for the social regulation of the Real's impact on individual and collective identity. Societal institutions, cultural practices, and linguistic representations provide a means through which the destabilizing effects of the Real can be contained and normalized. By ascribing meaning and coherence to the otherwise enigmatic manifestations of the Real, the Symbolic Order mediates the integration of these experiences into the broader narrative of identity, offering a semblance of stability and predictability amidst the turbulence of existential confrontation.

Thus, the interplay between the Real and the Symbolic Order in identity formation encapsulates a complex dynamic of negotiation, reinterpretation, and adaptation. It is within the discourse of the symbolic representations of identity that the disruptive force of the Real finds both containment and expression, intertwining with cultural expectations and individual experiences to shape the tapestry of human identity.

6. Transformational Experiences of the Real:

Transformational experiences stemming from encounters with the Real are pivotal moments in shaping an individual's identity. Such experiences often defy rational understanding and disrupt the prevailing symbolic order, catalyzing profound shifts in perception and self-awareness. These encounters can occur spontaneously or be precipitated by intense emotional or psychological events, prompting individuals to confront truths that destabilize established realities.

One common manifestation of transformation through the Real is the breakdown of familiar cognitive frameworks, leading to a reevaluation of one's fundamental beliefs about the self and the world. The ensuing disorientation and existential angst are often juxtaposed with moments of profound insight and clarity, challenging individuals to reconceptualize their place within the fabric of reality. As such, transformation catalyzed by the Real transcends mere cognitive reorganization; it encompasses visceral, emotional, and spiritual dimensions, underscoring the holistic impact of these experiences.

These transformational encounters bring to the forefront the porous boundaries between the conscious and unconscious registers, unraveling latent desires, fears, and anxieties that permeate the psyche. The unearthing of suppressed or unrecognized aspects of the self engenders a process of integration and reconciliation that enriches the individual's sense of wholeness. Consequently, the transformative power of the Real lies not only in the disruption it inflicts upon existing identities but also in the potential for personal growth, as individuals traverse the interplay between the known and the unknown.

The transformative force of the Real intersects with cultural and societal constructs, offering moments of rupture and critique against normative narratives. By destabilizing entrenched systems of meaning, individuals may find themselves empowered to challenge oppressive structures, carve out alternative pathways, and redefine their roles within broader social frameworks. This capacity for societal change underscores the far-reaching implications of transformational experiences, as they extend beyond the individual to cascade into collective movements and revolutions.

Critiques and Misinterpretations

1. Historical Misunderstandings and Their Impact:

Throughout history, the concept of the Real has been subject to numerous misunderstandings, often resulting in significant impacts on different spheres of human existence. One such historical misunderstanding can be traced back to the early philosophical discourse surrounding the nature of reality and existence. The tendency to conflate the Real with the concrete and tangible led to a reductionist interpretation, limiting the scope of the Real to merely that which is perceptible by the senses. This oversimplification marginalized the profound complexity and depth inherent to the Real, perpetuating a distorted understanding that prevailed for centuries.

The misinterpretation of the Real within religious and spiritual contexts further exemplifies the historical impact of misunderstandings. Many ancient belief systems and mystical traditions attempted to encapsulate the concept of the Real within narrowly defined dogmas and doctrines, constraining its boundless nature within rigid frameworks. Consequently, this restricted portrayal hindered individuals from accessing the transcendent and ineffable aspects of the Real, imposing artificial limitations on their spiritual and existential pursuits.

In addition to philosophical and spiritual arenas, the historical interpretations of the Real have also left enduring imprints on societal structures and cultural paradigms. The tendency to equate the Real with dominant power dynamics or prevailing socio-political constructs fostered an environment wherein meaningful dialogues and progress were impeded. By conflating the Real with oppressive systems and hierarchies, societies inadvertently perpetuated inequities and overlooked the genuine nuances of human experiences and aspirations.

2. Philosophical Objections and Counterarguments:

One of the primary philosophical objections to the concept of the Real stems from the inherent difficulty in defining and articulating the nature of the Real. Critics argue that the Real, by its very definition, resists symbolization and linguistic description. This ontological ambiguity has led to skepticism regarding the viability of incorporating the Real into philosophical discourse.

Another prominent contention revolves around the implications of acknowledging the existence of the Real. Some philosophers posit that embracing the Real may engender nihilistic tendencies, as the confrontation with an unmediated and unfathomable reality could result in a sense of existential despair and a loss of meaning. In response, advocates of the Real counterargue that confronting the Real enables individuals to grapple with fundamental truth and authenticity, leading to enhanced self-awareness and the potential for profound transformative experiences.

There are disputes regarding the relationship between the Real and language. Critics question whether it is possible to convey authentic experiences of the Real through linguistic representation. They argue that language, being intrinsically tied to the symbolic order, inherently distorts or oversimplifies the Real. Advocates, however, assert that while language may indeed fall short in capturing the full essence of the Real, it can still provide glimpses and evocative expressions that resonate with the ineffable nature of lived experiences.

Debates also arise concerning the relevance of the Real within the broader scope of philosophical inquiry. Some scholars contend that the concept of the Real, as expounded in psychoanalytic and literary contexts, possesses limited applicability outside these arenas. They question its significance for broader metaphysical, epistemological, and ethical inquiries. Proponents, conversely, advocate for the integration of the Real into these domains, emphasizing its potential to enrich philosophical investigations by introducing an unvarnished perspective on reality.

In response to these objections, proponents of the Real have articulated compelling counterarguments. They assert that the elusive nature of the Real does not diminish its import but, rather, underscores the limitations of conventional modes of understanding and representation. Furthermore, they contend that engaging with the Real does not necessitate succumbing to nihilism; instead, it invites individuals to cultivate a more nuanced and authentic relationship with thc world. Additionally, advocates emphasize that while language may be imperfect, it remains a vital tool for exploring and conveying the profundity of the Real, albeit through metaphorical and evocative means.

3. Psychoanalytic Debates on The Real:

Psychoanalytic discourse offers a rich terrain for the exploration of Lacan's concept of 'The Real', sparking compelling debates and critical investigations. Within this domain, scholars and practitioners alike engage in multifaceted discussions regarding the manifestation and elusive nature of the Real within the psychoanalytic framework. One pivotal aspect of these debates centers on the ontological and epistemological implications of The Real within the context of clinical practice and theoretical foundations. The juxtaposition of the symbolic and imaginary orders with the enigmatic terrain of The Real gives rise to profound questions about the nature of psychic reality and the unconscious.

Psychoanalytic debates on The Real delve into the significance of traumatic experiences and their connection to the irruption of The Real in subjective existence. This exploration examines the ways in which traumatic events rupture the fabric of the symbolic order, leading individuals into direct confrontation with the unmediated and often overwhelming force of The Real. Moreover, scholars interrogate the ethical implications of integrating The Real into therapeutic interventions, with some advocating for its acknowledgment and others cautioning against re-traumatization in the process of confrontational engagement with The Real.

Additionally, the topic of language and representation emerges as a focal point within psychoanalytic dialogues on The Real. Critics and proponents engage in rigorous discussions concerning the limitations and potential distortions of language when confronting The Real, fundamentally scrutinizing the efficacy of verbal and symbolic articulations in encapsulating an entity that defies categorization and symbolic translation.

Psychoanalytic perspectives shed light on how The Real intersects with concepts of desire and fantasy, prompting inquiries into the existential tensions between the pursuit of the Real and the allure of the imaginary register. These debates are marked by nuanced analyses of the ways in which desire interacts with The Real, yielding insights into the complex interplay between the drives, the ego, and the formidable presence of The Real.

4. Common Cultural Misinterpretations:

The pervasive influence of cultural narratives, belief systems, and societal constructs has often led to the appropriation and misunderstanding of Lacanian concepts related to the Real. One prevalent misinterpretation arises from the tendency to equate the Real with objective reality or empirical truth. This oversimplification ignores the nuanced theoretical underpinnings of the Real as an elusive, unattainable dimension that transcends the symbolic and imaginary registers. Furthermore, popular media and mainstream discourse frequently perpetuate misconceptions about the Real, depicting it as a tangible, concrete entity rather than a psychoanalytic construct deeply embedded in the human psyche. Such depictions contribute to the dilution of the concept's complexity and diminish its potential for profound philosophical and psychological inquiry. Additionally, disparate cultural contexts and value systems often lead to divergent interpretations of the Real, further complicating its understanding. These variations give rise to a multitude of misappropriations and oversimplifications, leading to a distorted popular understanding of this psychoanalytic concept. It is crucial to recognize and address these misinterpretations, as they have repercussions not only on academic discourse but also on broader societal perceptions of reality, subjectivity, and identity. Through rigorous examination and critical engagement, scholars and practitioners can strive to correct these misrepresentations, fostering a more comprehensive and accurate comprehension of the Real within both academic and cultural contexts.

5. The Real in Academic Discourses:

In academic discourses, the concept of the Real has garnered significant attention across various fields, including philosophy, psychology, literary studies, cultural criticism, and sociology. Scholars have engaged in rigorous debates regarding the nature of the Real and its implications for different disciplines. The intersection of Lacanian theory with critical theory has been pivotal in shaping these discussions, prompting a reexamination of fundamental assumptions about reality, representation, and language. Within philosophy, thinkers such as Slavoj Žižek and Alain Badiou have grappled with the implications of the Real for ontology, ethics, and political theory. Their analyses have spurred further inquiries into the intersection of the Real with time, existence, and the limitations of human comprehension. The contribution of psychoanalysis to academic explorations of the Real cannot be overstated. Freud's groundbreaking work provided a foundation for later theorists to delve into the subconscious manifestations of the Real, while post-Freudian developments, especially those by Jacques Lacan, formed the basis for a new wave of interdisciplinary inquiry. Moreover, the application of Lacanian concepts to literary studies has led to a profound reassessment of narrative strategies, authorial intent, and reader-response dynamics. In cultural criticism, the notion of the Real has been pivotal in deconstructing established paradigms and uncovering the underlying power structures that shape societal narratives. This has led to fruitful investigations into the intersections of the Real with race, gender, class, and other identity markers. Sociological perspectives on the Real have focused on its role in shaping collective beliefs, social constructs, and institutional practices. By examining the ways in which the Real operates within societal frameworks, scholars have sought to illuminate the mechanisms through which dominant ideologies are perpetuated and contested. The diversity of approaches within academic discourses reflects the multifaceted nature of the Real and its far-reaching ramifications.

6. Divergent Theoretical Perspectives:

Various philosophical, psychoanalytic, and cultural frameworks offer distinct vantage points from which to observe and interpret the nature of the Real. Within philosophical discourse, differing schools of thought such as phenomenology, existentialism, and post-structuralism present contrasting attitudes toward the ontological status of the Real. Phenomenologists emphasize the subjective experience of reality, positing that the essence of the Real is only accessible through lived human experiences. In contrast, existentialist thinkers delve into the individual's confrontation with their existence, often aligning the Real with moments of intense personal revelation or crisis. Post-structuralists, drawing from critical theory and deconstruction, interrogate the very grounds of reality and truth, deconstructing conventional understandings of the Real.

From a psychoanalytic standpoint, Freudian, Lacanian, and Jungian perspectives all contribute nuanced interpretations of the Real within the human psyche. Freud's emphasis on the unconscious and primal drives offers a foundational understanding of the Real as a disruptive force underlying one's conscious perceptions. Lacan, on the other hand, introduces the concept of the Real as an unattainable, traumatic kernel that defies symbolization and language, fundamentally shaping the subject's psyche. Meanwhile, Jung's conceptualization of the Real extends into archetypal images and universal symbols that tap into the collective unconscious, offering a different dimension to the understanding of the Real within psychoanalysis.

Cultural perspectives further enrich this exploration, with diverse global traditions offering alternative conceptions of the Real. Whether it be Eastern philosophies emphasizing interconnectedness and impermanence, or indigenous cosmologies rooted in animistic worldviews, these cultural vantages provide valuable insights into how the Real is understood and integrated within human societies. Additionally, contemporary discourses surrounding virtual realities, artificial intelligence, and cybernetic systems invite a reconsideration of the Real in relation to technology and digital arenas.

7. Distinctions within The Order Schema:

The concept of the Real, as expounded by Lacanian psychoanalysis, is imbued with layers of nuance that demand meticulous scrutiny. Re-evaluating the distinctions within the order schema becomes imperative to gain a more comprehensive understanding of this complex theoretical framework. An essential aspect of this re-evaluation involves delving into the relationships between the Symbolic, the Imaginary, and the Real orders. It necessitates a critical examination of how these registers intersect and diverge, shaping subjective experiences and societal constructs.

Within the context of Lacanian psychoanalysis, the Symbolic order is characterized by language, culture, and the rules and norms that govern human interactions. Meanwhile, the Imaginary order pertains to images, reflections, and ego formations. However, as we scrutinize these delineations, it becomes apparent that there are moments when these boundaries blur, leading to an intertwined interplay of the orders. These instances of ambiguity and entanglement can challenge conventional understandings of the distinctiveness of each order.

Re-evaluating the distinctions within the order schema allows for a deeper exploration of the ways in which the Real disrupts and subverts the Symbolic and the Imaginary. By closely examining the instances of rupture and dissonance, we can glean valuable insights into the enigmatic nature of the Real. This process unveils the inherent tensions and contradictions within the structure of the order schema, shedding light on the complex dynamics at play.

On the other hand, this re-evaluation calls for an interrogation of the hierarchical assumptions that often underpin discussions of the order schema. Instead of viewing the orders as neatly stacked layers, it becomes essential to consider the fluidity and permeability that characterize their interactions. This shift in perspective prompts a paradigmatic reformulation, fostering a more fluid and dynamic comprehension of the fabric of the human psyche and social systems.

IMPACT ON CONTEMPORARY PSYCHOLOGY & THERAPY

Integration into Cognitive Behavioral Therapy

Jacques Lacan's theories have made significant contributions to the field of psychology, particularly in their impact on contemporary therapy approaches such as Cognitive Behavioral Therapy (CBT). The integration of Lacanian concepts into CBT has opened new avenues for understanding and addressing complex psychological issues. By incorporating Lacanian principles, therapists can delve deeper into the unconscious structures that influence behaviors and thought patterns, thereby enhancing the effectiveness of CBT interventions. One key area of synergy lies in the exploration of the symbolic order and its implications for cognitive restructuring. Lacan's emphasis on language and signification aligns with CBT's focus on identifying and challenging maladaptive thought constructs, leading to more profound insights and sustainable therapeutic results. Moreover, the incorporation of Lacanian concepts into CBT enables a comprehensive analysis of the interplay between conscious and unconscious processes, enriching the therapeutic process and enhancing the depth of interventions. This integration provides a framework for therapists to address not only surface-level symptoms but also underlying symbolic meanings embedded in an individual's cognitive and behavioral patterns. Furthermore, by acknowledging the role of desire and the unconscious in shaping behavior, therapists can foster more holistic and enduring changes in clients undergoing CBT. Lacanian concepts also offer an alternative perspective on the nature of mental health issues, urging therapists to consider the interconnections between language, social dynamics, and subjective experience. By integrating Lacanian insights into CBT, psychological practitioners can refine their approach to addressing diverse concerns, including anxiety, depression, trauma, and identity-related struggles. In doing so, they can honor the complexities of the human psyche and provide more personalized and empathetic care that resonates on a deeper level with their clients. This fusion also encourages therapists to reconsider the very foundations of symptom formation and psychological distress, paving the way for a more nuanced and encompassing therapeutic landscape.

Influence on Humanistic Psychology Approaches

Humanistic psychology emphasizes an individual's inherent drive towards personal growth, self-actualization, and fulfilling their highest potential. The integration of Lacanian theories into humanistic approaches has brought about a significant paradigm shift in understanding the human psyche. By incorporating Lacan's concepts of the three orders—Symbolic, Imaginary, and Real—humanistic therapies have been enriched with a deeper understanding of the internal conflicts and dynamics that influence an individual's quest for self-discovery and authenticity. The emphasis on subjective experience and the exploration of the unconscious align remarkably well with Lacanian principles, contributing to a more holistic approach to humanistic therapy.

Lacanian insights have also influenced humanistic practices by shedding light on the nature of human identity formation and the role of language and symbols in shaping perceptions of the self and others. This has led to a reevaluation of traditional humanistic techniques, inspiring therapists to integrate symbolic and linguistic analysis to unearth hidden meanings and unveil unconscious patterns that hinder personal growth. Furthermore, the recognition of the Imaginary order's impact on self-identity and relationships has prompted therapists to delve deeper into the complexities of self-image, enabling clients to engage with and reconcile the dynamics of their inner worlds.

Additionally, the Real order, with its enigmatic and elusive nature, has sparked contemplation within humanistic psychology, provoking discussions on the limitations of conscious awareness and the significance of embracing the ineffable aspects of human experience. As a result, humanistic practitioners have utilized Lacanian principles to encourage clients to confront the 'Real' aspects of their existence, fostering a more profound level of introspection and acceptance of existential aspects that transcend rational comprehension.

Adoption in Systemic and Family Counseling

The incorporation of Lacanian theories into systemic and family counseling represents a paradigm shift in the understanding and treatment of familial dynamics. By embracing the concept of the unconscious, Lacanian principles serve as a cornerstone for delving into the interplay of individual psyches within a familial unit. This approach encourages therapists to explore how the unconscious drives intrafamilial interactions and shapes relational patterns.

Lacan's emphasis on the symbolic order offers a lens through which family counselors can decipher the complex web of meanings and signifiers that underpin family communication. Understanding the role of language and metaphor in shaping familial narratives is pivotal in uncovering deep-rooted conflicts and generational transmissions. Moreover, the application of Lacanian concepts such as the mirror stage and the Oedipus complex provides profound insights into the formation of familial identities and the dynamics of power and desire within the family structure.

The systemic perspective inherent in Lacanian theory underscores the interconnectedness of family members and the reciprocal influence they exert on each other. Therapists leveraging these insights can address relational imbalances and entrenched behavioral patterns by illuminating the underlying symbolic exchanges that perpetuate dysfunctional dynamics. By examining how the unconscious forces shape and perpetuate intergenerational scripts, systemic and family counselors are better equipped to facilitate transformative change within the familial system, promoting healthier relationships and emotional well-being.

The integration of Lacanian concepts into systemic and family counseling amplifies the scope of therapeutic interventions. It allows for a deeper exploration of family myths, collective fantasies, and ancestral burdens, enabling clinicians to untangle complex familial histories and liberate individuals from the grip of unconscious entanglements. Through traversing the symbolic terrain of family dynamics, practitioners can guide families towards a reconfiguration of their stories, fostering new narratives that empower and integrate diverse aspects of the self.

Relevance in Modern Psychoanalytic Practice

One of the primary contributions of Lacanian theory to modern psychoanalytic practice lies in its emphasis on language and signification. Lacan posited that the unconscious is structured like a language, incorporating the concept of the symbolic register as a key component of mental processes. This notion has revolutionized the understanding of how individuals communicate with themselves and others, offering therapists a framework to explore the underlying meanings and motivations behind their patients' behaviors and expressions.

Lacanian insights have shed light on the dynamics between the conscious and unconscious mind, providing practitioners with invaluable tools to manage the complexities of human emotions and desires. The proposition of the unconscious as the repository of repressed thoughts and desires has significantly informed modern psychoanalytic techniques, enabling therapists to guide their patients towards a deeper self-awareness and resolution of internal conflicts.

Lacan's reimagining of the Oedipus complex and his formulation of the mirror stage have deeply influenced contemporary psychoanalytic practice. These concepts have broadened the scope of understanding early childhood development and its implications on adult personality formation. Practitioners have integrated these ideas into their therapeutic approaches, fostering a more holistic comprehension of individuals' experiences and struggles.

Additionally, Lacanian theory has prompted a reevaluation of the traditional therapist-patient relationship, encouraging therapists to recognize the inherent power dynamics and transference phenomena at play within the therapeutic setting. This critical awareness has paved the way for more ethical and empathetic practices, leading to enhanced therapeutic alliances and improved treatment outcomes.

Contribution to Understanding the Unconscious

The concept of the unconscious as articulated by Lacan goes beyond traditional Freudian perspectives, emphasizing the linguistic and symbolic aspects of unconscious processes. According to Lacanian theory, the unconscious is structured like a language, characterized by a network of signifiers and signifieds that shape an individual's thoughts, emotions, and behaviors. This conceptualization has provided a rich theoretical foundation for exploring the complexities of the unconscious mind.

One of the key tenets of Lacanian theory is the idea that the unconscious is not a repository of repressed desires and memories, as posited in traditional psychoanalysis, but rather a site of conflict and contradiction. This departure from Freudian theory has sparked insightful debates and expanded the discourse on the nature of the unconscious. Lacan's emphasis on the role of language and symbols in shaping unconscious processes has also offered new avenues for understanding how meaning is constructed and represented in the unconscious.

Lacanian theory has contributed to a deeper understanding of the unconscious by highlighting the importance of the unconscious Other. The concept of the Other, central to Lacanian thought, refers to the external social and cultural frameworks that influence an individual's construction of reality and identity. Through this lens, the unconscious is not only shaped by intrapsychic dynamics but also by external socio-cultural forces, leading to a more nuanced and comprehensive understanding of unconscious processes.

The concept of the unconscious in Lacanian theory has led to innovative therapeutic approaches aimed at unraveling the symbolic and linguistic structures that underpin unconscious conflicts and dynamics. By exploring the symbolic meanings embedded in unconscious manifestations such as dreams, symptoms, and slips of the tongue, therapists have been able to engage with clients in profound ways, shedding light on their hidden patterns and struggles.

Role in Personal Development and Self-Realization

One key aspect of Lacanian theory is its emphasis on language and communication in shaping one's subjectivity. According to Lacan, the construction of the self occurs through linguistic and symbolic processes, which influence our relationships, desires, and aspirations. This insight has paved the way for a reevaluation of how individuals perceive and orchestrate their personal development journey. By acknowledging the role of language and discourse in shaping one's self-perception, individuals can gain a deeper understanding of their inner struggles and paradoxes, ultimately leading to a more authentic form of self-realization.

Lacanian theory has also shed light on the significance of unconscious desires and fantasies in personal development. The exploration of unconscious drives and repressed emotions can unravel the layers of an individual's psyche, offering profound insights into their behavior and choices. Through a Lacanian lens, individuals are encouraged to confront the hidden aspects of their mind, facilitating a transformative process that aligns with the principles of self-realization. By acknowledging and integrating these unconscious elements, individuals can embark on a journey towards holistic personal growth and genuine self-discovery.

The concept of the 'mirror stage' in Lacanian theory has implications for personal development and self-realization. This stage emphasizes the role of external perceptions and identifications in shaping one's self-image. In the context of personal development, understanding how early experiences of mirroring and recognition contribute to the formation of one's identity can help individuals chart their path towards self-realization more consciously. By deconstructing and reassessing these initial identifications, individuals can liberate themselves from the constraints of external expectations and societal norms, forging a more authentic and fulfilling sense of self.

Transformation of Therapeutic Techniques

The incorporation of Lacanian principles into contemporary therapy has led to a significant transformation in therapeutic techniques. By reimagining the nature of the unconscious and emphasizing the role of language, Lacanian theory has given rise to innovative approaches that diverge from traditional psychotherapeutic methods.

One of the central transformations lies in the way therapists approach the interpretation of patients' experiences. Rather than focusing solely on the manifest content of their narratives, practitioners trained in Lacanian thought are adept at recognizing the latent signifiers embedded within language. This interpretive shift allows for a deeper exploration of the unconscious processes shaping the individual's thoughts, emotions, and behaviors. Consequently, therapeutic sessions often involve an analysis of the symbolic meanings underlying seemingly mundane expressions and actions.

The therapeutic techniques derived from Lacanian theory underscore the significance of the therapeutic relationship itself. In contrast to more directive approaches, such as those found in traditional Freudian psychoanalysis, the Lacanian-informed therapist seeks to create a dynamic space for the unfolding of the patient's speech and associations without imposing predefined interpretations. This emphasis on free association and the co-construction of meaning between the analyst and the analysand fosters a collaborative and exploratory therapeutic environment.

The application of Lacanian concepts has brought about a reevaluation of the goals of therapy. While traditional theories often emphasize symptom reduction or adaptation to societal norms, Lacanian-oriented therapy focuses on fostering awareness of one's subjectivity and exploring the structures that underpin an individual's sense of self. This reorientation of therapeutic aims has led to a greater emphasis on encouraging patients to engage critically with their subjective experience and societal constructs, ultimately promoting personal growth and self-realization.

Comparison with Traditional Theories

In order to fully appreciate the impact of Lacanian theory on contemporary psychology and therapy, it is essential to conduct a comparative analysis with traditional theories that have dominated these fields for decades. One of the most prominent comparisons lies in contrasting Lacanian psychoanalysis with Freudian psychoanalysis, which serves as the foundational framework for many traditional therapeutic approaches. While Freud's emphasis on early childhood experiences and the primacy of sexual drives has traditionally guided therapeutic interventions, Lacan offers a unique perspective by focusing on the structuring role of language and the symbolic order in shaping human subjectivity.

The comparison extends to behavioral and cognitive theories, which have underscored the significance of observable behaviors and conscious mental processes in understanding and treating psychological issues. In contrast, Lacanian theory delves into the unconscious registers, challenging the reductionist tendencies of purely behaviorally or cognitively oriented approaches. This juxtaposition highlights the profound departure that Lacanian theory represents from conventional psychological paradigms.

When compared with humanistic and existential theories that emphasize personal growth, self-actualization, and the search for meaning, Lacanian theory introduces a critical dimension by illuminating the inherent lack and alienation in the structure of subjectivity. By traversing the interplay between the imaginary, the symbolic, and the real, Lacanian theory deepens our understanding of the complexities and contradictions within the human psyche, thereby enriching the discourse on personal fulfillment and existential authenticity.

Additionally, Lacanian concepts are juxtaposed with systemic and family theories, which prioritize the interpersonal dynamics and relational patterns within social systems. While systemic approaches accentuate the interrelatedness of individuals within their contexts, Lacanian theory uncovers the unconscious undercurrents that influence these dynamic interactions, providing a deeper layer of comprehension to familial and systemic dynamics.

Future Trajectories in Therapy

The future trajectories of Lacanian-informed therapy prompt contemplation on potential advancements and integrations with emerging psychological paradigms. Prospective developments may entail a more nuanced alignment of Lacanian concepts with neuroscientific findings, fostering an enriched understanding of the neural correlates of unconscious processes. Additionally, the burgeoning field of digital mental health interventions offers opportunities for integrating Lacanian insights into innovative technological platforms, thereby extending the reach of psychoanalytic perspectives to a wider demographic.

The evolution of therapeutic modalities could witness the integration of Lacanian tenets with somatic and body-centered approaches, acknowledging the embodied manifestations of unconscious dynamics and promoting holistic healing. This incorporation not only expands the scope of Lacanian influence but also paves the way for interdisciplinary collaboration among psychoanalysis, neuroscience, and somatic psychology. Moreover, the underlying essence of interpersonal dynamics within the therapeutic relationship calls for the exploration of Lacanian constructs in couples and family therapy, appraising their applicability in addressing relational conflicts and unconscious interplay between individuals.

Lastly, envisaging the future trajectories of Lacanian-inspired therapy necessitates a concerted effort to address its accessibility and inclusivity, fostering initiatives to make psychoanalytic insights available to marginalized populations and underserved communities. As we engage with the critiques and potentials of Lacanian theory, it becomes apparent that its relevance lies in the collaborative endeavors to bridge theoretical intricacies with pragmatic applications, thereby transcending the confines of traditional therapy and embracing the evolving landscape of psychological practice.

INFLUENCE ON MODERN THOUGHT

Psychoanalysis and Beyond

Drawing from Jacques Lacan's theories, the influence of psychoanalysis extends beyond the arenas of individual therapy and clinical settings, permeating into various disciplines and fields. This expansive impact manifests within the academic milieu through the integration of psychoanalytic concepts into diverse branches of psychology, sociology, and anthropology, not limited to its traditional domain of psychotherapy. Moreover, the inherent emphasis on unconscious motivations and desires in Lacanian thought has resonated profoundly with scholars seeking to unravel the complexities of human behavior and cognition.

Beyond academia, the influence of Lacanian psychoanalysis has pervaded popular culture, as evidenced by its incorporation into art, literature, and film. The notion of the unconscious as a repository of repressed emotions and conflicting impulses has fueled artistic creations that seek to delve into the depths of the human psyche. This integration of psychoanalytic themes within creative expressions serves to underscore the profound impact of Lacan's ideas on broader societal discourses surrounding identity, desire, and meaning.

The application of Lacanian principles to contemporary issues has expanded the frontiers of psychoanalysis, demonstrating its relevance in addressing evolving societal challenges. Concepts such as the mirror stage and the symbolic order have provided insightful frameworks for understanding phenomena related to self-image, representation, and social interactions, thus enriching dialogues on body image, social media, and interpersonal relationships.

In addition to its intellectual and cultural ramifications, the reach of Lacanian psychoanalysis extends to the domain of critical theory, where it has become a pivotal tool in analyzing power structures, language, and subjectivity. By unpacking the ways in which language constructs our reality and shapes our subjectivity, Lacanian theory has played an instrumental role in critiquing dominant ideologies and hierarchies, thereby contributing to the expansion of critical discourses across various domains of knowledge.

Impact on Contemporary Philosophy

In present times, the influence of Jacques Lacan's theories on contemporary philosophy has been profound and multifaceted. One of the key areas where Lacanian ideas have made a significant impact is in philosophical inquiry into subjectivity and the construction of the self. Lacan's concept of the divided subject and the role of language as a structuring force in the formation of individual identity has provoked rich debates within philosophical circles. Furthermore, his emphasis on the unconscious and its relationship to language has provided fertile ground for rethinking traditional notions of consciousness and rationality.

Lacanian concepts have also reverberated across various schools of thought within contemporary philosophy. Existentialist philosophers have engaged with Lacanian ideas concerning the nature of human existence and the experience of alienation, while phenomenologists have explored the implications of Lacan's understanding of perception and the constitution of reality. In addition, post-structuralist and deconstructionist thinkers have drawn inspiration from Lacan's insights into the interplay of signifiers and the elusive nature of meaning, leading to innovative reinterpretations of language, textuality, and interpretation.

Lacan's elucidation of the symbolic order and its role in mediating our relationships with others has sparked inquiries into intersubjectivity and the dynamics of social interaction. Philosophers have interrogated the implications of Lacanian theory for understanding power relations, ideological formations, and the construction of social norms. Additionally, the real as a domain beyond symbolization has prompted reflections on the limitations of linguistic representation and the enigmatic contours of reality.

The ongoing impact of Lacanian philosophy can also be discerned in the exploration of ethics and political theory. Lacan's emphasis on desire, lack, and jouissance has engendered critical reflections on the nature of ethical subjectivity and the challenges of moral agency. Furthermore, his reconceptualization of the unconscious has provoked reevaluations of freedom, responsibility, and the constitution of the subject in the context of contemporary political frameworks.

Lacan in Cultural Studies

Lacan's conceptual framework provides a compelling lens through which to understand the complex interplay between language, symbolization, and subjectivity within cultural productions, such as literature, film, visual arts, and performance. The application of Lacanian psychoanalysis in cultural studies has facilitated a deeper understanding of the ways in which meaning is constructed and negotiated within cultural texts. One of the central tenets of Lacanian theory, the notion of the symbolic order, has been instrumental in reshaping the study of culture. By emphasizing the role of language and symbols in shaping individual subjectivities, Lacanian analysis has illuminated the ways in which cultural artifacts convey meaning and contribute to the construction of identities. Moreover, the concept of the unconscious, as delineated by Lacan, has expanded the interpretive scope of cultural studies, enabling scholars to delve into the latent, symbolic dimensions of cultural products. This has led to a reconfiguration of traditional modes of interpretation, encouraging a more nuanced and multilayered approach to analyzing cultural texts. Lacanian thought has also engendered a reevaluation of the relationship between cultural production and the formation of societal norms and values. By foregrounding the role of fantasies, desires, and unconscious motivations in cultural manifestations, Lacanian analysis has reframed the understanding of cultural artifacts as sites of contestation, negotiation, and resistance. This shift has prompted a critical reexamination of dominant narratives and representations, fostering a more interrogative, reflexive engagement with cultural products. Furthermore, Lacan's emphasis on the process of identification and its connection to the formation of the self has offered new insights into the ways in which individuals engage with art and cultural expressions. This has spurred a reconceptualization of the audience's agency and participation in cultural meaning-making processes, challenging conventional notions of passive consumption.

Art and Literature

The concept of the Symbolic Order provides a lens through which to interpret and analyze artistic and literary expressions. In art, the symbolic refers to the use of visual elements to convey deeper, often unconscious meanings. Artists harness symbols and visual signifiers to evoke complex emotions and ideas, often tapping into the collective unconscious as theorized by Carl Jung. This interplay of symbols and their interpretation mirrors Lacan's understanding of language and the unconscious as central to the human experience. From Renaissance allegorical paintings to modernist and postmodernist works, the exploration of the symbolic in art reveals the relevance of Lacanian concepts.

Likewise, in literature, the symbolic takes on rich significance. Authors employ symbols, metaphors, and allegories to convey themes and motifs that transcend surface-level narratives. Lacanian theory enriches our understanding of these literary devices, highlighting their connection to unconscious desires, societal norms, and the construction of identity. The interplay between the conscious and unconscious, the signifier and the signified, becomes a fertile ground for literary analysis. By delving into the symbolic dimension of literary works, we gain insights into the complexities and contradictions of human existence.

Lacan's emphasis on the role of language in shaping subjectivity resonates deeply with discussions in literary theory and criticism. The linguistic turn in literary studies, influenced by structuralism and post-structuralism, aligns with Lacan's view of the Symbolic Order as the milieu of language and culture. Understanding how language structures meaning and shapes identities allows us to scrutinize texts with heightened awareness of the linguistic and symbolic dimensions at play. As such, the intersection of Lacanian theory and literary studies opens up new avenues for interpreting and engaging with diverse literary traditions.

Media Theory

The influence of Jacques Lacan's theoretical framework has extended into media theory, offering profound insights into the dynamics of the imaginary within popular culture. In contemporary society, the role of media in shaping collective perceptions and narratives cannot be overstated. Through the lens of Lacanian theory, we can discern how the imaginary order permeates a wide array of media forms, including film, television, advertising, social media, and digital entertainment.

Central to the application of Lacanian concepts in media theory is an exploration of the construction of idealized images and identities. The imaginary, as expounded by Lacan, encapsulates illusion and fantasy, which often finds vivid expression in popular cultural artifacts. From the portrayal of archetypal characters to the cultivation of aspirational lifestyles, media engages with the imaginary to shape desires and beliefs, thereby exerting a significant influence on individuals and societies at large.

The interplay between the imaginary and the gaze in media representation is a focal point within Lacanian analysis. The act of looking and being looked at, as portrayed and experienced in media narratives, underscores the pivotal role of the imaginary in constructing and perpetuating societal norms and values. This examination not only enriches our understanding of media dynamics but also offers a critical vantage point for analyzing power relations and identity formations within popular culture.

By delving into specific case studies across different media platforms, it becomes evident how Lacanian principles illuminate the underlying mechanisms that drive consumer behaviors, cultural trends, and the perpetuation of symbolic imagery. Through a rigorous application of Lacanian thought, scholars and practitioners in media theory can dissect the interplay between the imaginary, the symbolic, and the real, thus uncovering the deeper implications of media representations and their resonance with audiences.

Critical Social Theory

Power is an omnipresent force in societies, shaping relationships, institutions, and individual experiences. In the context of critical social theory, the examination of power dynamics is paramount to understanding and deconstructing existing systems of oppression. Drawing from Lacanian theories, it becomes evident that power operates within the symbolic, imaginary, and real orders, influencing and perpetuating social hierarchies and inequalities.

Within the symbolic order, power manifests through language, discourse, and social norms. Language serves as a tool for not only communication but also for the dissemination of ideologies that maintain power differentials. Lacan's concept of the symbolic highlights how linguistic constructs contribute to the construction of societal power dynamics, reinforcing certain identities while marginalizing others. Through an analysis of discourse, critical theorists illuminate the ways in which language is utilized to uphold hegemonic structures and perpetuate systemic injustices. Furthermore, the imaginary order intersects with power through the formation of cultural representations and images. Media, art, and popular culture play a pivotal role in constructing and disseminating imaginary perceptions that normalize power imbalances. Critical engagement with these cultural products unveils the underlying power dynamics, exposing the mechanisms through which dominant narratives are sustained by perpetuating illusions and idealized identities.

Moving to the real order, power operates at a palpable and material level, regulating access to resources, opportunities, and rights. Understanding the real as that which eludes symbolization, we recognize how power can manifest through embodied experiences of inequality and injustice. By examining the intersections between the real and power dynamics, critical social theory endeavors to address systemic oppressions that are embedded in the very fabric of society. Moreover, the exploration of the real allows for an analysis of how power relations are enacted through lived experiences, shedding light on the impact of power differentials on marginalized communities. By engaging with Lacanian frameworks, critical social theory unveils the multifaceted nature of power and its pervasive influence across the three orders, prompting actions aimed at challenging oppressive power structures and fostering social change.

Intersections with Gender and Identity Studies

Gender and identity studies have long grappled with questions of representation, power dynamics, and the construction of selfhood. Lacan's theories provide a rich foundation for examining these issues, as they emphasize the role of language, symbolism, and cultural norms in shaping individual identities. Central to Lacanian thought is the notion of the 'mirror stage,' which posits that an individual's sense of self is fundamentally bound up with external images and societal ideals of identity. This has profound ramifications for gender identities, as it illuminates how social constructs and expectations shape our understanding of masculinity, femininity, and non-binary expressions. Furthermore, Lacan's concept of the 'phallus' goes beyond biological determinism to encapsulate the symbolic power associated with gender and sexuality. By interrogating the phallus as a signifier of authority and privilege, gender and identity studies can unpack the dynamics of dominance and subjugation within social hierarchies. Additionally, Lacanian theory offers valuable insights into the formation of desire and the negotiation of sexual subjectivities. The interplay between the symbolic, imaginary, and real orders sheds light on the ways in which individuals traverse their desires, fantasies, and internal conflicts related to gender and sexual identity. Moreover, Lacanian psychoanalysis has been instrumental in critiquing heteronormative structures and expanding the discourse on LGBTQ+ experiences. By situating gender and identity within the broader framework of the three orders, scholars and activists have been able to challenge essentialist narratives and advocate for more inclusive understandings of human identity. Overall, the intersection of Lacanian theory with gender and identity studies enriches our comprehension of the complex interplay between social constructions, psychological development, and subjective experiences. It prompts ongoing dialogue and critical inquiry into the multifaceted nature of gendered selves, thereby propelling the evolution of modern thought.

The Real in Science and Technology Discourses

In considering the influence of Lacanian thought on modern discourses surrounding science and technology, it is crucial to delve into the notion of the 'Real' as proposed by Jacques Lacan. While traditionally explored within the domains of psychoanalysis and philosophy, the concept of the Real has also found resonance in the spheres of science and technology, prompting a reevaluation of traditional paradigms and frameworks. The interdisciplinary dialogue between Lacanian theory and scientific discourses has led to compelling insights into the nature of reality, human perception, and the limitations of our understanding.

One significant area of intersection lies in cognitive sciences and neurology. By intersecting with Lacanian concepts such as the 'unattainable Real' and the 'traumatic Real', researchers in these fields have gained a deeper understanding of the complexities of human consciousness and perception. The recognition of the inherent gaps and distortions in human cognition, as elucidated by Lacanian theory, has inspired new approaches to studying and interpreting brain functions, ultimately reshaping the discourse on the nature of reality and phenomenological experiences.

The impact of Lacanian thought extends to the field of artificial intelligence and robotics. The exploration of the 'Real' as a dimension beyond symbolic representation has challenged traditional AI models, prompting a shift towards more nuanced understandings of human-machine interactions. Additionally, Lacanian perspectives have engendered critical reflections on the ethical implications of technological advancements, particularly regarding the inherent human desires and fears embedded in the development and implementation of cutting-edge technologies.

The influence of the Real permeates discussions on quantum physics and cosmology, provoking contemplation on the very fabric of the universe. Lacanian notions of the Real as an elusive, ungraspable entity have catalyzed debates on the limits of human comprehension and the potential for alternative modes of perceiving fundamental aspects of existence. Consequently, the integration of Lacanian thought into scientific and technological discourses has fostered a rich tapestry of inquiry, fostering interdisciplinary collaborations and pushing the boundaries of knowledge and understanding.

Conclusion and the Ongoing Dialogue with Lacanian Thought

The ongoing dialogue with Lacanian thought continues to evolve and expand into new and diverse areas of study. The application of Lacanian concepts such as the Real, the Symbolic, and the Imaginary has proven instrumental in redefining traditional perspectives in fields ranging from literature and cultural studies to media theory and critical social analysis. Moreover, the interdisciplinary intersections between Lacanian thought and gender and identity studies highlight the versatile adaptability and impactful nature of Lacan's theories. These dialogues are not mere academic exercises but represent vital contributions to the continual refinement of our understanding of human subjectivity and society.

On the other hand, the ongoing dialogue with Lacanian thought has paved the way for a deeper exploration of the complexities of power dynamics, particularly in critical social theory. By offering a framework that delves into the unconscious drives and desires that underpin social structures, Lacanian thought encourages a more nuanced and penetrating analysis of power relations. This has profound implications for efforts to critically engage with and challenge prevailing systems of oppression and control.

The relevance of Lacanian thought in the contemporary landscape also extends to the interpretation of art and literature. By illuminating the symbolic functions of language and representations, Lacanian thought provides a rich framework for analyzing complex artistic expressions and narratives. It enables deeper insights into the ways in which meaning is constructed, interpreted, and contested, thereby enriching our encounters with cultural artifacts and texts.

In light of the multifaceted contributions and ongoing dialogues with Lacanian thought across various disciplines, it becomes evident that the transformative potential of Lacanian theory endures through its capacity to inspire continual reinterpretation and application. As new questions arise and existing paradigms are challenged, Lacanian thought remains a robust framework for grappling with the intricacies of human existence, societal structures, and the interplay of realities. The ongoing dialogue with Lacanian thought presents a dynamic and fertile ground for future explorations, collaborations, and innovations, ensuring its legacy in shaping modern intellectual inquiry.

50 STATEMENTS ON THE THREE LACANIAN ORDERS

On the Mirror Stage & Ego Formation

The ego forms through an image that the child takes as a unified self, even though their experience is fragmented.

Identifying with the mirror image gives the subject an illusion of coherence.

The Imaginary ego is a misrecognition—an alienated version of oneself.

The child's jubilation before the mirror hides a fundamental dependency on an external image.

The mirror stage shows that the self is constructed on an external form rather than an inner essence.

On the Imaginary Relations & Rivalry

Imaginary relations are governed by duality—me versus the other.

Rivalry and aggression arise from the subject's identification with images and the threat posed by others.

The Imaginary creates relationships marked by competition rather than mutual recognition.

The other's image is experienced as either idealized or hostile.

Fantasies populate the Imaginary, offering scenes in which the subject stages desirable or threatening identities.

On Limitations & Illusions of the Imaginary

The Imaginary cannot grasp the truth of desire because it is tied to images, not structures.

Ego knowledge is misleading because it relies on appearances.

The Imaginary gives coherence to the subject, but only by masking division.

Neurosis often emerges when the subject clings to Imaginary mastery.

The Imaginary must be traversed for the subject to enter the order of speech and law.

On Language & Structure

The Symbolic precedes the subject; one is born into the network of language.

Speech structures the unconscious because the unconscious is made of signifiers.

Words represent the subject before they can represent themselves.

The Symbolic order organizes relationships beyond images.

Meaning arises not from things but from the differences among signifiers.

On Law, Prohibition & the Father Function

The law that prohibits incest is the foundation of the Symbolic.

The paternal function introduces a limit that makes desire possible.

The Name-of-the-Father is a key signifier that stabilizes the subject's place in the Symbolic order.

The paternal metaphor replaces the mother's desire with a regulating signifier.

Psychosis occurs when the paternal signifier is foreclosed and fails to take its place in the Symbolic.

On Desire, Demand & Lack

Desire arises from the gap between what one demands and what one needs.

The Symbolic introduces lack, which becomes the engine of desire.

Every signifier implies another signifier, leaving desire endlessly metonymic.

What one says is never identical to what one wants, because desire hides behind the chain of signifiers.

The subject is represented by a signifier for another signifier, never fully present in speech.

On the Subject & the Unconscious

The unconscious speaks in the Symbolic through slips, jokes, and dreams.

The subject emerges where the signifier appears; it is an effect of language.

Symbolic castration introduces the subject into the order of desire.

Analysis works by reordering the subject's relation to the signifier.

The Symbolic reveals the structural truth behind Imaginary illusions.

On the Real Beyond Representation

The Real is what resists symbolization; it cannot be captured in language.

Unlike the Imaginary, the Real is not an image; unlike the Symbolic, it is not a signifier.

The Real is the impossible—what does not stop returning.

The Real is encountered as a limit where articulation breaks down.

Anxiety arises when the Real approaches the subject too closely.

On Trauma, Instability & the Impossible

Trauma marks the intrusion of the Real where symbolic mediation fails.

The Real emerges as a gap or rupture within the Symbolic order.

Fantasy functions as a screen that protects the subject from the Real.

The Real appears through moments of encounter where meaning collapses.

The Real is not the same as reality; it is what reality tries to cover over.

On the Knotting of the Three Orders

The three orders are distinct yet interlinked, each necessary for psychic structure.

The Real anchors the other orders by resisting both image and symbol.

The Symbolic ties the Imaginary into a network that gives it meaning.

When the knot loosens or breaks, the subject's sense of reality becomes unstable.

Psychoanalysis aims to re-knot the Imaginary, Symbolic, and Real so that desire can be sustained without collapse.

www.ingramcontent.com/pod-product-compliance
Lightning Source LLC
LaVergne TN
LVHW052257200926
848481LV00002B/398

9798232146450